*The Book*

The first work, set in the early eighties, of a young Englishman's life on the road. A tale of contrasts; as the hard toil of continental truck-driving finances the months of sun on the Riviera. A unique view of harsh winters in eastern Europe set against a Mediterranean beach bums way of life.

*The Author*

Christopher Arbon born 1953 in the village of Foxearth, England.
Working as a truck-driver since the age of 21, now living in Manitoba, Canada, and driving throughout North America.

Chris Arbon

# Roadtrip Ramatuelle

1st edition
march 2009
2nd edition
november 2009

**Part One**

**Chapter One**

I first met Rupert Machin on the beach in the summer of '81: Danny Rudd, I had known from the summer before; he had worked with two brothers who I had camped with the year before that. The beach had a way of bringing the same faces back, year after year. Danny spoke good French and was teaching himself guitar. He worked hard selling his toffee-covered peanuts on the beach. Rupert had ideas for the future and talked a lot. He had a beard like me and was the only other person I knew who wore Timberlands. Rupert was the first new friend I had made outside of school, work and the village in which I lived. Our conversations centred on world travel; the Magic Bus and going overland into Africa. Rupert told of ways to drive Peugeot 504's across the Sahara and sell them for use as taxis in Nigeria. Of how a good profit could be made from secondhand trucks, bought in Holland and sold in Baghdad. I had never heard such adventureous proposals, let alone being offered the chance to partake in enterprises that would make me rich while seeing the world.

Danny could not drive, so he did not share the enthusiasm. He sat, leaning back on an upturned dinghy, with his guitar on his lap; endlessly perfecting the intro to "a stairway from heaven", while slapping at the attacking mosquitoes. It was my last night of a four week holiday.

Sleeping on the beach, getting a best ever tan, and whizzing about on the 500. The three of us sat round the still-glowing coals of a long deserted barbecue. They said they were sorry to see me go. Rupert and Danny smoked, as we talked into the night and agreed to do it all again next year.

Rupert was waiting for money from England to pay for his fare back home. When it arrived, he was to stay until it was spent. Buying food, tobacco, wine and a small slab of dope; eventually hitching home to England. Danny had the address of a vineyard and the date that grapepicking started. It led to ten days work and enough money to get the train home.

I tore all the teeth off the back sprocket on the way home and limped over the Channel with chronic chain slip, cursing myself for showing off with all those wheelies. I went back to work determined to save enough money to be able to take off the whole of next summer, promising myself a season in the sun, on the beaches of Southern France. To realise my dream, I buried myself in my work from the moment I got back.

I was driving on general haulage, with a Mercedes 1626 unit pulling a 40 foot flat trailer. It was all roping and sheeting: leaving Monday, getting home Saturday morning - carrying anything that could be tied down, but mostly farm machinery or fertiliser from ICI. It suited me as I was still living with my parents, it suited the boss as I was young and fit, didn't mind the nights away or long hours. The governor even turned a blind eye to the late starts and odd bit of running off route.

Most of the detours centred on Chelmsford and nearly always on a Friday. The county town of Essex had a lot going for it at the time: a big truck park, right next to the public baths, a friendly pub that did good food and, most importantly, a Country and Western Club that had a surplus of women. If it was reckoned that a truckdriver had a girl in every town, then he would probably have three or four in Chelmsford.

Illegal Citizen Band radios had just started to get popular and word soon spread that Chelmsford was the place to be on a Friday night. The truck park would start filling up from 2.00 o'clock in the afternoon - the same faces every week, and the same routine: down to the off-licence for some cold cans of lager, then over to the baths for a clean up; not to swim, but to pay for the use of the bathroom-type baths that the old establishment still retained. 30 pence gave you the use of the detachable, hot tap handle and a shave, shampoo and soak was always accompanied by a cold beer. Everybody then dressed in the last of that week's clean clothes, which had been saved especially for the big night out.

It was only a short walk to the "Three Cups" public house; a bar meal with a few pints, before going through to the back room that was the home of the Blueberry Hill Country and Western Club. It was always packed out, regardless of the quality of the live band, but most importantly, the women out-numbered the men two-to-one. All the drivers employed the same pulling tactics. That was: to stand at the bar, drinking steadily, making comments and only venturing onto the dance floor for the slow dances.  Some even played hard to get, only dancing if they were asked and then only accepting if it was a smooch. This is how I met Sheila, who had come with her friend, who was the regular girl of a Ferrymasters' driver.  It was her first visit to the Club and she looked good in her tight jeans and checked shirt.  Sheila said that she didn't get the chance to get out much, so she was determined to have a good time.  We were still dancing together when the band finished at the end of the night.

"Do you want to come back to the truck for a kiss and a cuddle?" I asked, as we stood together on the emptying dance floor.

"No truck, no way.  Let's get a taxi back to my place," replied Sheila.

The kissing and cuddling went from the taxi to the kitchen and half a cup of coffee later, we were in bed. Considering it was our first time together, it was good; we had both drunk just the right amount of alcohol.  At least that was how I saw it. Sheila asked me to stay for breakfast, but I refused, as I feared the truck would get blocked in by cars if I didn't get back to the truck park as soon as possible. It was only when I pulled the front door shut, as I stepped out into the foggy dawn, that I realised I didn't know where the hell I was.  I had spent out, so calling a taxi was out of the question. It was a council estate, like any council estate, and with the fog, I had no sense of direction. How I regretted snogging in the taxi all the way back to her place.

A paperboy directed me to the main road and I waved down a milk tanker, coming out of a side turning. The driver laughed when I told him my story, but he did give me a lift down to the ring road. From there, I strode off into town and caught a glimpse of the truck park through the fog, on the other side of the river. I cut back along the riverbank to the first available bridge, from where I made my way along the opposite bank, towards the trucks - only to find that the fun fair was in town and it was not my truck park. Determined not to break into a run, I continued my search and, after what seemed hours, and miles of walking, I tracked down my vehicle: the last truck left on the park. Fortunately, the thoughtful Saturday morning shoppers of Chelmsford had encountered the situation before and had left me a wide path to the exit. As the nights grew shorter and less cold it became easier to motivate myself as the end of the work came closer.

The Falklands' conflict was brewing in the early summer of '82 and, as the task force headed south, I made my plans to go in the same direction. I decided against taking the 500 - saving on its expense and preferring to make a life as a true beach bum. There was plenty of money; I had saved over the winter, but I aimed to put myself at the bottom of the social ladder. When it looked like you had nothing to loose, you didn't had to be so defensive, although this had the effect of making others frightened of you. After a lot of thought on what to take, I settled on a large sports bag in preference to a rucksack. In it, I put a sleeping bag, towel, toothpaste and brush, swimming trunks, jeans, cut-offs, tee-shirt, denim shirt, thick woollen jumper, bomber jacket, two pairs of socks and a sun hat; a Swiss army knife and lightweight, one-man tent completed the load, which was not heavy and didn't fill up the bag. As I had never had much luck at hitchhiking, I reckoned that going by train was the best way to get to the South of France, quickly and easily. After catching the ferry from Dover to Calais, I was looking forward to my couchette experience, but it was a mistake to take so many cans of lager; too many long treks to the toilet during the night ruined what should have been a peaceful journey.

When I disembarked at St Rapheal on a warm Mediterranean morning, I made straight for the beach and headed westward, along the coast. Going barefoot on the sand, eating baguette and Camembert, drinking a fizzy bitter lemon called "Pshitt" which tasted as good warm as it did cold, unlike Coca Cola. I didn't even try hitching, I just walked, laid in the shade when the day was at its hottest, swam in the sea to keep clean and slept on the sand – taking care not to establish an obvious camp, but to just unroll my sleeping bag when I was ready to sleep. At St Maxime, I did contemplate taking the water-taxi across the bay to St Tropez, but in the end I saved the fare by walking all the way. Three days after getting off the train, I arrived at Pampellone Beach.

Pampellone is the largest, uninterrupted stretch of sand on the French Riviera. Nine kilometres long, it faces east, and is the beach at St Tropez that everybody goes to. It has no road running behind it as a promenade and is reached by a series of tracks that fork off left from the St Tropez to Ramatuelle road. The sand is split up into public areas and private beach clubs in a ratio of about 50:50 – the more expensive beach clubs being closer to St Tropez; the less pretentious were along towards the lighthouse on Cap Camarat, at the end of the beach where the seaweed tended to be washed up.

It was here that I intended to make my base for the summer.

The first person I spoke to was Ronnie. He was working his first day as a beach seller, selling cold drinks out of an icebox. He had bought the drinks at the local campsite supermarket, put in a six franc lump of ice and was walking up and down, shouting "Boisson fraiche". Ronnie had sold a few when I met him, so we sat and discussed the prospects for the season.

Soon, he had offered me a partnership, taking it in turns to walk up and down the beach. I took him up on his offer, thinking it would give me something to do and a bit of 'beach bum' creditability. First impressions of Ronnie were quite favourable: he was fit and strong, aged about 19, enthusiastic about the work and thought the beach was a great place to spend the summer. I was a bit put off by the amateurish tattoo proclaiming his undying love for Fiona, but that was just the start.

On the first evening, after everybody had gone and the sun was setting over the hills behind us, Ronnie showed me his kung-fu rice flails and gave an impressive display of swirling them at lightening speed around his body. He then told me of the great opportunities offered by unattended cars in the car park and unoccupied holiday homes. It was then that I started thinking of ways to dissolve our partnership. The answer came to me the next day, not that I thought about it - it just happened. I was in the sun for far too long, burnt myself everywhere, heated up my blood, had a stomach ache and a headache. Ronnie was unsympathetic and said I was a whimp. I was ill for three days. I told him I wasn't cut out for beach selling and that he had better go it alone. He replied that he was giving up beach selling in order to work for Stefan, the Belgian, who had a whole gang of beach sellers. Ronnie was going to become his minder. He offered to sell me his icebox, but in the end, he just left it with me.

The one good thing to come from knowing Ronnie, besides getting the use of his icebox, was that I met Liz and Kate: two British girls who worked as shelf-fillers in Les Tournels Campsite supermarket. They were both students, studying French, and had just finished their middle year as English teachers at Rouen, from where they had arranged their summer jobs. Liz had been conned by Ronnie, the same way I had, and she was as pleased as I was when he moved to Cogolan to camp with Stefan's mob. It was only when I told the girls how glad I was to see him go that they became friendly towards me.

During these first four days, the number of people sleeping on the beach mushroomed dramatically: Rupert arrived; Danny Rudd and his mate Roger turned up in Roger's Mini; Len from Sheffield returned for another summer; Dave Anson and Ray Brennan were combining drink selling with chasing the two Dutch girls who worked in the campsite reception; Robert and Axel from Berlin said they had stolen a Porsche, which had been chased by police all the way to the Riviera; and, finally, Mick and Rob, the West Ham supporters, with the Commer van, were working the hardest, selling drinks by day and syphoning petrol by night.

Rupert had spent the winter on the dole, living at home and working odd days on the black, mostly painting and decorating. Together with some hashish-dealing that had financed an adequate supply of dope for himself. Rupert was his usual upbeat self when he talked of past and present; with even more enthusiasm for the future.

"We have the beginnings of a good scene here, man. The same faces, the beach, the weather. We could really make it happen. This is the place to be," said Rupert in a way that, intenionally or not, made everyone think they were part of something special.

Danny Rudd's winter had also been mostly workless. Getting up after midday, spending most of the time in his room, listening to music or playing his guitar. Eventually

Danny had to take a job at Casey Jones, a new burger-bar on a mainline station in the center of London. It had the bonus of free rail travel, as it was part of British Rail. Danny told of how the management had sent him a letter when he left, thanking him for his hard work in setting up the operation. I was surprised that he had mixed feelings about leaving the job. Danny did not strike me as a team player; rather the observer watching other people's actions and storing it all away without comment. Those on the beach offered Danny safety in numbers but he did not need them like Rupert did.

Miraculously, the day after Ronnie left, I felt well enough to work again. I bought a dozen Cokes and a block of ice from the supermarket, started walking the beach at 1.00 o'clock, sold out by 4.00 o'clock and had only drunk two cans myself. There was 50 francs profit – enough to pay for food and wine for the day. Most of the other sellers were doing similar business, except for the good looking Axel, who sat on the gay beach, expecting people to come to him, which they did. He always sold out, without doing any walking.

Day Two of the post-Ronnie selling was completely different. After my first sale, I came across Liz and Kate who had come down to the beach in their lunch hour break. We sat and talked for ages, until Liz said she had to go back to work. Kate stayed on the beach as it was her half day and we were still sitting on the sand, talking, at 7.00 o'clock, as the beach became deserted. Kate only left to go back to the caravan as it was her turn to cook dinner for Liz, because she had only worked half day. She asked me if I would like to eat with them. As we walked back to the campsite, along the dusty tracks, through the vineyards, it suddenly struck me that this superbly tanned little Scottish girl might be looking for a bit of romance.

After the spaghetti bolognaise, I offered to wash up and took the pots, pans and dishes up to the sinks, at the toilet block. Kate came up, shortly afterwards, to give me a hand.

"Would you like to take a shower with me?" asked Kate unexpectedly.

"Yeah, sure," I replied, unhesitatingly.

"Oh great, it will be nice to have someone to press the button, so that there is an uninterrupted flow of water," said Kate as we left the worst of the pans to soak.

As it was a hot day in early season, all the hot water had not been run off, so I was able to give myself a real good soaping.

"This is the first time I've had a shower with someone and not been fucked", remarked Kate.

"This is the first shower I've had a week, " I replied, "you want me clean, don't you?"

"It's nice to know you've got good standards of hygiene," murmured Kate, as she went down on her knees and took me in her mouth.

The shower was not the ideal place to first make love, especially for two people of such differing heights. But Kate didn't complain, even with the cold ceramic tiles pressed against her back, and all the time I was trying to think of something that would keep the hot water running without continually pressing that damned button.

Afterwards, we went back to the caravan, with the clean dishes and had coffee, before I left to go back down the track to the beach. It was past midnight when I got back to where everybody was lounging around on the sand. Most of the crew were lying in half-open sleeping bags, bottle of wine in one hand, roll-up in the other. The only movement was from the tobacco and papers as they were thrown from sleeping bag to sleeping bag.

"How many you sell today then, Chris?" came a voice from the dark.

"One," I replied.

"Bad day for you then."

"No. Probably one of the best days in my life" I announced proudly.

"Oh, my God. Chris is in love," shouted Rupert, to

a chorus of cheers and whistles.

Ignoring them all, I pulled my sleeping bag out from under an up-turned dinghy, climbed in and lay back, with my hands behind my head.

"And I don't mind if I am" I thought to myself.

The next four weeks saw my life fall into a pleasant routine, based on selling cold drinks, together with making love to Kate. This involved a lot of walking, usually bare foot, from beach to campsite to supermarket, with the occasional trek up to Ramatuelle to check for mail at the post office. The village was about four kilometres from the beach, perched half way up the hillside that rose from the narrow coastal plain, about two kilometres inland. The major part of the village was arranged in circular, fortified style, with a dominant church tower. Newer additions branched out from the maze of narrow streets that were the original medieval formation. The market in the village square on Thursdays and Sundays made it a popular place to visit, while the many restaurants, with tables outside on the pavement, attracted a lot of people during the evenings. For me, the attractions were that the village supermarket was cheaper than that of the campsite and that you could have letters delivered to the Poste Restante, to be collected on production of your passport, although I always felt that the post office staff rather begrudged giving this service.

These were the longest days of the year, scorching hot, with never any rain. The drink selling never made me more than 50 francs a day, but I rarely spent more than that. Kate spent most of her free time with me. Her days off from the supermarket were either spent lazing on the beach, or making love in the caravan; the evenings, either sitting round a camp fire on the beach, or at the local discotheque. Both discos were free to enter: Tuesdays and Fridays at Les Bronzes on the beach; Wednesdays and Saturdays at Les Tournels bar, next to the supermarket. The same tactics applied to both: walk in, start dancing and they won't ask you to buy a drink; stop dancing, walk out and find the bottle of red wine that you had stashed away earlier. Good fun, cheap, plus the bar owners didn't want the hassle of dealing with the beach bums anyway.

The biggest thing for me at this time was the sex. I had never met anybody like Kate before. She had no inhibitions. Kate liked making love, wasn't ashamed that she liked it and wanted to do it as much as possible. Kate's first lover had been her French teacher, when she was still at school. He had certainly given her a good education.

We did it everywhere: the caravan being the most frequent, and most comfortable; in the showers; on the beach; in the vineyards; at the water tower, and on the climbing frame in the playground at 3.00 o'clock in the morning. It was after the climbing frame adventure, when I had wandered back to the beach, that I got a surprise. Nobody was asleep on the beach. The place that normally accommodated up to 20 persons was deserted. I found my gear in Roger's Mini, that stood alone in the car park, but with its old-style sliding windows, I had no problem breaking into the car to get my sleeping bag. Just as I closed the window and shut the door, Roger came walking back, from the direction of the campsite.

"Where have you been?" I asked, expecting an explanation for everyone's disappearance.

"I've been up at the campsite with Janine, the French girl who sells donuts, but it was so uncomfortable in her tent I've come back to sleep on the sand. Hey, where is everybody?" exclaimed Roger.

"I dunno, I just got back myself. Either they're messing about, hiding in the rocks or they've gone off to some party we don't know about," I said, as the two of us settled down for the night.

It was only as the sun came up that Roger and I found out what had happened to the others. Slowly, everybody came trudging back to the beach, with their backpacks and sleeping bags. Rupert, Dave Anson and Robert from Berlin had been up at the campsite supermarket sometime after midnight. They had been robbing the bottle store - as they had done several times before, not full bottles, but empty ones that were kept in a wire mesh compound at the rear of the supermarket. The lads would take as many empties as they could and hide them in a nearby ditch. Then, in the morning, they would take them back into the shop and collect the money on the bottles. This time, however, they had walked into a trap.

Rupert escaped by running off into the darkness but the other two were arrested, along with everyone else who was on the beach when the police came down to fetch Dave and Robert's gear. Everybody was put in a van, taken to the police station, cautioned, then driven up to Gassin la Foux and told to hitchhike home – all except the two bottle robbers, who were given 30 days in Draguinun prison. Rupert hid out in the campsite shower block where he bumped into the girl who served on the supermarket cheese counter. Spending the rest of the night back at her caravan was an ideal alternative to a month in the nick.

It was later that day, five German girls from Regensburg arrived on the beach in a big green Mercedes van; also Kate told me the news that her boyfriend from Rouen was coming to stay for a week and Carlisle Eddie, who was the dishwasher at Club Tropicana told me that the private beach next to his place was looking for a plagiste. He said it might be a good idea to invest in some smart satin boxer-style swimming shorts, instead of going for the position in cut-off Levis. Good advice it was too, as I got the job, which paid 100 francs a day and meals.

L'Esquinade was a friendly, family-run business with a Norwegian lady, Madame Edna, in charge of the staff. Her husband, Roger, who had flown Spitfires for the RAF during the war, cooked the food with the help of his daughter, Carola. Manuel, the son, waited at table. Edison, from Brazil, was the barman and Mahmood, from Morocco, washed the dishes. I was replacing an

Argentinean called Luis as plagiste. I was responsible for the sand area of the private beach. It was my duty to rake the sand every morning, in order to sift out all the litter such as cigarette ends, ice cream wrappers, cocktail umbrellas and so on. The best time to start was at the crack of dawn, before the sun got too hot, so that all the mattresses on the sun loungers, the little drinks tables, together with the big shady parasols were in position without too much sweat. My other task was to collect everything up in the evening, or at a moment's notice, if it came on to rain. To do a good job it took me three hours in the morning and half an hour at the end of the day.

Lots of helpful hints on sand sifting technique and mattress carrying were given to me by the plagiste from the neighbouring Club Tropicana. He was working his fourth season caring for sand, having done the previous three at L'Esquinade. He had the physique of a body builder and wore leopard skin swimming trunks. His name was Yves, but he liked people to call him Tarzan. He was tall, blonde, clean-cut and in his mid-twenties. He spoke French, English, German and Dutch, but when asked where he came from, Tarzan would only say it was from an area where the borders of three countries met – very mysterious.

When Kate and Liz's old flames arrived from Rouen, I had resigned myself to a quiet week with some welcome early nights. But I hadn't reckoned on the arrival of Vero into my life. She came from the French country town of

Gap, where she worked as a beekeeper. I first noticed Vero in Les Bronzes disco, where I saw her looking at me with her smiling eyes. We were dancing apart, but when I smiled back, Vero came over to dance in front of me.

At the first slow dance we just fell together. When the music speeded up, we left, hand-in-hand, to walk barefoot along the beach. Without a word to each other we came to L'Esquinade, where we stopped and kissed passionately on my excellently sifted sand. As we kissed, Vero spoke softly to me in French.

"Beignet," whispered Vero.

"Oui," I murmured, wondering what donuts had to do with it.

"Oui," whispered Vero, as she started to undress.

It wasn't until we had both taken off our clothes and gone into the sea that I realised it wasn't "beignet" meaning "donut" but "baigner" which was "to bathe".

This was the first time I had ever made love to a French girl, also I had never before done it in the sea. But that night I did both to someone I had known for less than an hour. It was a fantasy come true. After we came out of the water, it was Vero's turn to be amazed, as I led her across the sand to the mattress store. There, I reached up to get the hidden padlock key, before unlocking the door, so that I could find my towel amongst all my other stuff. I rubbed Vero dry and laid down with her on the mattresses, pulled my sleeping bag over us, then made love to her again.

During the day, I never saw Vero at all, we never ate together and we never spoke much more than two words to each other, but late in the evening she would turn up at the disco or on the beach. Almost straightaway we would go off to the mattress store to make love. Vero never suggested doing it in the sea again, but that was understandable, because you couldn't beat those mattresses for comfort, especially after you had been sleeping on the ground.

After Kate's friend from Rouen and Vero from Gap had finished their holidays, things never returned to how they were before. Kate had been away from home for a long time and, understandably, she was keen to get back to Scotland before the end of the summer. The two students handed in their notice at the supermarket and we spent most of the last week as a foursome, with Liz's Dutch boyfriend, Eric. Using Eric's car, we spent a couple of evenings in St Tropez. The four of us wandered round the port, looking at the expensive yachts, then walked round the streets, looking in expensive shops. First impressions of Eric were that he was as arrogant as the worst Germans, but when you got to know him, saw his command of languages, his superb physical fitness and his sharp mind, it was only his honesty in telling you about himself that was off-putting. Eric and I became good mates during the last few days of the girls' stay and impressed them more than once with our combined cooking talents on the caravan stove. I was sad to see Kate go, but we exchanged addresses, phone numbers and promised to keep in touch.

Everybody was still scratching out a living by selling cold drinks to the sun-worshipping public. Roger and Steffi, the driver of the big green Mercedes van, had fallen madly in love, only for Steffi to find out she was pregnant from before the holiday started. Roger took her to London, on the train, for a termination, while Rupert took to chauffeuring the rest of the German girls around in the van, as none of them could handle a vehicle that big. Les from Sheffield looked after Roger's Mini for him. One lunchtime, Stefan, the Belgian beachmaster, turned up with Ronnie, to demand that everyone stop selling drinks on his beach. When nobody agreed to his wishes, he told Ronnie to deal with it and stormed off. All the independent sellers were sitting on their iceboxes, ready to go to work, while Ronnie stood there, waiting for someone to make a move.

"Ronnie, go home," said Axel, who was practising his yoga on an upturned dinghy.
Ronnie thought about it for well over a minute, before he walked away down the beach and was never seen again.
A couple of days later, one of Stephan's sellers turned up at the beach in his van and announced he was joining the independents. His name was Robin, although

everyone called him Speedy.   It turned out that he had lost his long-time girlfriend to one of Stefan's lieutenants. Speedy and I had passed each other many times while selling our wares, also I remembered meeting him when I was walking back from Ramatuelle one morning.  He was standing beside his van, with the bonnet up, after it had boiled over.  Sensibly, he was waiting for it to cool down a bit before he topped up the radiator with cold water.

"Hi!   Thing's overheated a bit" I observed sympathetically.

"Yeah.  It's always doing it.  That's why I carry spare water," said Speedy, holding up a big plastic container.

"Could be the thermostat stuck," I suggested.

"No. I think it's the water pump. I took the thermostat out last week," he replied dejectedly.

It was an old Renault 4 van, previously owned by a television rental company.  It should have been just the thing for bumming around France – it looked like Speedy was down on his luck.  It was a coincidence that Roger's water pump on his Mini had also packed up.  He had brought a reconditioned one back from England when he returned with Steffi. The German girls' holiday was now over and they had to get the van back to Steffi's brother-in-law.   Rupert volunteered to drive the van back to Regensburg, while Danny Rudd and Irish Danny went along for the ride.   Roger and I changed the water pump on the Mini, using the cardboard from a pack of Kronenbourg as a gasket.  Two days after the girls left, we followed in the Mini.  Roger thought that I might come in handy as a mechanic and a navigator.

We left late one afternoon, heading east along the coast, towards Italy.   At Monte Carlo, we tried to drive the Grand Prix circuit, finding plenty of red and white painted kerbs around the track, but Roger never completed a full lap.   Compensation came in the form of the Chinese entry to the Monte Carlo Annual Firework Competition.  The whole principality came to a standstill for something which Roger and I agreed was truly spectacular.  Afterwards, we pushed on into Italy, to have a night sleeping on an Italian beach, just for a change. Next morning, we left the coast, continuing east in the general direction of the Brenner Pass, keeping off the autostrades in a bid to save money on tolls.   It probably didn't help the economy that much, due to wrong turns and extra mileage, as well as making a lot of work for the navigator.   Our second night of the trip was spent on the shore of Lade Garda, near Trento, where I persuaded Roger to use the toll motorways.   In the morning we made much better progress.  The Mini was up and over the pass by lunchtime, out of Austria by teatime and into Regensburg before dusk.  The Mini had done well, but both front tyres were now completely bald.

After a couple of phone calls, it was arranged to meet up in a bar.  All the girls were coming, along with the two Dannys.  Rupert was already on his way back to London.

Roger and I had a lot of trouble finding the bar and ended up down a blind alley with a blind drunk German barring our exit. I could not believe he was going to mug us, not one onto two, but he shaped up with some karate moves and chopped Roger on the back of the neck. As he turned towards me, I pointed over his shoulder, said "Police" and swung my right foot up between his legs whilst he looked around. The mugger went down like a sack of spuds. Roger threw a nearby bicycle on top of him, but we all went off asking ourselves what the hell the prat thought he was doing.

The bar was close by in the next alley. The girls were so upset that we should be mugged in their home town that they bought all the drinks, all night. The two Dannys and I slept the night in the park and spent the next two days looking around the town. Claudia, who had the hots for Danny Rudd, brought some sandwiches that she had made at home. We all had a nice picnic on the banks of the Danube. But there was really nothing for me in Regensburg, so I decided to head back to England the next day. Danny Rudd and Danny Oakes hitchhiked back to the beach. Ingrid gave me lift in her car to a spot at an autobahn junction which she assured me was the best place for hitchhiking west out of the city. I found a note written on the back of a nearby road sign, it read: "No hope, no dope, no ride, we died". After two hours waiting, I had my suspicions about being in the best spot for getting out of Regensburg, but then two lads in a BMW stopped to give me a lift all the way to Cologne.

It was evening by the time I was dropped off so, on seeing signs for a campsite, I made my way along the banks of the River Rhine to sleep my first night of the summer in my tent. I was put off hitchhiking by the daunting prospect of crossing Belgium with its fast motorways around Brussels. Instead, I chose the railway and was at the station bright and early to catch the train straight through to Ostend. It was the Vienna-Ostend express which had stopped at Regensburg just after midnight, on its way westwards. A ferry to Dover, a train to London, the tube across the capital and another train out into Suffolk brought me home that same day. But not for long. With the distinct possibility of some grape-picking work, I was eager to get back to the beach. All that I had come home for was my 500-cc motorcycle. With the harvest in the countryside, I would need some transport. As I would be earning a good weekly wage, I figured it would be okay.

# Chapter Two

After the drive chain problems of the previous year, I took it easy getting back to the beach on the 500. The main change since I had been away was the arrival of Billy Carroll and his girlfriend, Vicky. Billy was a six-foot Dubliner, with blonde, spiky hair that made him look three inches taller. He was the main man as far as picking grapes was concerned. Billy and Vicky had picked the grapes in the vineyards surrounding Les Tournels Camping last year. The vendangeur, Monsieur Francis Boi, had moved to Vidauban since then, where Bill and Vicky had called in to see him on their way to the beach. Francis had given Billy the job of recruiting a team of pickers for the harvest at his new domaine. At our first meeting, Billy offered me a job. He reckoned there was three or four weeks' work and it would start during the first week in September, which is early for grape-picking in France, but we were in the far south. This gave everybody ten days to fill, before the exodus inland to Vidauban.

The weather was more changeable now, with a distinct 'end-of-season' feel to the beach. The year before, at this time, Billy, Vicky and the other Irish boys had squatted in an old abandoned villa for the duration of the work. Billy insisted that it was dry, comfortable and a damn good place for parties, so everybody on the team moved from the beach to the villa. The place was just as they had left it. The villa was situated on the road to the lighthouse on Cap Camarat. You could not see it from the road as it was set back down the hill, but it was still high enough to give panoramic views of the beach and the Med. It was difficult to tell if the building had ever been lived-in, as it seemed equally half-finished and half-dismantled. There was no water supply or electricity, but the roof was good, along with an excellent fireplace in the main open-plan living area. Of the two bedrooms only one had a door, so Billy claimed it for himself and Vicky, saying it was the same situation as last year. Everybody else either slept on the roof, if it was warm, or in front of the fire, if it was cold. In the ten days of residency, the numbers varied from between 12 and 20, with Billy Carroll very much in charge.

"It's 30 francs a day per person,: 10 francs for food, 10 for wine and 10 francs for dope," said Billy, before doing the shopping every afternoon. "But if you haven't got 30, just give what you can."

There was always plenty of food, either rice, pasta or potatoes, with a vegetable sauce. Also, more than enough of the cheap red wine that came in the two litre plastic bottles. The cooking was done in the fireplace, over a wood fire, with the back flap of a supermarket shopping trolley providing a stand for the pots and a rack for the baked potatoes. Lighting was by candles and music came from the stereo in Paddy Botley's VW Variant or Danny Rudd's guitar. "Just Can't Stop" by the Beat was the most popular cassette, with everyone dancing right through to tracks such as "Mirror in the

Bathroom". Danny Rudd played mostly obscure tunes by people such as John Martyn, but he did do Clapton's "Wonderful Tonight" and Led Zep's "Stairway to Heaven". However, everyone's favourite 'live' song was the Jam's "That's Entertainment" where the whole crew joined in with the words. In spite of the noise from the music and the constant foraging for firewood at our neighbours' woodpiles, nobody gave us any hassle in the whole time we were at the villa. It was an easy life, in an idyllic spot, absolutely rent-free. Nobody was looking forward to moving up to Vidauban to start the hard work, although we all needed the money.

When it came to leaving the villa, the big problem was the transport. The Commer van of Mick and Rob, the West Ham supporters, had finally given up the ghost. As it was the biggest vehicle, this was a great disappointment. Danny Rudd had organised some grape-picking for himself, Roger and Les in the Beaujolais region, south of Lyon, so that was the Mini spoken for. That left Paddy's VW estate, Speedy's Renault 4 and my 500. There were sixteen of us, plus all the rucksacks, which made everything overcrowded. On the evening of the first Saturday in September, we all set off in a convoy, stopping at the Geant Casino supermarche at Gassin Le Foux for petrol. I spent my last 30 francs on half-filling the bike's tank, then continued, with both Helen and Petra riding pillion. There were seven in the VW, six in the Renault and three on the 500.

It took an hour and a half on the country lanes to

reach the Domaine de Ste Genevieve. It was a good job Billy was navigating from the passenger seat of the VW, as I would never have found the place in the dark. Fortunately, Francis was expecting us and had arranged for two old military buses to be towed up from the local scrapyard. These vehicles, minus their seats, were filled with old mattresses, which converted them into quite comfortable dormitories. Everybody slept in the buses, except for Speedy, who used his van, while Rupert and I pitched our tents. Sunday morning dawned fine and clear to reveal our home and work place for the next month. The house of the owner, Monsieur Cordier, the house of Francis, plus the winery, were all joined together in a collection of old stone-built buildings. A one-roomed, single storey dwelling was the home of Gasen, the full-time farm worker, and adjoining that was the kitchen, dining room, lounge, bar and meeting room of the grape-pickers.

This one room contained a cooker, a refrigerator, three tables and 12 chairs, plus an assortment of pots, pans, plates, cups, knives and forks. Outside, there was a toilet, two picnic tables, the buses, plus all the usual farm equipment of tractors, trailers and sprayers. Other machinery was scattered about the yard and in the smaller, tumble-down farm buildings. This was definitely not the image I had expected. I had been anticipating a long tabled dining hall and bunk-bedded sleeping quarters, set round a courtyard of a neat and tidy chateau. It also came as a shock to learn that we were to cook for ourselves too.

As everybody was flat broke, Francis agreed to give us all a 'sub', so that we could eat on the Sunday. He had enough experience of the English and Irish to make it large enough for food, but small enough so that nobody could go into town and get blind drunk. Billy also worked out a kitty system with Francis whereby he received a lump sum every day that would buy enough food for everybody's meals. Each weekend, each worker would be paid half of their wages, less their share of the kitty: the other half of the earnings would be collected at the end of the harvest. The hourly rate of pay was the French legal minimum wage: 30 francs an hour. The hours were from 08.00 in the morning until midday and from 2 until 6 after lunch, Monday to Friday. No pay if we didn't work due to bad weather.

Francis told Billy who was the best baker in town and suggested that we placed a regular order for our bread. Fetching the dozen loaves first thing in the morning became my job, which I usually enjoyed because I could treat myself to a "café au lait" in the Bar Tabac – to this day, some of the best cups of coffee I have every had. As we lazed around on the Sunday, I was surprised just how eager everybody now was to start work. It must have been the thought of the money, as I am sure the prospect of all the back-breaking toil in the hot sun didn't appeal to me. It was only the hope that I would get a job as one of the porters that gave me any comfort that I would see the whole thing through. Billy said the tallest and the strongest would be porters; I put myself at number two on the list. Carrying buckets of grapes and tipping them into a trailer was a darn sight easier than being bent double with a pair of secateurs in your hand for eight hours a day.

8.00 o'clock Monday morning, we all assembled, ready to start work. The 16 in Billy's team, four local Tunisians, the eldest two of Francis' five daughters and Marcel, a cousin from Marseilles. Marcel was to drive the tractor; Billy, Rupert, Keith Connery and myself were to be porters, while the other 18 paired themselves up ready to start picking the first nine rows of vines in the field at the back of the winery. As the pickers moved down the rows, the porters exchanged their full buckets with the two empty ones that they carried. These were then emptied into the trailer, which was parked down the middle of the nine lines.

Marcel moved the tractor and trailer along, ahead of the pickers, then at the end of the row, we all moved across to the next nine rows and worked back the other way. A tried and tested method that worked well, with only the slight snag that not everybody picked at the same speed. The four Tunisians who worked as two pairs, and Francis' daughters, Bridget and Celine, always finished their rows first. The Tunisians tended to stop for a cigarette at the end of their rows, whereas the French girls came back to help the slowest of the others. When Francis started to order them back to help the English and Irish, the North Africans soon realised they need not work so fast and soon mastered the art of finishing only just in front of everybody else.

Most of the pairings that started together on the first day stayed established for the whole harvest.    Claudia and Petra, the sisters from Karlsruhe, worked opposite each other, chatting away in German.    Ray Brennan, from Dublin, and his Dutch girlfriend, Marlene, always worked the row next to West Ham Mick, who went with Marlene's friend, Helen. Vicky, Billy's girlfriend, worked with Marianne, who was previously at the cheese counter of Les Tournels camping supermarket.    Vicky wanted to improve her French and Marianne her English.    The others sometimes swapped around to avoid boredom, but usually to be with someone who had tobacco and papers.    The porter's job was not at all difficult, as the full buckets were not that heavy.    We split up the rows between us, changing from inside to outside at every turn.    There was plenty of walking, but it was pleasant countryside and after the morning dew had dried during the first two hours, it became hot enough to take your shirt off in order to top up the suntan.    The A7 autoroute to Italy ran through the fields, about one kilometre away from our farm.    I soon adopted the habit of watching for passing British trucks, as they sped by.

Marcel, the cousin of Bridget and Celine, was a city boy who had little idea of tractor driving;   he was okay on the straights, but did not know about the trick of braking the inside back wheel independently to help get him round the tight corners at the end of the rows. Marcel had also never reversed a trailer before.   This was a major problem for him as when each trailer was full, he had to reverse it up a ramp in order to tip the grapes into a pit, from where it was augured into the winery. The ramp was not much wider than the tractor, which was loosely coupled to the trailer, making steering difficult. Gassen, the full-time worker who was operating the grape-pressing machinery came to Marcel's rescue every time – with his experience, he made it look easy. Everyone felt sorry for Marcel as they all realised how tricky the manoeuvre was. Nobody else wanted the tractor-driving job, but I told Billy that someone who had been professionally trained to reverse trailers would have no trouble with the ramp. Billy told Francis that I was experienced with articulated vehicles, so when the next load was ready, I was asked to take it. Francis was eager to get the trailers tipped and back in the field quickly, so it was make or break time if I wanted to get the driving job for myself. It was a problem that I had not driven anything more than a motorcycle for over three months. Fortunately, I remembered what I had been taught on the windswept Mendlesham airfield all those years ago: start off from the best possible position, move the trailer slowly, the steering wheel fast and above all, concentrate one hundred percent.

Francis was watching from across the fields as I swung round at the bottom of the ramp. Gassen came to stand by the pit to see if I was any better than Marcel. I lined the tractor up with a small angle, so that I could turn in slowly as the trailer went up the slope. With reverse gear engaged, I adjusted the hand throttle so that the engine would not stall and it went up with no trouble at all. It was a bit out of shape as I reached the top, but when the trailer wheels hit the low wall at the edge of the pit, they straightened themselves out perfectly. I jumped off the tractor, undid the retaining clamp on the trailer, dumped the grapes into the pit, did the clamp back up, climbed on the tractor, nodded to Gassen and drove back to the field. I had done it in one and was now the new tractor driver – Marcel went to portering. For the last load of the day, Francis stood at the bottom of the ramp to watch. Again, I reversed up the slope in one go. Although Francis said nothing, he could see I knew what I was doing.

Breakfasts on the farm consisted of coffee with marmalade sandwiches. Lunch was nearly always cheese salad sandwiches, but dinner was always complicated. Billy, as fair as ever, implemented a rota system: four different people each day – two to cook, two to wash up. Four groups of four, alternating between cooking and cleaning, which meant everyone only cooked once every eight days. The menu was sorted out in the field during the day, but was either pasta, rice or potatoes, with a sauce that was called chilli, curry, bolognaise or ratatouille, but always tasted the same. A pot of home-made popcorn was a popular starter, while pancakes were everybody's favourite dessert. There was, of course, ample wine to drink before, during and after dinner.

Everyone found the work exhausting, but worked through the aches and pains during the hard first week. The worst thing to happen was when Speedy's van caught fire. It did not burn out, but all the electric wires behind the dashboard melted into one multi-coloured blob of plastic and copper. It would not start after this, which was a shame, as it was only a week since Speedy had fitted a replacement water pump.

The weekend came with everyone having the same idea: go into a Vidauban bar and stay there all day, drinking. It was not something that was done in French society – going out to get deliberately drunk; so the town bars were very wary of the hard-drinking foreigners, although they welcomed the extra trade. Over the next few weekends, it was something Vidauban was to get used to. Nobody gave the locals too much trouble. But Keith Connery took things a bit far when he borrowed a builder's pick-up truck to get back to the farm one Sunday evening.

During the second week, most pickers acquired a level of fitness that let them cope easily with the work, whilst I had the tractor driving down to a fine art. Billy, who would discuss anything with Francis to avoid emptying buckets, had run out of things to say and was now pulling his weight. Rupert, who had paired up with Petra, wanted everyone to pool their wages in order to buy one of the buses and take it overland to Mombassa. Some people were keen on the idea, but those who knew Rupert well, warned against such romantic schemes.

Rupert and Petra were sleeping in the tent next to mine. It was a surprise when, one night, I heard her voice when I was just falling asleep.

"Can I sleep with you tonight?" she whispered.

"Yes, of course you can," I replied, after looking out to check that Petra was talking to me.

"What's wrong?" I asked, as she spread out her sleeping bag and lay down beside me.

"Rupert does not like me any more. He makes fun of me with the others. He speaks about Petra and Blue Peter. I do not understand."

"Ah well, Blue Peter is a television programme and they had a little puppy called 'Petra' on the show. It was a very famous dog and everybody's favourite pet," said as tactfully as I could.

Five our of six German girls had names that ended in 'a'; one was always called Claudia, while another was nearly always a Petra.

"Do you like me?" asked Petra, after a short silence.

"Yeah, 'course I do," I replied, as I propped myself up on one elbow and leaned over to kiss Petra on the lips. The young German girl did not resist my advances. She put her arms around my neck and pulled me down on top of her. We made love carefully, rather than passionately, trying not to draw attention to the tent. It was enjoyable for both of us, but I think Petra got more out of the long close cuddle we had before falling asleep.

Unlike her confidant, street-wise sister Claudia, Petra seemed vulnerable and lonely out in the big wide world for the first time.

Next morning, it wasn't long before Rupert came over for a chat as we pottered away in the fields.

"Did Petra sleep with you last night?" he asked in a friendly manner.

"Yeah. She was upset about you taking the piss," I replied.

"What? Was she on about Blue Peter? Germans have got no sense of humour."

"She's a sensitive girl. She needs love and affection."

"She's too clingy," retorted Rupert.

"She thinks a lot of you" I said finally, as we went back to emptying buckets.

From then on, Petra divided her nights between Rupert and myself. On some occasions she even went to both tents, before going to sleep. I never questioned Petra about it, while Rupert and I deliberately avoided talking about the German girl's love life.

One of the most amusing moments of the harvest

came one day when Marlene and Helen were chattering away in Dutch, while filing their buckets with grapes. It concerned Rupert, who had a name that the Dutch girls had never heard before.

"Shall we call you 'Rupert', 'Rupe' or 'Ru'? they asked.

"Oh, Rupe will do," replied Rupert, as he wandered away, after changing the full buckets.

From then on, Rupert was known as 'Rupelldo', first by the Dutch and then by everyone else.

On the second Sunday, I decided to take a run out on the 500. Petra said she would come too. We went to the Gorge du Verdun, the 'Grand Canyon' of Europe. It was about an hour's ride north of Vidauban. We left at about half past ten, after coffee and croissants with the others, in Bar Tabac. First stop was at the shore of the Lac de Ste Croix, where the river Verdun came out of the gorge into the lake. It was spectacular country, in the late summer sunshine. As we sat on the gravel beach, watching the hang-gliders high above us. Petra rolled a joint with the dope she had scored in town. Not being a smoker myself, Petra had it all to herself and promptly got as high as the hang-gliders. We left the lakeside road to take the single track lane that climbed to the top of the gorge and ran along the edge of the south-facing cliffs. Petra was well out of it. I could see I had trouble, as I glanced down at our shadows on the road.

My passenger was sitting on the luggage rack, leaning back with her arms outstretched. The 500cc trail bike was prone to wheelies at the best of times, but going uphill with so much weight over the back wheel made it nearly impossible. I had to lean forward, over the petrol tank, with the peak of my helmet nearly touching the speedometer, to keep the front wheel down. Taking it very steady, we managed to arrive safely at the half-way point round the gorge where the road crosses from the north bank to the south, at the Pont d'Artbury  Here we stopped, to have a beer at the roadside café. Afterwards, I wandered out across the bridge and looked down on the small stream, some 200 feet below – that was the main tributary to the lake. Petra had rolled another joint by the time she joined me in the middle of the bridge. Without a word, she climbed onto the three foot high, nine inch wide safety wall and started walking back to the bike at the end of the bridge. Quickly, I walked ahead of Petra, not wanting to know what was happening. I sat on the bike, looking away. Just as I thought I had better turn round, Petra climbed on the pillion behind me. I kicked the engine into life and we made straight back to the farm, with Petra holding tight around my waist for the whole journey.

Should I have told Petra to get down? Should I have told her what an idiot she was? Was she testing me, or just testing herself? Petra was not showing off, as there was no one else there at the time. Did I take the easy option by not wanting to know, or would my watching have made things worse? Petra and I never discussed it.

Half-way through the next week, Paddy rolled his Volkswagen on the way back from the supermarket in the evening. No one was hurt, but the car was a write-off. It was lucky that there was only four in the car at the time. Normally, twice that many crammed into the estate for the trip into town and it was not unusual to have two people sitting on top with their feet through the sun roof. The car still ran after the crash, but was in such a state that Paddy only took it down the lanes to the outskirts of town and walked the rest of the way.

At the end of the week, Rupert had done enough hard work for his liking and decided to take off with Petra to Paris. The couple drew their money on the Friday night, planning to catch the lunchtime train from Les Arcs on the Saturday. Everyone went into town for a farewell drink, sad to see them go, so they stayed in the bar until evening. But inside a week the pair had spent out: Rupert went to London, while Petra hitchhiked back to Vidauban to ask for her job back. Claudia was really pleased to see her.

Meanwhile, Rob, who knew a bit about car electrics, was spending all his spare time fixing Speedy's Renault van. He borrowed my Haynes manual for the 500 to help him wire up the car like a battery-less motorbike, using the diagrams in the back of the book To everyone's amazement, Rob got the van to go again, but it had no lights or indicators and the battery would not charge when the engine was running. These little problems didn't bother Speedy who, with Rob and Irish Danny, began to make plans to drive down to Morocco when the work had finished.

If anybody ever asked to borrow the 500, I always let them have it – on the condition that they could start the engine with no help from me.  The reason for this was because if someone was going somewhere, I wanted them to be able to get back.  As the single cylinder 500cc engine only had a kick-start, there were few borrowers. The high compression engine had no valve lifter, so there was a definite knack in getting it to fire up.  Only Speedy, who had plenty of experience with old British bikes, never found starting a problem.  He often used the bike to run up to Le Luc, the next town along the RN7.

These frequent trips were made in the evenings, when Speedy went to buy drugs for the rest of the crew. On his way back one night, he hit a patch of gravel on the last corner before the farm.  In a valiant attempt to avoid doing damage to the bike, he kept his leg under the machine as he slid off.  Speedy lost all the skin off his right knee, incurred severe gravel rash to his right arm and shoulder, while burning his left leg on the hot exhaust pipe.  The bike was completely unharmed.  Heroically, Speedy pushed the bike back to the farm, unaided, with his knee a mass of blood and grit.   Luckily the son of Monsieur Cordier, the patron, had done some medical training in the French army, so he was able to clean up the wound and dress it.  Speedy rested for two days, but was back at work on the third, saying he was bored sitting alone up at the farm all day.  It was too soon to make a come back, as all the leg bending hindered the healing. His knee was still in a mess when all the grapes had been picked. The work went on into a fifth week, as more and more time was lost to bad weather.

The days became shorter and the nights cooler. Petra and I packed up our tent in order to move into a bus, as the cold and wet kept us awake at night. Paddy bought an old VW van from a local quarry, with the intention of importing it into the UK. It was a good, strong vehicle and just the thing for living in when touring Europe.

When the work finally ended, Francis was happy enough with our performance to invite us all back again next year. Everyone exchanged addresses and telephone numbers, while agreeing to meet on the beach, before doing it all again. With all our hard-earned wages, we went out separate ways: Billy and Vicky caught the train to Barcelona; Speedy, Rob and Irish Danny set off for Morocco in the Renault 4; Marlene and Helen, the Dutch girls, took their boyfriends back to Holland; while Paddy had a van-load of passengers going back to England via Marianne's farm in the Dordogne. Petra wanted me to take her to Greece on the bike, but I said the 500 wasn't made for two-up touring, so I left her to go back to Karlsruhe with her sister.

It was the middle of October when I got home, having spent three days riding and two nights in smart hotels that I would never had patronised if I did not have a pocket full of money.

## Chapter Three

The first thing I did when I got back to the UK was to buy a Volkswagen van. It was a 'nearly-new', white, windowless panel van with a two litre, air-cooled engine. I gave a lot of thought to the interior design and finally chose a 'do-it-yourself' kit from the Reading-based Richard Holdsworth Company. The kit consisted of: a bench seat that folded flat to form a double bed; a plywood unit which contained a sink, double gas burner with grill, along with two cupboards underneath. Also, there was a wardrobe that had a fold-out, rear-facing seat attached to it; a single legged table that fitted in a socket sunk in the floor and all the foam cushions, complete with their check dralon covers. For in-car entertainment, I fitted a Pioneer radio cassette with 120 watt amplifier, hooked up to a pair of aluminium bodied cabinet speakers that were only just capable of handling the power. The walls, floor and ceiling were all covered in the same tan-coloured carpet, a short pile, waterproof product with a rubber backing – primarily used in kitchens and bathrooms. The whole lot was put together in less than a week. The Holdsworth equipment was a good quality and fitted perfectly, as well as saving me a lot of time. For a test run and to try everything out, I telephoned Kate in Scotland, to arrange a visit on the next weekend.

Kate seemed keen on the van and quickly organised a tour of some of her old school friends, scattered around the country. We visited places as varied as Drumchapel and Inverness.

Drumchapel, the over-spill new-town, reputedly the hardest place in Scotland, where I couldn't understand a word anybody said; Inverness, a traditional Scottish town where English is spoken better than in England. Autumn was a great time to be in Scotland. The colours of the scenery in the highlands were at their best, with the constantly changing cloud formations reflecting on to the surfaces of the lochs. Loch Ness was particularly impressive, with castle ruins on its shore; it was hard not to keep looking across the legendary water whilst driving alongside.

Kate made no secret of the fact that she was using my visit as a chance to see some of her friends. The poor student had no car of her own and very little money. I didn't mind being a chauffeur, as everyone we met was very hospitable and a guided tour was better than being alone. Of course, sleeping with Kate again was what I had really come for. There was a vast difference from the warmth of the south of France, but with two sleeping bags and an assortment of blankets, things were warm and cosy – just as enjoyable as the summer. It was term time at the university, so Kate had to be back in Glasgow on Monday afternoon for a lecture. This cut short the touring, but I stayed another night at her flat, just off Sauchiehall Street, before I made my way back south to look for a job.

Although newspapers and job centres are good ways to find truck-driving jobs, I have always found the best way to get work is to drive round the haulage yards and knock on doors.  If you look like a professional driver, they tend to remember you, even if they haven't got anything for you at the time.   This method paid off on this occasion, when I met a guy who I had worked with several years before.  He was now working in the office as a transport manager for another company.  We had been talking for ages when Ivan Merrick came in to discuss the purchase of a company vehicle.  I knew Ivan from when we had both competed in motorcycle trials in the late '70s.

"You was on for Bartrums last time I saw you.  What are you up to these days?" asked Ivan, in his usual friendly manner.

"Not a lot.  I've been working over in France.  Just got back and I'm going round looking for work," I replied.

"I didn't know you had Continental experience.  I'm looking for a driver to do weekly Germans for me – are you interested?" enquired Ivan.

"Yeah.  I'm probably just the man you're looking for," I said, omitting to say that my international driving had been done on a tractor.

"Well, I'm supposed to be taking one out on Sunday afternoon.  If you could do it, that would let me catch up on all the damn paperwork.  What do you say?"

"Sure.  No worries," I said casually.

"Okay then. Meet me in the Routemaster truck park. Midday Sunday and you can take it from there," said Ivan, with the air of a man who had just got lucky.

I prepared for my maiden voyage the best I could. I bought the best road atlas of Europe that I could find; food and clothes for a week were assembled, with my tools, sleeping bag and other bits and pieces. Ivan volunteered to look after the van while I was away. I promised to look after his truck. The boat left Felixstowe at 4.00 o'clock and I had just enough time to get the cab organised before my departure. What I wasn't prepared for was the five hour crossing in rough seas – I was violently seasick several times. All my time was spent either in the toilet or on my bunk. This was time I had planned to utilise by talking to other drivers about Customs' procedures and which was the best route to take. Ideally, I hoped somebody was going my way and that I could tag along. Almost every other driver had the same travel sickness problem as me. Anyone not in their cabin seemed to be on their way to the toilet and definitely on receptive to the approaches of an ignorant 'first-timer'. When I drove off the ferry at Zeebrugge, on a windy Belgian evening, I felt terrible and had no idea what to do. At the end of a long row of trucks, I parked on the quayside and went straight to bed.

When morning came, I felt a lot better. I muddled my way through the Customs' paperwork, while concentrating hard on what was done to what and by whom. Next time, I did not want to look such an idiot.

The driving on the wrong side of the road had never been a problem for me, so the three and a half hours it took to cross Belgium on the motorways came as a welcome relief before I came to the German border at Aachen and had to tackle the whole Customs' paperwork nightmare again. A Dutch driver who, like most of his countrymen, spoke fluent English and German, helped me through the maze of forms, permits, tank scheins and carnets. It was then that I realised the best way to tackle the situation was to tell someone that it was my first time and to ask them to show me what to do. Conning Ivan Merrick into thinking I knew what I was doing was alright, as it got me the job that I had always dreamed about, but now I was only fooling myself. After Aachen, I always adopted the "Can you help me, please?" technique, but never forgot my first time at a fresh border and tried to help other drivers, even if they never asked.

This first trailer load of exports had three consignments: one for delivery in Nuremberg and two for Munich. The biggest foreseeable problem seemed to be in finding the location of the delivery addresses. So I decided to invest in street maps of the two cities, which I was able to buy from an autobahn service area. With the help of the maps I had made all three deliveries by Tuesday afternoon and had telephoned Ivan in England to find out the re-load address for the goods to take back. A load of fridge-freezers was waiting for me at Bingen. So I drove over on the Tuesday evening, in order to be at the factory for first thing Wednesday morning. Three men with sack barrows filled up the trailer in less than half an hour so, with a more confident approach to border crossing, I was back at Zeebrugge to catch the night's boat to Felixstowe. The ferry docked first thing in the morning and after clearing Customs, the agent telephoned the delivery warehouse at Watford to arrange for unloading that afternoon. When I called Ivan that night, he seemed very impressed with the way things had gone.

"You done that quicker than I could have done it," remarked Ivan.

"Yeah, not bad trip. No problems really," I lied.

Little did he know of the stress and anxiety I had suffered, not to mention physical discomfort. He went on to give me a loading address for Friday, saying the truck would be booked to ship out on the Sunday afternoon to Zeebrugge.

The weekly trips to Germany continued up to Christmas and into the New Year. The paperwork became easier, as I learned the border checks off by heart. I got used to the boat crossings, where I saw the same faces every week, doing similar runs to mine. On one re-load, I went to collect a load of rocket sticks for Standard Fireworks, from a wood yard in the hills, east of Regensburg. I took the chance to go into town and see how Steffi and the others were getting on. Steffi had finished with Roger, but was pleased to see me. We went out for a meal and talked about the summer. She dropped me off afterwards, back at the truck, where she gave me a big goodbye kiss, right in front of two German drivers, parked nearby.   As Steffi drove away, one of them shouted something I did not understand.  It could have been either a friendly "You're a lucky bastard" or a confrontational "Leave our girls alone" but, whatever it was, I just shrugged my shoulders as I unlocked the cab door. They laughed, and said something else – this time, with a smile.

Ivan Merrick's truck was a big Fiat Vee-eight, painted red with gold and green stripes running round the middle – not the best colour scheme, if you wanted to pass unhindered through British Customs, but it had a 350 horsepower engine, which was more than enough to cope with 32 tonnes. It was ultra reliable, but the big 18 litre motor used a lot of diesel. Ivan had plenty of work for the unit and trailer, but he had a problem getting the essential permits for travel in Germany.   This shortage always occurred to new companies trying to break into the Continental haulage market.   Ivan overcame this by borrowing permits from friendly, established companies and by purchasing forgeries from someone who lived in Southend.   The counterfeit paperwork was very good, with the correct colour paper, only the printed stamp gave the game away.   However, the Germans did not realise there was a shortage problem for English hauliers and never gave anything that I presented to them a second glance.   In January, Ivan took on trips to Switzerland.  Once again, I had new borders to cross and new procedures to master, as it seemed Switzerland was trying to discourage imports by putting unnecessary obstacles in the way of foreign truck drivers. Fortunately, Ivan arranged for me to run with one of Maritana's drivers to learn the route. Maritana was the company that sub-contracted the work to Ivan and, as they were based in Felixstowe, the arrangement worked out well. It was convenient that all the Swiss work was centred around Basle, in the north-west corner of the country. After a few weeks, I knew the run as well as I did the journey down to Bavaria. The main difference was the increased cost of living in Switzerland. A meal, followed by a few drinks in a bar afterwards, could easily cost over £48.00 per person per night.

With Basle being situated near the borders of both France and Germany, it was possible to go from Zeebrugge in Belgium via either country. The most economic route was through Luxembourg, where diesel fuel was at its cheapest in Europe. From Luxembourg to Basle, the road passed close to Karlsruhe so, on one occasion, I took the opportunity to call in and see Petra and Claudia. They were surprised to see me, but Claudia took me from the house to meet up with Petra, who was working as a barmaid on the other side of town. It was a bar frequented by lots of American soldiers based in the area. Claudia left me drinking with them while I waited for Petra to get off work at closing time. Its amazing how many Americans who you have never met before and never likely to meet again give you their complete, in-depth life story in the time it takes to drink a couple of beers. I was eventually rescued by Petra, when we went for a pizza. She told me what she had been up to since the end of the grape harvest. Petra was pretty keen on going back to the beach in the summer, but seemed pretty cool about taking up with me again. I got the impression she thought I was a bit boring, not doing drugs and getting drunk every night – Petra was looking for more adventure. After our meal, a taxi dropped me off back at the truck, before going on to take Petra home. Although I passed Karlsruhe several times again that winter, I never stopped again.

## Chapter Four

In February, Kate took a week off from her French and Fine Art studies at Glasgow University, to catch the train south. We met at the station on the Saturday morning, before I took her to my parents' home, where I was living at the time. My Mum and Dad ran a shop in the town. They were at work, so in no time, Kate and I were in the bath together, with far too much water and an extravagant amount of bubble bath. The floor was flooded as we did it every way that a bath tub will allow.

"Go on. Push it up my bum. It'll be nice and tight for you," said Kate, as she knelt in front of me.

Kate didn't seem to mind at all and had obviously done it like that before. She never ceased to amaze me with her enlightened attitude and insatiable appetite for sex. Kate taught me a lot more than any other woman I had met before. After the bath, we finished up in bed for the rest of the afternoon, only just managing to get downstairs, in front of the television, before my parents came home.

Next morning, we set off for Switzerland, where we disastrously ran out of diesel before we got on the boat. Luckily, a truck belonging to Carter's of Woodbridge stopped to help. The driver went back to his depot to fetch five gallons of fuel in a drum. He wouldn't take any money for the diesel and we would have missed the boat without him helping out. I told him I owed him one. Kate took the diesel problem, the docks, the ferry crossing and the whole truck-driving experience in her stride. She was not the least overawed or excited by any of it. The student had brought along a copy of Tolstoy's "War and Peace" to read. Kate spent most of the time I was driving with her head in her book. She didn't look out of the window, was not bothered whereabouts we were or how far we had to go. It seemed to me, Kate only came on the trip so that she could go back to her mates in Scotland and tell them she had been to Switzerland and back in a truck.

Kate did enjoy herself more in Basle, particularly when we parked up for the night near to another British truck, which contained the driver and a barmaid from one of the pubs in Dover. We all went out together for a meal in the town of Muttenz. The restaurant served good food and we all drank plenty of beer. All four of us ended up completely drunk – it cost a fortune. The next day, I still had a couple of deliveries to do, as well as two collections for export to the UK. I had an almighty hangover, while Kate felt much the same, although she was able to spend the whole morning crashed out on the bottom bunk, while I drove around. The last pick-up point was in a small village, just outside Basle, where I had to back into a narrow gateway. It was a busy street and the opening was on my blind side, so I asked Kate to get out, in order to watch me reverse without hitting anything. Reluctantly, she agreed to get out, only to promptly disappear from view. Traffic began queuing up both ways along the street, as the truck straddled both lanes. I couldn't see Kate, or where the back of the trailer was positioned, so I had to get out and have a look. Kate was looking in the window of a nearby chocolate shop.

"I thought you were going to watch me back in," I said.

"It's embarrassing," answered Kate, not even looking away from the window.

Astounded, I got back into the cab and drove off up the road, leaving her admiring the confectionery. The idea was to turn round, so that I could come back with the gateway on my offside, which made it easier for me to reverse into the opening, as I could see where I was going. While I was turning round in a handy lay-by, I thought I would teach Kate a lesson for her unhelpful behaviour. I sat there for ten minutes. The time it took to read three pages of "War and Peace", before I returned to the village and backed into the gateway, first time. Kate was still looking in shop windows, but by the time I had finished loading, she had got back into the cab.

"Have you moved my book mark?" she asked.

"No, I haven't," I lied.

Kate went straight back to Scotland after the trip with only vague plans being made to meet up again on the beach, sometime during the summer. It was a strange relationship that seemed to work well when we were together, but there was no desperate urge from either of us to see more of each other. We both saw others between times and both never bothered about it.

The one girl I did see a lot of that winter was Candy. Her mother was a regular at Chelmsford's Country and Western Club. Candy had recently broken up with her long-term boyfriend and her mum was trying to cheer her up by taking her out on a Friday night. Country and Western was not Candy's sort of music, but she liked the club atmosphere where she found she was mixing with men for the first time – at discos she only ever met boys. The night we met, I was with Ben, an old friend and drinking partner. We both drank Bacardi: Ben's with coke, mine mixed with lemonade – that way we never got them mixed up. The drink count was well into double figures when we went through to the club. The place was packed, everybody was in town to see George Moody and the Country Squires. Ben knew Candy's mum from before he knew me and soon all four of us were wedged into the corner, at the far end of the bar; handy for drinks, but with no chance of getting on the dance floor. This didn't seem to bother Ben who, at the first slow dance, was smooching. I just managed to put my glass down before I was in Candy's arms. By the end of the number, her tongue was further down my throat than any tongue had ever gone before. I was well on the way to being very drunk indeed. Candy, who was also drinking Bacardi, did not need as much to make herself noticeably tipsy. Violet, Candy's mum, didn't want to be left out, so she changed to white rum.  With a round of four shorts, it seemed we began to drink even faster.

At the end of the night, everything was a blur.  Candy and I staggered out into the street as everyone came piling out of the club, shouting, firing Colt 45s and tumbling off the pavement as they tried to cross the road.  I remember Candy getting into a taxi with her mum, before spending ages looking in her handbag for a pen and paper so that she could give me her 'phone number, then she was gone. Ben was discussing with some other drinkers whether we should go for an Indian or a Chinese, when the barmaid came out of the club to give me the bottle of Champagne cider I had won in the raffle and had left on the bar.  In the Chinese restaurant, I had an omelette and chips, as always.  Halfway back to the truck park, our waiter came running down the road with my bottle of cider, which I had stood down by my chair.  Back at the truck, I stood the bottle on the diesel tank, while I had a pee.  When I got up in the morning to have another one, it was still there.  I put it in the cab, even though I don't like cider.  I gave it to my Dad when I got home.

At 6.00 o'clock, Saturday evening, I rang Candy's number, figuring it was probably the best time of the week if you wanted to catch anyone at home.  We talked for ages, in which time, Candy easily persuaded me to drive over to her place that night.  The directions for a small village in the wilds of north Essex were a bit vague, but I threw a few things into the van, in case I had a few too many to drink, and set off for an unexpected date.

Thinking that I was a married man looking for a bit on the side, Candy was suspicious of me at first, so she had arranged for us to go down the village pub with her mum and her brother. Possibly not the ideal first date, but they were all good fun, as we played darts and pool, while drinking plenty more Bacardis. At 11.20 p.m. we all staggered, drunk for the second night running, back to the house for coffee.

When we were left alone on the sofa, things soon got very steamy. Candy was so passionate and loved to kiss. In no time we were all over each other with every piece of clothing undone. I was so horny, I was seriously thinking of having her there and then on the hearthrug. I am sure Candy was up for it, but we were stopped when her younger sister came in from her Saturday night out. I suggested that we go out to the van, which was in the car park at the end of the terraced council houses. Candy was a bit reluctant, but when I told her it was kitted out as a camper, with a big bed, she agreed to take a look.

"Okay, but just for a few minutes."

The clear moonlit sky meant it was a freezing cold night, with everything covered in frost, but Candy and I generated so much heat by rubbing our bodies together under the covers, we never felt the wintry weather. It was so cosy that a few minutes turned into all night. We were still asleep when someone knocked on the van door in the morning. I had a vision of Candy's mum standing outside in her dressing gown, with her arms folded. I expected to hear her bellow "Have you got my daughter in there?" Incredibly, it was Candy's sister with toast, coffee and a big smile on her face. Suddenly, it was 11.00 o'clock in the morning and I was booked on the 1600 sailing out of Felixstowe.

I made the boat in time. I made the trip down the Essex country lanes a lot more times as well. If I was not going to be at Chelmsford on a Friday in the truck, I would go over in the van. Candy often stayed overnight, as I parked the little Volkswagen in amongst the trucks. We spent our Saturdays shopping together in town. It was impossible to make it every week, but the love-making with Candy was so good, I made it if I could. One Saturday night, we went over to Ipswich for the engagement party of a work-mate. Candy looked great that night. It was the only time I ever saw her in a dress, as she always wore jeans. It was red, with an asymmetrical hem and two thin straps holding it over her shoulders. I couldn't wait to get her home that night. Candy couldn't wait either. We only made it as far as the truck park in Chelmsford, where we were the only vehicle on a Saturday night out. Candy was amazing that night. It was 3.00 o'clock in the afternoon when we went for breakfast at a Little Chef. Luckily, I had not been able to load up on the Friday, so was not booked on a ferry.

A couple of weeks later, all of a sudden, things went wrong between Candy and myself. We had been together all night at the Country and Western, but when we came out, Candy and I became separated in the usual mass of merry music fans. I did not know then, that Candy had been seeing the landlord's brother and had gone upstairs in the pub. As I stood waiting for her, I started talking to Candy's friend called Jenny. After waiting a while, we eventually walked off down the road together, in the direction of the van. Like every Friday night, I was drunk, but can remember a goodnight kiss turning into a full blown snog up against the side of the van. It was one of those situations when not a word was said. Jenny and I soon went from against the side of the van to inside the van and on the bed. She was wearing stockings and suspenders, with matching bra and panties in Burgundy red. When Jenny took off her black dress my eyes nearly popped out of my head. The whole encounter was based on lust. A feeding frenzy of a sixty-nine was followed by me taking Jenny from behind. When I came, I collapsed down beside her and fell asleep almost immediately.

I never did find out if Candy had asked Jenny to look after me when she went with the guy at the pub, or whether Jenny went with me just to be spiteful to Candy. We never went out together again. Jenny made me angry, not only because of what she did to split up Candy and me, but when she got up and left, sometime during that night, she left the side door of the van open.

Nothing was taken, but when I woke up, freezing cold, it was 10.00 o'clock in the morning and I was surrounded by cars whose occupants must have all looked in to see me crashed out, naked on the bed.

It was springtime now. Ivan sent me off to Italy, while he went down to Baghdad with his other truck. He left me half a dozen Italian and French permits, while arranging for his sister, Elaine, to see to the running of the money and wages. The permit shortage for Italian trips was even more acute than for German. The normal practice was for drivers to bung the Italian frontier officials 30,000 lira, not to have their paperwork stamped, so that they could use it week after week. With the second-rate forgeries I had been given, I had to give a bribe of 30,000 just to get mine stamped.

The Italian trips were certainly a challenge. It was a long drive down to Milan that sometimes had to be completed in one day. The climb up to the Mont Blanc tunnel and down the other side to Aosta, called for concentration together with skill. Finding your way about in cities such as Milan and Turin was not easy. Also, Customs clearance never took less than half a day, but at least that gave you a chance to get some rest. There was always the risk of having your load stolen, or the cab broken into. On my first night in Milan, the German truck parked next to me had his tilt slit and half his load of video recorders vanished into thin air. I was glad I was only carrying 18 tonnes of shampoo. About the only good thing on the Italian run was the food: excellent grub at the routier stops in France, along with cheap and plentiful meals at the restaurants near the Italian Customs' clearance compounds.

As the weather warmed up and the days lengthened,

I was faced with the dilemma of staying at work or heading off to the beach. Did I remain doing a job I liked and had always wanted? Or did I go off to the south of France and use the van for what it was intended? Although I didn't toss a coin, it was that close. I chose the beach. There was enough money in my bank account to see me through until the grape picking. Now I was an experienced, international truck driver, I did not envisage having any problems getting work in the autumn.

# Chapter Five

On the 1st June, I loaded up the van, put my windsurfer on the roof and headed down to Dover. In France, I only used the sections of autoroute that I knew were toll-free. Taking it easy, I made it to the beach by the evening of the third day. At Aix-en-Provence, I picked up a Dutch hitch-hiker who appreciated the ride right down to the coast. He then spent his whole two week holiday sleeping on the beach for what he reckoned was the best time of his life.

The first person I went to see was Tarzan. He had spent the whole winter living on the beach as the caretaker of Club Tropicana and L'Esquinade private beach clubs. There wasn't any pay to go with the job, but it gave him rent-free lodgings; also, it guaranteed Tarzan the job of plagiste during the summer. This year, he was back working at L'Esquinade.

I took round a duty free bottle of Blue Label Smirnoff. Tarzan supplied the glasses, the ice and a jug of fresh orange juice. We finished the bottle that night, as Tarzan told me of his winter and all the reading he had done. He recommended that I read Nitzsche, offering to lend me his copies. The books were in English, which was not Tarzan's first language, so it must have been heavy going. Tarzan also kept himself fit through the winter months, but from the way he talked non-stop, there could not have been many people around for him to chat with. When the vodka bottle was empty, it seemed as if I had told Tarzan nothing of my travels.

The next day I met the people sleeping on the beach – the same place as the year before, but with different faces and all speaking with Irish accents.

"Do any of you guys know Billy Carroll?" I asked.

It was like knowing a secret password as they all began to treat me as a long lost friend, asking questions about selling drinks and picking grapes. There and then, I envisaged how Billy Carroll must have returned to Ireland and held court in the pubs of Dublin, telling tales of beaches paved in gold and grape picking with unlimited free booze. Billy's stories had fired the unemployed imaginations of a whole generation of young Dubliners who all seemed to come from large families where prospects were grim. The problem was, all the lads were so broke, they did not have enough money between them to buy an ice box, the ice and the drinks to get started as beach sellers. They were only surviving by thieving, shoplifting from the supermarkets, taking vegetables from fields and stealing wine from tents on the campsite. This way of life was fraught with danger. Two guys were beaten up by supermarket security guards after being caught eating Mars Bars in the store. A farmer chased them down the road with a six foot length of wood sticking out the side of his pick-up truck. Everyone had to dive into a ditch to avoid being wiped out. Even nicking a five litre bottle of white wine from outside a tent did not work out as planned, for when the lads got it back to the beach they found it was full of sea water.

The robbing of the empty gas cannister cage at the supermarket also failed to yield any financial gain. When two Camping Gaz bottles were taken to the shop in the morning, the Dubliners found that they could only be exchanged for full bottles and not for cash as they had hoped. For a while after that there were half a dozen empty gas bottles lying in a ditch beside the road to the beach. I took one to have as a spare in the van and five other camping cars soon did the same. I was a bit worried about my stuff in the van, so it was a relief when Danny Oakes turned up. Irish Danny took to cooking for everybody, on the stove in the van, while making sure the others treated my things with respect.

Danny was a hero to all the Dublin boys as he had been and done it all before. He compounded his status by telling colourful stories of how he, Speedy and Rob went to Morocco in a beat-up Renault 4. The old TV rental van had done remarkably well with its re-built electrics. No lights meant that they could not drive at night, but they overcame the eventuality of a flat battery by swapping them with other cars' - of course, this was done without the consent of the owner. Danny even told of occasions when the donor car owner had returned to find their vehicle had a dead battery, while the van was still parked nearby. Speedy always took great delight in helping to push start the disabled car. Danny didn't know if it was because Speedy felt guilty, or he just enjoyed foreigners thanking him so profusely. Speedy once talked the other two into having a drink, seated outside a café, just to be on hand when a distressed motorist needed them. The three adventurers left the van in Algercias when they caught the ferry to North Africa, but when they came back, two weeks later, it had gone.

A few days after Danny, Claudia from Karlsruhe returned to the beach, where she took up with the Dutch hitch-hiker before he went home. After that, Claudia moved into the van, where she made a point of doing all the washing-up and keeping everything spotless. I was concentrating on my wind-surfing, after telling everyone there was not enough people on the beach to warrant any drink selling. Claudia came and went as she pleased, both day and night. We had only made love a couple of time in a week before she told me I was boring and moved out to share a sleeping bag with Big Mick Cummings.

Big Mick was from Dublin and had been a resident on the beach before I arrived, but had gone back to Ireland to pick up a cheque for £5,000 which was compensation for injuries he had suffered in a motor-cycle accident. Along with Liam McNally, Big Mick had returned with three and a half grand, intending to spend the cash making sure everyone had a good time. He was an answered prayer to his penniless countrymen, which took a lot of the responsibility of providing for them off my shoulders. Big Mick bought endless jugs of wine from the local Co-operative – all the Irish were drunk all the time. Claudia soon tired of this and when Rupert arrived from England in Paddy's Volkswagen van, she moved in with him. It had been another winter in which Rupert had failed to make any contribution to the coffers of the Chancellor. This time the odd days of decorating had been supplemented with income earned by using the VW for light haulage. For the second year running, I found it remarkable that Rupert could be such a buoyant mood when he reflected on such barren times.

In the same week as Rupert returned to the beach, I had some bad luck when I went shopping in Ramatuelle. I returned to the van to find it had been broken into. Amongst other things, the stereo speakers had been stolen. It was totally unexpected, as I thought that I was mixing with the dregs of society. I did not think anybody would steal from me because they all thought I was out to take from them. Being at the bottom of the social standing ladder has the advantage that you can be carefree as you have nothing to loose, but I had not realised that I was now a few rungs higher than the year before and now a target of opportunists. With a piece of wood in place of the broken quarter-light, I hoped villains would see it and think that everything had already been stolen. When I couldn't play the Irish boys U2 tapes any more, I didn't see much of them in the evenings as they got stuck into spending Big Mick's money.

To finance a new pair of speakers, I went back to

selling cold drinks. My music now came from the two discotheques: Club des Bronzes on the beach and the bar behind the campsite supermarket. It was here that I met Laurence: dressed in white jeans and dark red polo; she was slim, tall, with short blonde hair, cut in a neat layered style. Laurence looked like a boy. At first, when she kept looking at me, I wondered if she was. But the way she smiled across the dance floor led me to conclude she was a girl. When we moved closer together, Laurence spoke to me in German, thinking it was my native tongue. This made me think that she was German. Quite a bit of confusion followed, before we both spoke English, and I found out Laurence was French. My new dance partner was camping with a group of friends who turned out to be members of the Versaille ladies basketball team - some were French international players. I thought some of them had bought cold drinks from me on the beach, but I didn't remember Laurence buying one. We talked about wind-surfing. I offered to loan my board to Laurence so that she could look after it while I was selling my drinks. The basketball players already had one windsurfer between them, with the use of mine, they could now hold races. I had hoped to go for a sail, as a break from selling, but found the competitive sportswomen were always somewhere out at sea with my board.

Laurence and I met every night to dance or to go to Ramatuelle, but at the end of the evening I never got more than a peck on the cheek. I discussed the situation with Rupert.

"It's obvious, she's a lesbian, isn't it?"

"How do you know?" I enquired.

"Women's team games, always lesbians. Well known fact – especially the French," stated Rupert.

The next night, after the disco, we drove up to Ramatuelle. In the car park above the village, I made a pot of coffee as we sat looking out over the Med and the circling light of Cap Camarat. I put my arm round Laurence and tried to kiss her. She pulled away, turning to face me as she wriggled free.

"What's wrong?" I asked.

"I don't want to do that," said Laurence firmly.

"Maybe you prefer girls," I said, looking the other way.

"Maybe. Why do you say that?" asked Laurence.

"It's just that I find you very attractive, I want to be close to you," I replied, while turning my head to make eye contact.

There was a long pause in the conversation in which, I hoped, Laurence would admire my forthright honesty and throw herself across the front seats in order to smother me with kisses. It did not happen.

"Can I drive the camping car back to the campsite? I have never driven from the right side before," asked Laurence, finally.

"Sure you can," I conceded.

I gave up any hope of bedding Laurence after that night, but still danced with her at the discos; we even raced each other on the windsurfers.

Veronique, the beekeeper, returned to the beach during this time, which eased my frustration. It was the same as the year before: no drinks or talking together, just going off somewhere to make love, not in the mattress shed this year, but in the van. It was whilst making love to Vero one night that I sensed someone was watching. I looked up to see Laurence leaning in the half-opened side door of the van. She just stood there, looking at us. I stopped what I was doing, but Laurence still stood there, saying nothing.

"Can you give us five minutes?" I asked.

Laurence casually raised her left hand with five outstretched fingers, gave a little wave and left.

"Do you think she wanted to join us?" asked Vero. I was too gob-smacked to answer.

When Laurence flew back to Paris from Toulon, she asked me to drive her to the airport. I agreed. So, to say thank you, on her last night, Laurence took me to one of the open air restaurants in Ramatuelle. She wore a bright yellow number; it was the first time I had seen Laurence in a dress. She looked stunning with her blonde hair and dark brown tan. I wore my best clothes: that was, my cleanest clothes. It was good French cuisine, with a complimentary liqueur at the end of the meal, when the patron told us what a perfect couple we seemed to be.

"All the world expects the normal boy-girl relationship – they know nothing," said Laurence angrily.

"They see a man and a woman enjoying themselves – what are they supposed to think? I said.

"But on that first night, did you think I was a boy or a girl?" asked Laurence.

"I didn't think about it. I just saw you and felt an attraction," I answered, trying to appear sophisticated.

"And the girl the other night?" continued Laurence.

"I know her from last year. She just comes to me for sex."

"She must have a very open relationship with her boyfriend."

"What boyfriend?" I enquired.
"They are near us on the camping. He has been

going with Dominique," replied Laurence.

"Oh, that boyfriend," I said, trying hard not to seem bewildered. We had another glass of liqueur.

"Why do you go with me if you know we will not have sex?" asked Laurence, as the alcohol loosened her tongue.

"Sex is not everything. It's good just to be your friend. It has been fun," I lied, as Laurence sat there, looking a million dollars and all I wanted to do was get in her knickers.

"It has been good to be with you, too. It has stopped the others making a pass at me. I promised my girlfriend that I would be faithful. You are a good friend."

"I'm glad to have been of assistance. That's what friends are for," I said without a trace of sarcasm.

Laurence pulled some paper and a pen from her bag in order to scribble down her address. After she handed me the paper, Laurence came out with a photograph of her and the girlfriend, with her long dark hair, she contrasted well with the blonde sitting opposite me. Both were wearing top hats and tails: Laurence in trousers, her friend in fishnet tights. They both carried canes. It was a stunning photograph.

"If I had a dollar for all the lips I should have kissed,

If I had dancing lessons for all the chances I have missed
I'd be a millionaire
I'd be Fred Astaire." I quoted.

"Your poetry?" asked Laurence.

"No. Martin Fry of ABC."

"I like it. Please write it down on the back of the photograph."

If there had been some loudspeakers in the van, I would have dug out my "Lexicon of Love" cassette and played it to Laurence on the way back down to the campsite. The next morning, after I had dropped my passenger off at the airport, I went into Toulon and bought a new pair of speakers.

A couple of days later, it was Bastille Day, 14 July: the start of a six week period when most of France took their holidays. In the evening, I took a van-load up to Ramatuelle from the beach. Later, Rupert brought up another van-load, after stopping at the local wine co-operative so that Big Mick could buy enough wine to get everyone plastered. I had gone off the local red, which was always too warm and left my mouth unfit for human consumption on the morning after. My liquid refreshment for the evening was a bottle of vodka, mixed one-to-one with bitter lemon. A band was playing on the stage in the village square. Everyone drank and danced, as the whole village turned out for the party. I was drinking from my litre bottle of bitter lemon when Vero turned up. In no time at all we had swigged down the whole bottle. We then went back to the van in the top car park, via the passage with the 76 step climb. Halfway up, Vero and I stopped to kiss, with her one step higher, we were face-to-face, two steps higher and my head nestled between her breasts. I undid the buttons on Vero's long flowing summer dress, slid it back off her shoulders and smothered her with kisses. Then I pulled up the back of the dress, cupping my hands around the cheeks of her bum to find that Vero was wearing no underwear whatsoever, top or bottom.

A middle aged couple, making their descent to the street party, stopped us making love on the staircase. I held Vero close to me as they wished us "Bon soir" and gave a knowing smile. At the top of the steps, our passion resumed: first against the side of the van, then on the bonnet of a nearby Peugeot 505 that was parked in the shadow of the street lamp.

After we had made our way back to the music, Vero matched me, swig for swig, from the second bottle of half vodka, half bitter lemon. The news that Speedy had been hit by a car, while hitching up to Ramatuelle, had just reached everyone at the dance. He had been taken to St Tropez hospital with blood pouring from a head wound, but as he was still conscious everyone decided he would be okay and carried on partying. It was only Speedy's second day back on the beach – the guy had the worst of luck.

When the alcohol was finished, Vero and I realised we couldn't match the stamina of the band, so we retired to bed, just after midnight, with the music and dancing still in full swing. We made love slowly and gently, before I thought it might be a good time to test my theory about alcohol influencing the left side of the brain – the side that governed the aptitude to speak foreign languages. I wanted to question Vero about her boyfriend.

"What does your boy friend think of me?"

"He thinks you are an animal."

"Oh yeah. What kind of animal?"

"He did not say, but I think you are a bear."

"Is he angry with me?"

"No. We agreed to take lovers on holidays."

"He is sleeping with Dominique, the basketball player, isn't he?"

"Yes. Last night my boyfriend asked me to sleep with Dominique and him."

"Was that okay with you?"

"Yes it was okay. Dominique is a very nice person."

I was still thinking of something to say to this when there was a knock on the van and Rupert opened the side door.

"Heh man, we're all ready to go back down to the beach."

"Oh Rupert, I was thinking of staying parked up here for the night," I moaned.

"What? There are 20 people waiting for a lift. They're all too scared to walk after what happened to Speedy."

"You'll have to do two trips then," I suggested.

"The hell I will," said Rupert, slamming the door, then packing everybody in his Volkswagen and doing it in one go. It was a good job it was all downhill.

## Chapter Six

There were a few days left of Vero's holiday after Bastille Day, which I spent windsurfing and selling, while spending the nights making love to the beekeeper from Gap. Selling cold drinks was easier than it had ever been. There were plenty of thirsty customers on the beach and the Irish sellers were still spending Big Mick's money, so they couldn't see the point of working. Most of the Irish spent their days at the Cannibale snack bar, which was set back in an area of sand dunes, known as the gay beach. The place was run by Doobie, a tall, skinny, mop-haired Frenchman of great intellect. He spoke four languages fluently, while serving customers and playing chess at the same time, never losing a match. He was under-achieving, but it was a long-held ambition of his to run a snack bar on the beach and he was making a big success of it as well. The Irish boys spent all day eating plates of chips and drinking cold beer, which made the Cannibale look popular. This attracted the gays and others, who soon gave Doobie so much work that he had to employ staff to cope with all the unexpected trade.

Every other evening, I made a trip into St Tropez to visit Speedy in hospital. Rupert drove in to visit on the other nights. Speedy had suffered a fractured skull in the accident when the car hit him. He had spun round and his head had gone through the windscreen. After a couple of days he was back to his chirpy self, but was told he would have to stay in bed for three weeks. Speedy had a problem in that: he had no insurance or money to pay for anything, but this did not prevent him from receiving first class treatment. There were plenty of visitors willing to travel in with either Rupert or myself, as there was usually a free coffee and a supply of clean clothing. One of the Irish boys stumbled on a laundry cupboard, while looking for the toilet and soon everyone was wearing hospital issue smock tops. These came in light blue, vee-necked with short sleeves and most importantly, clean. Nobody wore their shirt on the ward, but dumped it in a handy soiled linen bin on the way in, taking a clean one in exchange on the way out. The hospital staff never once questioned why Speedy's visitors were always bear-chested men, or girls in bikini tops. When the time came for Speedy's discharge, the hospital administration kicked up a fuss about the payment of the bill, but in the end Rupert drove round to a side door, picked up the fully recovered patient and brought him back to the beach. The hospital still had his passport, but his didn't seem to bother Speedy, as he was the sort of bloke who only took one day at a time.

During the latter days of the hospital-visiting, Sally moved into the van and became a great fan of the light blue medical wear which she wore as a very sexy mini dress. Sally was on holiday with her best mate, Hannah, who had come down to the south of France with Sally's parents for a two week stay in a caravan at Les Tournels campsite. The girls liked the beach life so much that they persuaded the mum and dad to leave them on holiday when they returned to Wales.

Both Sally and Hannah were 18 and due to go to university in the October, so had no pressing reason to go home. Another reason was that Hannah had fallen madly in love with Keith Connery, Rupert's old school friend, who was back again for another summer – this time in an old Austin Maxi. The car had expired in the car park behind the Cannibale snack bar, but such was the design of the Maxi that it provided an excellent double bed for Keith and Hannah, as well as a place to store their gear. I wondered if the main reason for Sally sleeping with me was because she wanted to match the comfort of her friend, and didn't fancy the beach, after having to give up the bunk in the caravan. However, Sally was quite affectionate and although we never had the same sort of relationship as Keith and Hannah, we had some good times, even if we were only sleeping together for convenience.

For the occupants of the camper vans, the time that you got up in the morning was usually governed by how much the sun heated up the inside of the vehicle. A normal Riviera summertime morning, you hads until about 9.00 o'clock before the temperature made it unbearable to lie inside with the doors closed. There then followed the brewing of the coffee, with discussions on the plans for the day with all the regular crew. This routine was broken one morning by Rupert bursting in at the crack of dawn. He had been in conversation with Doobie, the previous evening, and had learned of a place in the mountains where it was possible to find gold. Get-rich-quick schemes always appealed to Rupert and he had spent a sleepless night with Claudia, planning how to spend his new found wealth. Rupert was so excited, he just had to tell someone. His plan was for the two Volkswagen vans, with hand-picked crew, to take supplies into the mountains, where we would search for the gold in the riverbed of the river Verdun. It was the same place that I had taken Petra, Claudia's sister, the year before, during the grape harvest. Sally was enthusiastic, while I thought it might be good to get away from the beach for a few days.

We decided to leave that morning, after settling on a maximum number of 14, which allowed for seven in each van, and did not overload them.

It was a truly international team that we put together: Rupert with Claudia from Germany; myself with Sally from Swansea; Keith Connery with Hannah, also from Wales; Big Mick Cummings from Dublin and his English girlfriend, Julie; West Ham Mick and Helen from Holland; Davy Breitner from South Africa with Veronique, who was French; the guitarist, Danny Rudd and a Geordie, nicknamed Badger. Davy Breitner got to come because he was in on the conversation with Rupert and Doobie the previous night. Davy and Veronique worked at the Cannibale, but Doobie gave them the time off.

There were a few people who didn't get invited and were a bit upset, but when they saw that it was mostly couples, nobody complained. By 11.00 o'clock we were ready to roll. At the hypermarket outside St Tropez, we stopped for supplies.   My van bought the food:   rice, pasta, vegetables, etc.  Rupert and Big Mick just bought a vast amount of red wine and beer.

Although the vans had different registration letters: they had the same "Y" suffix and similar numbers – Rupert's 603 and mine 602;  both were white, but 603 was left-hand drive, whereas 602 was right;  603 had a side door which was nearly impossible to open - 602's side door was difficult to shut.  Rupert solved his door problem by taking it off and leaving it at the Cannibale. At the first town we passed through, 602 was stopped by the police because the side door was open.  603, with its opening on the other side, went passed untroubled, with no door on at all.  But apart from that, it was an uneventful journey to the Lac de Ste Croix.

The Volkswagens reached the lakeside in the early evening, as most of the day-trippers were leaving.  We set up camp on the north-side of the lake, a stone's throw away from where the river Verdun came out of the gorge. Most of the car park was deserted, except for a few camper vans over-nighting, under the oak trees.  It was a spectacular setting, as the crystal clear water of the lake reflected the thousand foot high cliffs that rose straight up out of its edge.   After a swim in the warm, unsalted water, there was a meal and wine at the vans, before everyone wandered onto the bridge to watch the sunset. The bridge marked the end of the gorge and the start of the lake.  The modern concrete, two lane structure stood 100 feet above the surface of the water.

Big Mick was the one who suggested jumping off the bridge and wanted to know who was going to do it with him. As an ex-army man, Big Mick had done a few parachute jumps which enabled him to give everyone some simple instructions on jumping into water from a great height: point toes, tuck in chin, arms straight against your sides. After a long debate, it was agreed to leave it until the morning as, by then, it was too dark to get a decent descent photograph.

"Are you going to jump?" asked Sally, as we lay in bed that night.

"I dunno. See what the weather is like in the morning," I said, uncertainly, as if the weather had anything to do with it.

"Keith is going to jump to show his love for Hannah. Will you jump for me?"

"Sure, no worries," I blurted, resisting the urge to add, "A jump for a jump."

Everyone had sobered up by the morning except for Badger, but the jump was still on. Straight after coffee, we all moved onto the bridge: Big Mick, Keith and myself were soon joined on the wrong side of the four foot high railings by Danny Rudd and Rupert. West Ham Mick couldn't swim; Badger could hardly stand up and Davy Breitner said he didn't do that sort of thing. Sally and Hannah took the camera and moved onto the rocks, at the side of the bridge, to get a better angle for the photograph.

"So you're doing this for the love of a woman then Keith?" I asked, as we stood holding on, with our back to the rail.

"No, I'm only doing it because you are doing it for Sally," replied Keith.

"What? I'm only doing it because of you!" I exclaimed.

"Oh no, we've been set up," we both said together.

It was too late to pull out. Big Mick ran through his instructions again.

"Go on my count of three: one, two, three," said Davy Breitner, before I stepped forward and followed instructions.

My vision was all a blur, as I was in the air for less than three seconds. The most noticeable thing was the whistling sound, like that of a kettle, caused by my passage through still air – unlike its normal occurrence, when air passes quickly through a still object. Hitting the water was painless, but my entrance speed caused me to descend a lot deeper than I expected. I stopped, without finding the bottom of the lake and had an amazing split second of complete stillness, before I felt myself rising to the surface.   Without hardly any propulsion from me, I accelerated upwards until I burst through the surface, to rise up almost clear of the water before falling back and looking up at the bridge above.  Rupert and Danny Rudd still stood on the waterside of the rail;  Big Mick and Keith were in the water beside me.   We heard Davy's count again before Rupert and Danny dropped down into the water.

"Good job I remembered I still had my wallet in my pocket," said Rupert, upon surfacing.

"Just wanted to see how you got on first," offered Danny Rudd.

"Rupert, you have not left your wallet up there with Claudia have you?" quipped Keith.

"Come on.   Let's get out of here," said Rupert urgently, and we all started the 200 metre swim to the first available exit out of the water.

It soon became obvious that we could not do any prospecting from our camp beside the bridge.  The river conditions needed for gold hunting had to be shallow water, tumbling over rocks with gravel banks at the bends.  This is where the nuggets would be found, not in the silt, many fathoms under the bridge.  We left the lake shore to take the narrow, zigzagging road that climbed to the top of the gorge, before it ran along the sunny, south facing cliffs.  Numerous dead-end roads ran down to the edge of the gorge, but they all ended at viewing platforms and picnic areas. It did not appear possible to take the vehicles down to the water's edge. Everyone was eager to get started, so as soon as a pathway was found that ran down the side of the cliff, we parked the Volkswagens and set off exploring by foot. Luckily, it was an ideal spot where the water depth was wadeable and there were numerous banks of gravel containing our fortunes. The advance party climbed back up with the good news and soon all the equipment needed for the day was taken down the path, leaving Badger, alone with his jug of wine, to look after the vans.

Nobody had done any panning for gold before. All our ideas on how it was done were based on what we had seen in old cowboy films. Our pans were the hub caps from the Volkswagens which, as hub caps go, were probably the best design of cap suitable for panning. This gave eight of the 13 a chance to work, while the others looked on in anticipation. After the hope and endeavour of the first few hours had subsided, when the easy riches were not forthcoming, it became clear who was going to stick with it and who was going to take it easy. The sun had risen in the sky, the chill of the shaded canyon floor was replaced by the burning heat of high summer. Sally and Hannah, whose holiday was coming to an end, took the opportunity to top up their tans, stripping off to stretch out on a suitable flat topped rock. Claudia and Julie soon joined them. Big Mick and Keith worked together on the same bank, while keeping a five litre jug of wine cool in a specially dug channel of cold water.  The Mick and Helen pairing, along with Davy and Veronique, seemed to be the only ones still working at their starting pace – everyone else had slowed, looking forward to a lunch break.

Even less prospecting was done after lunch; sunbathing, sleeping, exploring and drinking occupied our time.  This list would have included swimming, but the water was straight off the mountains and freezing cold, when compared to the sun-warmed shallows of the lake.  Not one single piece of gold had been found by sunset, when the hub caps went back on the van wheels.  Nobody, except Rupert, was too disappointed, as it was a beautiful place to spend a few hours;  also, with having done the bridge jump in the morning, it was a memorable day.

The next morning saw a half-hearted attempt to find some gold, but as supplies dwindled, especially the wine, it was decided to return to the beach.  Both van loads were back at the Cannibale that night, telling tales of rivers, lakes and bridges:  making everyone else feel as if they had missed out.

# Chapter Seven

Regine and Pascaline were two school teachers from Nancy who had spent a couple of weeks camping at Les Tournels in July. They were regulars at the discotheques where I got to know them well, as Pascaline went out with Eric from Amsterdam. A week after going home, Regine returned to St Tropez with her dog, Virgile. The Latin teacher had the long summer school holidays, so when Thierry, the friend of a friend, asked her if she would like to stay with him at his parents' holiday apartment, Regine jumped at the chance to come back. However, Thierry was a bit miffed when Regine refused to sleep with him and even more upset when Virgile started messing in the flat. When we came back from the Gorge du Verdun, Regine was at the Cannibale and somehow talked me into looking after the dog for her. Sally liked the dog, who slept on the floor of the van at night, while having the run of the car park during the day. Thierry treated me as his new best mate because of what I did and was over the moon when I introduced him to an English girl called Carolyn. Regine, meanwhile, had taken up with Badger's Geordie pall called Kevin. I was amazed when they all went out for a meal together in Ramatuelle. My circle of friends grew bigger, month by month.

The O'Malleys were drawn into the circle at this time, which was unusual, because of the fact that they were a family: husband and wife, Pat and Maggie, plus the two kids: Sean aged eight and Alice, five. Pat was

Irish, so he was drawn to the Dublin boys, especially Liam. Home on the beach for the O'Malleys was an old ambulance that Pat had converted into a very practical camper van, with hot water heater, shower, fridge, four burner hob and oven, plus four beds. It was not luxurious or fast, but had everything the family needed, including a 50 gallon water tank and all Pat's tools. He was a motor mechanic by trade, although Pat had trained as a doctor at University College Dublin for a few years. He now lived and worked in the West End of London, servicing the prestige cars of the wealthy. This freelance occupation enabled Pat to bring the family away to France for the whole of the English schools' summer break. Pat's great passion, after eyeing up the women on the beach, was his beer drinking. He was never without a litre bottle of Kronenbourg – from just after breakfast until he went to bed, Pat always had a red and white labelled lager close at hand; even when driving, there was a bottle propped up between the dashboard and the windscreen pillar. The main problem Pat had with his beer was in keeping it cold. The fridge in the camper van only needed four litres of Kronenbourg and it was full. This meant Maggie's perishable foods were out in the heat, which annoyed her immensely. As fast as Pat stocked up the fridge with beer, Maggie would throw them out again. It seemed to be a never-ending, day-long battle that Maggie usually won because Pat drank all his beer, warm or cold, and had nothing left to continue the argument with.

On a rare day of bad weather, when it rained all morning and was cloudy in the afternoon, Pat came up with the idea of the Beach Olympics. There was nobody on the sand that day, except those who slept there and those who slept in the car park. All the beach bums had crammed into the camping cars during the morning rain and Pat's sports scheme was his idea for getting everyone out of his vehicle. Pat was master of ceremonies and once all the competitors had assembled on the deserted beach, he announced the events. There was to be a 100 metre sprint, long jump, high jump, javelin, discus, shot putt and marathon. Scoring was on the Formula One system of ten; six; four; three; two; one, with a first prize of 100 francs for the overall champion.

I scored a few points in each of the sprint and the long jump. The jumping being particularly difficult as you had to take off from sand, as well as land in it. In the high jump, I came first – when I was the only one to get over a metre high bamboo cane, held up by two clothes pegs attached to a pair of upright bamboos. The javelin was another bamboo cane, which I could not throw to save my life, but I did score a point in the discus – which was a Frisbee in normal life. The shot putt was an old petangue boule that Pat's kids had found in the car park. After a lot of argument about what was a putt and what was a cricket ball throw, I was credited with another point for sixth place. With only one event to go, Rupert, who had won the long jump, while being consistently good throughout, was in the lead by two points. I was second, with Danny Rudd and his brother Paul tying for third spot, two points further back. Anti-post favourite, Keith Connery, was well out of it, both in a points scoring way as well as physically. He and Big Mick had really been knocking back the wine during the rainstorm and could hardly stand.

It was all down to the marathon, with anyone of our four being the possible winner of Pat's 100 francs. The race was a 500 metre run along the shore, a swim out to the 200 metre buoy, the swim back to land, finishing with another dash along the beach to the finish. As it was, Rupert led from start to finish. I only got close to him when he started swimming too early, while I continued wading in the shallows. I got nothing for my second place and Danny Rudd got the same for third. But fair play to Rupert, who went straight up to the wine Co-operative with his prize money and bought enough Ramatuelle Rosé to keep everybody going for the rest of the day. Pat stuck to his Kronenbourg, but was so impressed with the success of his idea that he said the next time it rained, we should do it all again.

There was a period of changeable weather towards the end of August, during which time Sally and Hannah went back home on a coach. A lot of the Irish boys moved on, after Big Mick's money was exhausted. It was a similar situation to that of the year before, as things slowed up, as we all waited for the grape picking to commence. As usual, Rupert was restless, so he planned another gorge trip, with a lot of the crew coming from those who had missed out on the first expedition. Speedy and Irish Danny were keen, as was Danny Rudd's brother, Paul. He had been mugged in Italy, while hitching hiking his way north, on the road from Greece. Paul was bitter and depressed when he arrived, penniless, on the beach, but was gradually pulling out of it as he saw the money from grape picking as a way of getting back on his feet.

The Volkswagens made a late start to the journey up to the gorge, mainly due to Rupert's failure to find a donor car from which to syphon petrol. It was nearly dark when we reached our destination. A lot of the gloom was due to overhead storm clouds and the whole atmosphere was one of imminent downpour. In the lull before the storm, we drove up the south side of the cliff top road, just in time to witness the most amazing display of thunder and lightening with lashings of rain. The climb up the twisting mountain road had taken us into the clouds, where forks of lightening criss-crossed the canyon, as thunder echoed around us. It only became dangerous when someone mentioned that if the van was hit by any of the bolts of electricity we would all be brown bread. For safety's sake, we stopped in one of the many tunnels cut into the rock, high up on the north facing cliff. No other traffic passed while we sheltered and before the weather eased, we were able to eat our evening meal in the dry.

A ventilation shaft of the tunnel, opened directly out of the rock face where you could watch rain falling downwards in the split seconds of electric illumination.

After the rain stopped, it was far too wet for the crew to camp or sleep rough. Luckily Danny Rudd said he remembered a cave that he had found whilst exploring on our previous trip. So, after a short drive round the gorge, everyone was able to troop off, to shelter for the night. In the morning, it was dry, but overcast – ideal weather conditions for the strenuous work of gold prospecting. Eagerly, the crew climbed down the path to the river, with the hub caps and high expectations, but were met by a raging torrent, where before there had been a trickling stream. The water was running at least six feet above normal and the crystal clear flow had been replaced by a dark, muddy soup, boiling with an unfriendly rage.

Rupert called a strategy meeting in his van. Marianne, the cheese seller at the campsite supermarket and at the Domaine Ste. Genevieve for the vendange was now working as a shepherdess. Rupert was due to look after Marianne's farm while she came to pick the grapes, so he suggested that we all trek over to the Dordogne for a few days, before our work began. I thought the cost of petrol would be too much for my budget, especially as I would be driving straight back, almost immediately. Some of the others were keen, so we split up, 50:50, with Speedy and Irish Danny going with Rupert, while hoping Marianne would give them a lift back to Vidauban.

Those who stayed at the gorge spent the day exploring the footpath at the river's edge. A short way along the path, heading downstream, we came across a group of French school children who had spent the previous night camping at the bottom of the gorge. They were all in a wet and sorry state, but could not do anything about it as they were trapped on the far side of the river. The children, with their leaders, had camped on a flat grassy area, surrounded by sheer cliffs – not a problem when the water could be forded by stepping stones, but the overnight rise in water level had caught them out. We had just worked out a rescue plan, using a pine tree that had been washed downstream, when the local mountain rescue team arrived. The professionals were armed with ropes, tools and a rubber dinghy, but to our satisfaction, used our pine tree to effect the rescue of the French city kids. We all sat on nearby rocks, as we stayed to watch the show. The expedition had another night in the mountains, when we camped on the shore of the Lac de la Ste Croix, but by the afternoon of that day, everyone was back on the beach.

For no particular reason, almost everyone was in Ramatuelle village that night – just hanging around in the square, drinking wine and watching the world go by. One of those present was Gerry Turner, another of Rupert's old school chums, who had come down to the beach with his former classmate, in the Volkswagen. Gerry had brought a bicycle with him in the van, which had given him a certain amount of independence, not having to rely on those with vehicles and, for most of the time, he had gone his own way.

When we all came to return to the beach, Gerry found he had forgotten his cycle lamps, as he had ridden up to the village before it had got dark and had not intended to stay so long. I offered to drive behind him, so that he could ride in the beam of the van's headlights. As we set off, down the narrow twisting road, I took it easy, as I had a van full, as well as a skin-full. Keeping in second gear, I let the engine do the braking, but Gerry sped away at great speed, disappearing out of the pool of light and round the bend. When he came back into view, Gerry was bouncing off the rock face at the right hand side of the road, before cartwheeling with the bicycle, down the hill. Gerry came to rest in the middle of the road, a twisted mess of arms, legs, wheels and bicycle frame. I slammed on the brakes as hard as I could and only just managed to stop before I ran him over. The next car down the hill turned round and went back up to Ramatuelle to telephone for an ambulance. Gerry was still unconscious when it arrived, so the hospital visits started all over again. It was another fractured skull, but Gerry also had a broken collar bone to go with it. Unlike Speedy, Gerry had an E111 form from the Department of Social Security, so his hospital bill was paid for by the British Government. Towards the end of his stay in hospital, Speedy came back from the Dordogne, with Marianne and Irish Danny, to visit Gerry in the same ward as he was in two months' earlier. The nurses recognised him instantly, but never told the administration about his return, which meant Speedy avoided any questions about his unpaid bill.

## Chapter Eight

Finally, on the first weekend in September, the waiting was over and everyone made their way to the Domaine de St Genevieve to start work. There were lots of familiar faces: the same Arab workers; Francis' two daughters, Marianne – this time with her brother, Pierre; Bill and Vicky; West Ham Mick and Helen; Irish Danny; Speedy and Keith Connery. these had all done it the year before. Danny and Paul Rudd, Dubliners: Larry, Tony and Eddie, Irish girls: Nicola and Sheila, Badger and a fully recovered Gerry Turner were working at Vidauban for the first time.

Quickly, I fell back into the old routine – up early every morning to go into Vidauban to have a coffee and collect the bread. The lady in the baker's recognised me and even remembered how many baguettes I had bought the year before. The tractors and trailers were the same. The fields looked the same, with no noticeable growth to any vine. Meal times were as chaotic as ever, but the wine consumption was markedly up on last year. A 20 litre and a 15 litre container were both filled with red wine as soon as work for the day was finished, and the Irish boys made a point of drinking every last drop, before going to bed. Most of the girls only had a couple of glasses with their meal. I rarely had more than half a litre, so some people were drinking between two or three litres of wine a night, every night. Danny Rudd and his guitar gave us live music most evenings, with Frank

Zappa being the main influence to his style; although Danny could sometimes be persuaded to play the sing-along tunes we all loved so much. Rod Stewart's "Baby Jane" was the favourite, closely followed by "The Boxer" – Simon and Garfunkel's classic, where everyone could be a cymbal.

During the day, all the talk in the fields was on what to do and where to go after the work had finished. Larry, Tony and Eddie wanted to go to Crete. Gerry Turner and Speedy, the head-bangers, planned to visit Barcelona, where Gerry fancied his chances of making money as an English language teacher. Billy had a job working for Vicky's dad, back in England, so they were treating the grape picking as a working holiday. At the weekends, the couple went to stay at local country hotels and enjoy themselves. Danny Rudd, Keith Connery and myself fancied Israel. We thought we would pool our earnings and catch the ferry from Venice. We hoped we could get some work on a kibbutz, stay the winter in the warm climate and come back to the beach in the summer.

After three weeks' work, Danny, Keith and myself went to the Gorge du Verdun for the weekend, as a sort of dummy run for the Israeli trip. We camped at our usual lakeside car park and, although the nights were colder, it was still scorching hot in the noon day sun of late September. Most of the tourists were French day trippers, in local registered cars. It was good to spend a couple of lazy days away from the farm and the Irish accents. Keith commented that we were all starting to speak Irish, using such phrases as "Is it that you're going out after coming in?" and "Fair play to you".

On the way back to the farm, all our plans changed. There was heavy traffic coming away from the gorge. As it had just got dark, I was content just to move along with the flow. Nobody seemed to be in a hurry, except for the guy from Marseilles, in a Simca. The first I saw of him was when he flew up alongside the van and cut in from the left. He hit the offside front corner of the Volkswagen, forcing it off the road and into a ditch. The momentum of the vehicle carried it along the ditch at a 45 degree angle, until the top corner of the windscreen on the driver's side hit a telegraph pole. Everything in the van came crashing down into the front, including Keith, who had been dozing in the back. The Simca was far more spectacular. After hitting the Volkswagen, it spun round, climbed the verge on the other side of the road before rolling over twice and finishing up on its roof. Amazingly, the three people in the car crawled out, unaided, with only scratches and bruises. Out of the three of us in the van, only Danny complained of a banged knee.

The police came and took statements. Danny spoke good enough French to put over our side of the story, while a couple of witnesses from the cars following behind made it clear that the Simca driver was the cause of it all. The man, in his 50s, had his wife and teenage stepdaughter with him and didn't seem too upset as it wasn't his car. Two tow trucks turned up and, while one craned on the written-off Simca, the other pulled the van out of the ditch. All the driver's side panels on the Volkswagen were squashed flat: the rear view mirror and the door handle had been ripped off; the windscreen was badly cracked; the rear wheel was buckled and the tyre had blown. On seeing all the damage, I went into a severe state of mental depression. The van was then reverse towed back to the farm for the fee of 500 francs – which was all I had on me.

"Do you have the Simca driver's address?" asked Danny Rudd, as we sat in the tow truck's crew cab, going to Vidauban.

"Of course I do. You wrote it out for me. Don't you remember?" I replied.

"Can I have a copy when we get back?"

"What for?" I enquired, rather puzzled.

"Well, that girl, you know, the one in the Simca, she kept giving me the eye. I think I could be in there," said Danny.

"Quick, get this man to a hospital. He must have bumped his head. Gone into shock or something. I can't believe Danny Rudd has finally discovered girls," laughed Keith, as our gloom lifted monetarily.

I didn't feel like work on the Monday morning, so

I spend my time cleaning up the broken bits in the van. After putting the spare wheel on, I went for a drive and was pleased that the Volkswagen still handled okay, but I was feeling low and could not face the grape picking any more.

In the afternoon, I drove back to the beach at Ramatuelle. Doobie was still running the Cannibale snack bar. He was very sympathetic, as everyone at the farm had been. Sunbathers were few and far between on the beach. The only people I knew well were Davy and Veronique, along with Kev from Peterlee, Regine's boyfriend. It was a good place to be and a good time to be there, so I hung around for a few days, but I did not appreciate it as I was so fed up about the condition of the van.

At the Cannibale, we played cards most afternoons and evenings. I had a crib board in the van and the lads were quite keen players.

On the second afternoon, Davy taught Veronique how to play, so from then on the four of us played doubles. It was amazing how quickly the French girl picked up the skills needed to play crib well. Although she was quiet and rarely spoke to anybody except Davy, Veronique often became quite animated during our games and showed an unexpected competitive streak. After one particular game when Kev and I had pegged nine, while Davy and Veronique had died in the hole when it was their first take, they had a full blown row in French.

"Chris wasn't as upset as this when that pratt run him off the road," said Kev, trying to lighten up the atmosphere.

"I know now exactly how bad he feels," snapped Davy.

"The way I'm feeling, if anybody had pegged in from that far behind to win it from me, I'd go and top myself," I said dejectedly.

After the best part of a week at the beach, I made up my mind to go back to England and sort out the insurance claim for the damage to the van. The winter trip to Israel was cancelled. Kev asked for a lift and offered to chip in some francs to help with the cost of petrol. We called in at the farm, to say goodbye to the workers, before driving north. Both of us had the address of Regine in Nancy so, as we went along, we discussed whether to call in on our way past. First, I was keen, while Kev was not bothered; then I wondered if it was the right thing to do, as Kev became more enthusiastic about the idea. Maybe the visit would be awkward for Regine, so we decided to telephone first. No answer. Further up the road, we rang again. Still no answer. This happened all the way to Nancy, where we took a chance and called round her house, but there was no one in. Kev and I didn't know what to do, so in the end we just got back in the van and continued on to Zeebrugge.

# Chapter Nine

Back in England, my priority was to get the van fixed. It was only covered by third party insurance, so I would have to get the money for repairs out of the French insurance company. I took the Volkswagen to an old water-skiing mate of my brother's. The panel beater reckoned there was about £900 worth of damage, so he typed out a proforma invoice for £4,200. I posted it off to France and waited for the cheque. As time passed, I became accustomed to the state of the van, which drove perfectly well and was still fully usable.

Archie Frederick's of Ipswich gave me a job. He did European and Middle Eastern haulage, but employed me, to start with, on the UK side of his operation. It was mostly container work, out of Felixstowe, and I was soon back into the Friday night at Chelmsford routine.

In no time at all, it was Christmas, and when a card came from Regine, asking if I could visit, I gave her a ring to arrange a New Year stay in Nancy. There was no work to do, as practically everywhere was shut down. It seemed a good way to fill the boring days between Christmas and the New Year. To save money on the ferry ticket and to cut petrol costs, I took the 500 Honda. Zeebrugge to Nancy was about a six hour drive in a truck, so I thought I would beat that easily on a motorcycle, but I didn't reckon on the weather being so cold. It started snowing when I got off the ferry at 8.00 o'clock in the morning and snowed off and on all the way through Belgium, Luxembourg and France. The journey took ten hours, as I could not do more than an hour in the saddle without stopping for half an hour to thaw out. I was wearing a good set of wax cotton waterproofs, but it was not long before freezing cold water was trickling down my neck and soaking through the seat of my pants. I arrived in Nancy wet through, freezing cold and with my nose running like a tap. Regine was pleased to see me, as was Virgile, the dog, but she could not understand why I chose to come on the bike, in the middle of winter. It now seemed crazy to me, too.

Regine had a beautiful flat, which was on the first floor of an old terraced house in the city centre. With its high ceilings and tall windows, the place was light, even in the dull mid-winter. The decoration was very tasteful, with lots of art deco influences. Like most French city girls, Regine had style: from the way she walked, to what she wore, to how her home was laid out – everything about Regine was class and sophistication.

The next day, after I had thawed out, Regine gave me a guided tour of her city. To most English-speaking people, the only remarkable thing about Nancy is its name; the locals pronounce it "North Sea".

But when you have somebody who knows everyone and everywhere worth visiting, it gave me a good insight into the heart of a city that considers itself the second city in France, after Paris.

The impressive Place de Stanislas must be a hive of activity in summer, with tables and chairs out on the pavement, but in the snowy depths of winter, it was bleak. Everybody was crossing the square as quickly as they could, to get to their favourite café. Every other building seemed to be a bar, restaurant or café, with crystal chandeliers, wood panelling and huge coffee machines in brass or copper that dominated the area behind the bar. Regine and I visited three of these establishments in the morning of my first day. They were all full, with hardly a vacant table in any of them. Regine knew the occupants of practically every other table, where she stopped to say hello and do the little kisses on the cheek thing. I was introduced to everyone, which meant hundreds of handshakes, loads of kisses and a whole load of names that I instantly forgot. It took an inordinate amount of time just to get across the room to a free seat. I thought that if this happened every time I wanted a coffee, I would look for somewhere quieter, but Regine relished the situation and was in her element.

In the third café, we were joined at our table by Laurence – no, not the basketball player, but anther Laurence, who was an outstandingly beautiful woman: tall, slim, with classic features and an immaculate bob hairstyle. If you had seen her photograph in any international woman's magazine and asked to guess her nationality, everyone would have said Laurence was French. As an art student, studying the history of fashion and design, Laurence made all her own clothes, which gave her a unique 'look' that was certainly different, although some would say, weird.    Laurence had the model body to carry this off and, in the mind of most men, plus quite a few women, was 'drop dead gorgeous'.

Regine had told Laurence all about me.  It seemed she was trying to throw us together, for Laurence came everywhere that Regine and I went during my stay.  Three things stopped this match-making succeeding: first, was the language problem – because Laurence spoke no English;  then there was the fact that I couldn't believe such a beautiful woman would want to have anything to do with me;  and, finally, I had the worst cold I could ever remember having.  My runny nose needed constant wiping, which had soaked both of my handkerchiefs so much, it was embarrassing to get them out.

For New Year's Eve, Regine, Laurence and I went to the home of George and Pascaline.  I had met Pascaline in the summer, and George was her new man.    He was a qualified architect, but also very much a 'nature' boy.   His home was a one roomed shack in the woods, beside a lake;  it had no electricity, just one cold water tap, over a sink, and was heated by a bottled gas fire. The room was lit by candles and the food was cooked by George, on a two ringed gas stove, but we had an excellent meal of roast duck and vegetables.  The two ducks had been swimming on the lake since before Christmas, but had been fattened up especially for the New Year celebrations.  It was a very cosy atmosphere in the candlelight and warmth from fire.  By midnight, I had drunk enough brandy to finally forget I had a cold.  The dinner party was a great way to finish the year. George put the radio on at midnight and everyone sung "Auld Lang Syne" - they all knew the words better than I did. I stayed another day, to get over my hangover, leaving Nancy on the morning of the 2nd. It had been a good time. I was sad to be leaving, not because I thought I could get somewhere with Laurence, but because I was not relishing the ride back to England in the freezing weather. Even now, whenever I drive through the rolling hills of south-east Belgium, it sends shivers down my spine.

It was back to work and back to Chelmsford: same faces, even the same music. Then, one Friday, a strange affair started when I arrive late one evening. Bernard Mullinger came up to have a drink with me in the bar.

"There's a good looking female in the club asking about you," said Bernie.

"Why is she asking you?" I wondered out loud.

"It's the one you danced with before Christmas when we were drinking Bacardi," replied Bernie.

"Red dress and long black hair?" I queried.

"Yeah. She's got the same dress on tonight. Come on, let's go through," suggested Bernie.

When I saw her again, it all came back to me. We

had danced and talked. She had told me she had four kids under five and was living in a battered wives' refuge. I had rung the telephone number that she had given me, but had been told that no one called Julie lived at that address. Julie spoke too posh to be in a refuge, so I had put it all down to her being a wind-up merchant.

Julie was pleased to see me, although she was dismayed to hear that I had telephoned. She explained that all telephone callers were told that whoever they wanted to speak to was not there. It was a tactic employed to deter unwanted partners from tracking down their women. If I had called again, straight away, Julie said she would have answered herself. So, the battered wives story was true, but the four children was a wind-up. As we drank and danced the night away, Julie pointed out the other residents of the refuge. It was now a regular Friday night out for them, with a rota for the babysitting. The women came team-handed, to protect themselves if they were found by their violent partners, but the threat of trouble did not stop them from letting their hair down and having a good time. However, as soon as the last dance had finished, all the residents went off together, straight back to the refuge. Julie had just enough time for a kiss and a cuddle before she gave me her 'phone number again.

Julie was certainly different, not only from the other refuge women, but from the normal country and western loving girl: the way that she spoke such good English, the way she conducted herself were very upper class.

Julie was a classy lady who had obviously been through tough times. It would be interesting to hear her story.

During the next week I telephoned the refuge again and on my second call I spoke to Julie. She seemed keen to come out for a ride in the truck, not even being put off by the prospect of staying away overnight. We rendezvoused early one morning, which was ideal for Julie as she was able to get away before the others were up. All the other women at the refuge had children with them, so breakfast time was an endless barrage of noise, as mothers made demands on their offspring and the kids made ceaseless demands on their mums.

Apart from an early verbal exchange, Julie became quiet and withdrawn, content just to look out of the window as we went along. I did not ask questions, thinking it would all come out in due course, anyway, I liked the situation as it was. Julie was quite good looking and no trouble – perfect in fact.

On the first night we slept together on the bottom bunk of the Scania.

"Do you want me?" asked Julie, in an unenthusiastic tone that suggested that she was resigned to making love if I wanted to do it.

"Of course I do, but this is not the time or the place," I said, in a genuine caring way.

"Thank you," was all she said, as we cuddled together for love and affection, as well as for warmth on a bitterly cold January night.

The longer Julie stayed with me in the Scania, the more her self-confidence started to return. Day by day I was able to put together the jigsaw of my passenger's past life. Julie was brought up and went to school in Cheltenham, which explained the accent. When she was still a teenager, Julie left home to live in London, where she flat-shared and partied her way around the capital for the next ten years. Most of her work was as a secretary and then as a PA, mostly with advertising agencies which is where Julie met her man. He was a talented artist who was responsible for a lot of successful television commercials, before he set up a company of his own. Julie was a partner in the venture, where she did the administration side of things. Soon the profitable enterprise allowed the couple to live the champagne life-style with a penthouse in Chelsea and a Rolls Royce. Julie told me that, one day, out of the blue, her fella decided to liquidate the company in order to move to the country where, he said, he wanted to concentrate on painting pictures. In a big, old north Essex farmhouse their relationship fell apart. Probably because they had too much time of their hands. Most of the abuse Julie took was mental. She referred to it as his 'mind games'. But whatever it was, it certainly got her down.

As a couple, Julie reckoned they were worth well over a million pounds, so was suing for half – even though they had never married. This had made her man very angry, which was the reason she was hiding in the refuge. It was even better for Julie to be out on the road with me. Her self-confidence, which had risen already to my level, soon streaked ahead, almost to the point of domination. Julie spoke of buying a truck in which we could do Continental haulage together. She spoke of finding a cottage and setting up home, but most scary of all, Julie wanted to marry me on the 29th February – less than a month away.

I was never one to argue, so I went along with what Julie said. This type of woman was a completely new experience for me. Maybe I should have said something, but how was I to know it was not just all talk? Julie was good to be with: intelligent and good looking. She made people stare when they saw her getting into the truck. I have to admit, it made me feel good to have her around. The sex was good too. Julie knew how to please a man. She gave me the impression that she had done things I had not even thought about, but this could have been half her problem, so I kept the love-making simple, with plenty of kissing and cuddling. Pretending to be naïve probably made me more attractive to Julie, as she often called me her 'bit of rough'.

So why didn't it last? What went wrong? Why didn't I marry Julie, even if it was only for half of her money? The fact that she was older than I was, or that Julie was a heavy smoker, did not turn me off. One reason why I finished our relationship was because I thought I was being used. I had visions of Julie going to her ex-boyfriend and saying: "It's over. I'm never coming back to you and there's nothing you can do to me now. If you do try anything, my husband will come round and sort you out. He's a truck driver who will eat you for breakfast."

The other nagging doubt I had was that the marriage would not last. Julie was a high flier who had come back from the depths of despair since he had known me. She was still on the way up. How long would it be before I became an embarrassment? What would happen when Julie met someone who could keep her in the manner to which she was accustomed? I saw myself as a stepping stone on her route back to where she belonged. As for the money, maybe I missed a chance of easy riches – my ship was about to come in, but then sailed on by.

Archie Fredericks gave me an escape route, which let me make a clean getaway. The French truckers had been staging one of their regular blockades and Archie had a truck caught up in it. The driver had sat with it for ten days at Cluses, near the Italian border. The load was for Milan, but the driver had got so fed up that he caught a train back to England and jacked in the job. The blockade was lifted the same weekend that the driver returned the truck keys to Ipswich. Roger Tripp and I were asked to take the company Volkswagen Golf over to France and find the truck. When we found the vehicle, I was to then take over and run through to Italy, while Roger came back in the car. We left Ipswich at midday on Saturday, to go via Dover-Calais. Hammering the Golf non-stop along the autoroutes, we found the Mercedes truck at lunchtime on Sunday.

The truck and trailer were still all in one piece and started easily, but because of the French weekend truck curfew, I could not drive until 10.00 o'clock in the evening. As I had been driving all night, I climbed on the bunk to have a well-earned sleep. The work was for the same company that Ivan Merrick was sub-contracting for the year before, so when I got to Italy, I knew the Customs agent and the re-load address. By Tuesday evening, I was coming back through the Mont Blanc tunnel, which impressed Archie Fredericks so much that he sent me straight back to Italy. Archie sent an unaccompanied trailer over to Zeebrugge and gave instructions that I was to leave my trailer on the Belgium quay, in order to take the other back to Milan. This was a common practice that saved on ferry costs, but left me with a shortage of running money. However, it did keep me out of the country for a few more days.

I spent the weekend at Carisio, a small Italian town on the autostrada, mid-way between Turin and Milan. There was a restaurant with a huge truck park, a few hundred metres from the motorway exit. It was a popular place with British drivers and anyone week-ending in the north of Italy always knew they could find a drinking partner at Carisio. Monday morning saw me at the Milan Customs' clearance compound, ready to delivery two consignments in the afternoon. Tuesday was taken up by collecting two pick-ups, before clearing Customs, late in the evening. The drive up to Mont Blanc tunnel and most of the journey across France accounted for Wednesday. The rest of France, plus the ferry-crossing, brought me back to Ipswich late on Thursday evening.

"A bird called Julie 'phoned up quite a few times while you were in Italy – sounded a bit posh. What's she doing chasing a bloke like you?" asked Archie, with no hint of any thanks for all my hard work.

"I've dumped her. What did you say to her?" I replied.

"We had quite a few long talks. She knows quite a bit about trucks, you know. I was thinking of offering her a job in the office," stated Archie.

"You do that and she'd be running the company within a month, She's a bit too bossy," I warned.

"Well, that's worth thinking about," said Archie, with a lopsided grin.

Julie never telephoned him again. I saw her for the last time on that weekend. She tried everything she could to get me to resume the relationship: pleading, begging, ordering, bullying and promising everything. Julie went through them all. I tried not to be nasty by saying she deserved someone better than me. The talking went on and on, with both of us going over our point of view, again and again.  In the end, Julie got fed up with my stubbornness.

"If you cannot see what a good relationship we could have together, then you do not deserve to be with someone like me," said Julie, as she realised she was wasting her time.

There was a couple of letters during the weeks that followed.  Julie went to stay with her parents in Cheltenham and by the second letter, she was flat-sharing with some girls in Gloucester.  I didn't write back, but hoped she would be alright.

## Chapter Ten

The trips to Milan continued at one a week for the next month. It was work I could handle pretty well, so I kept my head down and got stuck in. Friday was my usual day to visit the office for wages and instructions.

"I want your passport, boy. I'm sending it up to London for a Polish visa," said Archie, one Friday morning.

"Poland! That'll make a change from Italy," I said, trying to sound unconcerned.

"Yeah. You ship out Wednesday night, weekend in Warsaw, re-load in Germany: back here the following Wednesday. Don't worry, you'll have an escort."

On the Monday, I tipped and on the Tuesday, I re-loaded the Italian trailer for somebody else to take to Milan. First thing Wednesday morning, I was at an old RAF airfield, near Royston in Hertfordshire. The aeroplanes had long gone but the buildings were still used by the Ministry of Defence for storage. The people who were paying for the truck to go to Poland was a Charity called "Medical Aid for Poland", who raised money to buy hospital equipment, which it then shipped out to the Communist state. Archie Fredericks had done some work for them before and, this time, the charity had purchased a load of nurses' uniforms from Government

Surplus. One of the security guards at the store reckoned the stuff was from the Second World War, and had been kept at Royston for longer than he had worked there. The thousands of brown paper parcels containing the uniforms were all neatly tied up with string, but the two car loads of charity workers got stuck into loading and passed the parcels into the trailer, loading it to the roof, from front to back. All the helpers were Polish or sons of Poles who lived in Britain. I wondered which one was going to be my escort. It came as a shock when Mr Bronsky, the top man, told me my escort wasn't at Royston, but that she would meet me at Dover.

When the trailer was loaded, I was given instructions that the vehicle was booked on that evening's Dover to Ostend ferry. The arrangements gave me plenty of time, so I took it easy, plodding down to the Channel port. On the A2 dual carriageway, a silver Cortina came alongside, flashing its headlights and blowing its hooter. The passenger was gesticulating that I should pull over. Thinking that there was something wrong with the trailer, I pulled in at the first opportunity, which happened to be a transport café. The young guy from the Cortina came running over to ask if I was going to Poland. It then clicked that my escort had seen the Fredericks' truck and thought it would save time if they could get me to stop.

My escort was the passenger of the car, not at all what I had been expecting. Irena was well over 60 years old. Over a cup of tea, I found out the lady had been born in Poland, but had lived in Britain since the end of the Second World War. The car driver was her grandson. This was Irena's fourth trip as an escort for "Medical Aid for Poland" and she seemed quite at ease with the prospect of sleeping in a truck cab. My escort was keen to spend Saturday and Sunday with old friends in Warsaw, so she was pleased to hear I wasn't in any particular hurry to complete the trip – visiting friends was the only perk from the unpaid escort's job.

It was an uneventful Channel crossing, which disembarked at just after midnight. I parked on the quay at Ostend for the night. As I had slept in my cabin during the voyage, I was up early and across Belgium before dawn. Transiting Holland did not take long either, as we made our way east, entering Germany at the border town of Venlo. The Mercedes truck made good time across the flat terrain. The nurses' uniforms did not weigh much, which suited the 260 horsepower v-eight engine.

It looked as if we would just have enough driving time to cross into East Germany on the first full day. Even with a complete vehicle search at the East-West German border, my plan looked to be on schedule; but, when I came to stop for the night, Irena was most upset.

"You cannot stop here, not in Germany. I hate the Germans. You must continue to Poland. I will not sleep a night in Germany, especially East Germany," exclaimed Irena.

"But I have driven my permitted hours. We have

to stop for nine hours," I explained, taken aback by the strength of the lady's protest.

"You do not understand.  I was in Auschwitz concentration camp during the war.  I cannot stay in Germany longer than necessary," continued Irena, in the same distraught tone.

"Okay.  We'll have a coffee and then push on to the Polish border," I replied.

"Thank you," sighed Irena.

You have a have a pretty good excuse to break the tachograph laws.  The situation would take a lot of explaining, if I was caught;  but this was good enough for me.  The last thing I wanted, was to argue with Irena and after what she had said, going against her wishes was unthinkable.  During the evening, as we drove on towards Poland, Irena told me about Auschwitz and how she went there as a Jewish teenager, from Warsaw.  The only reason Irena had survived was because she spoke German and was used as a translator.  The escort trips on behalf of the "Medical Aid for Poland" charity were the first time since the war that Irena had been to Germany, or spoken German.  The way Irena had been able to rise above the hatred and do something positive for the people of her homeland was remarkable.  That night, I felt humble to be in the company of someone who had been through so much and was still willing to do her bit for a country she had left 40 years ago.

Fortunately, East Germany was not a wide country and was crossed in a few hours. Although the state of the road from Berlin, eastwards, to Frankfurt am der Oder was terrible, the concrete slabs that made up the dual carriageway all seemed to have subsided at one end, which gave the truck a back-jarring jolt every two lengths that it travelled. At the Polish border, the East German formalities were quick and easy, as it seemed the authorities did not expect anyone would be trying to escape into Poland. However, it was a different story two hundred yards up the road, on the Polish side. Irena took charge of things so, as she went off with the paperwork, I thought I would catch up on some sleep. But I was soon woken up and told to drive into a Customs' examination shed. It seemed that a charity truck from Holland had been caught trying to smuggle in a printing press and, since then, every aid shipment was completely unloaded for a thorough check. It looked like a squad of young Polish soldiers had been especially roused for the job. They did not look very happy. Irena told me to get some rest, while she kept an eye on things to make sure none of the nurses' uniform went missing.

I slept well, as I was tired enough not to notice the rocking of the trailer, but I woke to find Irena was still supervising the Polish army, as they tried to get all the packages back on the vehicle. Why they needed more space than the loaders at Royston, I do not know. When the boy soldiers had finished, the canvas canopy of the trailer looked like a sack of spuds. We got underway as soon as possible after the examination. The sun was coming up, as Irena reclined on the passenger seat, to get some well-earned rest. The lady slept all morning, as I drove eastwards, on the poorly surfaced, single carriageway. There was no need for maps, as Warsaw was sign posted all the way from the frontier. Traffic was light, tractors and trailers shared the road with local Polish trucks. There was the occasional west-bound, Russian registered TIR outfit, but not many cars. Most Polish cars seemed to be 124 Fiat look-a-likes that spent most of their life parked beside blocks of flats in drab Polish towns. Progress was steady, rather than spectacular, while I soon learned to slow down to a walking pace when negotiating level crossings. They were anything but level, with sections of wooden sleepers between the tracks often missing. With just one stop for lunch, it was still after dark when we reached the outskirts of Warsaw. I had not expected it to take so long; but on taking a second look at the map of Poland in my European road atlas, I realised, not only was Warsaw three-quarters of the way across the country, but the Polish map was drawn to a smaller scale than that of Germany and the rest of Western Europe

Irena then produced a street map of Warsaw from her handbag and, while telling me the story of how she had acquired this rare item, she showed me our final destination. It was a Catholic church, on the banks of the river, opposite the zoo, upstream from the third road bridge. I found it with no trouble. The church was at the centre of a complex that included a convent, a school and a meeting hall. There was just enough room to reverse into the playground beside the school. The unloading of the trailer had been arranged for the Saturday morning so, while Irena went off to stay with her friends, I was given room in the convent. It was smartly furnished with a bed, wardrobe and desk. A decorative star-shaped light-fitting illuminated the room. There were places for five bulbs, only one of the three worked. That summed up Poland perfectly.

An enthusiastic crew of helpers turned up in the morning to unload the uniforms. Great fun was had by all, throwing the brown paper parcels off the trailer and into the church hall, through an open window. I did not know Poland had so many talented Rugby players. In the afternoon, I wandered around the city. It was overcast and cold: the weather was the same. Warsaw seemed to have little to offer, or was I in the wrong part of town? Dressed in an old bomber jacket and jeans, I thought I would blend in with the crowd, but so many people stopped me, to ask if I wanted to exchange any dollars for zlotys, I took off my jacket to check if someone had chalked USA on the back.

My meals at the convent were brought to my room by the nuns - big portions of meat and vegetables that I knew they would not be having themselves. It was a difficult situation. I wanted to tell them I did not want special treatment, that they should not give all their rations to me, but I did not want to seem ungrateful or waste anything. I tried to make the nuns feel happy, by eating everything up and thanking them profusely. The fact was, I had three weeks' worth of food in the truck and had not been expecting a bed, let alone full board.

When I was washing the truck on the Sunday morning, Irena came to see me, in order to discuss our departure time. She talked me into staying the Sunday night so she could see more of her friends. The couple drove Irena round to the church in their beat-up old Polish Fiat. The old man had fought with the RAF during the war and could have stayed on to live in Britain, but had chosen to return to his native Poland. He was a nice bloke, who spoke perfect English. He could have certainly done better for himself than a rusty Lada clone if he had been like Irena and so many other Poles who settled in Britain after 1945.

My three friends were pleased to hear that I did not intend to move out until Monday morning. I figured that I could drive to the East German border by Monday night and cross, first thing Tuesday, load in West Germany in the afternoon and the get across, into Holland, by the end of the day. This plan, I hoped, would keep Irena happy: in and out of both East and West German in one day. It was not a plan of which Archie Fredericks would have approved, as it did not make for good economic transport operations, but sitting about on a Sunday was the least I could do for someone like Irena. As it was, the plan worked perfectly, even with a hiccup of a broken fuel pipe. German efficiency in repairing the engine and in loading the trailer at Hannover meant that we were able to catch the midnight fright ferry from Zeebrugge to Dover.

When I got back to Ipswich, after tipping in Leicester, Archie asked why I had taken so long.  I told him about the Dutch printing press and the full turnout at the border, which seemed to satisfy his curiosity.

## Chapter Eleven

Later in the week, Archie Fredericks won the contract to take 300 tonnes of chemicals down to Rumania. My passport went off to London for Czech and Hungarian visas and I went off to Scotland, tipping the trailer at Blackburn on the way north. I arrived at the polythene factory, on the outskirts of Glasgow, at about 4.00 o'clock in the afternoon.

"Hello mate. I've come for the load to Baghdad," I said.

"It'll be in the morning now, Jimmy," said the forklift driver predictably.

"Can I leave the trailer here for the night?" I asked.

"Aye. Stick it on the waste ground, round the back. It'll no be in the way there," the forklift driver helpfully replied.

In no time at all, I was bob-tailing my way across Glasgow in the unit, wondering if I should give Kate a ring before turning up, unannounced, on her doorstep. I telephoned, but there was no answer. Undeterred, I parked the Mercedes right opposite the flat in St Vincents Crescent. Kate's flatmate answered the door when I rang the bell. She had come home since I telephoned and reckoned Kate was due back shortly. I said I would call back later and asked the flatmate to tell Kate I had called.

After popping up the road for some fish and chips, I sat in the cab to wait for Kate. At 9.00 o'clock, I was fed up sitting and waiting, so I climbed onto the bottom bunk. At nearly midnight, I was awoken by somebody climbing into the cab. I had forgotten to lock the door, which was a stupid thing to do as I was only a stone's throw away from Sauchiehall Street. It was a good job it was only Kate. She had been in the pub all night with a boyfriend. They had just pulled up in his car, when Kate saw the truck. The Ipswich address on the door told her it was probably me. The boyfriend was not too pleased when Kate got a sudden headache.

"You had better come up and take a shower," said Kate in a matter of fact way that was so unsexy and different that it somehow became a huge turn on.

The love-making between us was as good as it had ever been – so exhausting that it did not matter that we were sleeping in a narrow, single bed. I awoke, feeling refreshed, but as it was still dark, I tried to get back to sleep again. Kate was also awake.

"What time do you have to load your truck?" Kate asked.

"About half past eight," I replied.

"Well, you have missed that by a long way. It's nearly 10."

"It can't be. It's still dark outside," I stammered.

"It won't be, if I open the shutters," laughed Kate.

"Shutters! Your windows have shutters. You never told me you had shutters!" I exclaimed, jumping out of bed.

"Well, there are builders working opposite – you know how it is," explained Kate.

After stopping long enough for toast and coffee, I raced across Glasgow to get back to the trailer. The rolls of polythene were loaded by midday, so I told the traffic office I would be back in the yard first thing in the morning. It was one of those times when there was so many other things going on in the company that nobody noticed I was running well behind schedule.

Rumania was my next destination, with 54 drums of insecticide used for spraying fruit trees. Archie Fredericks had another load of the same drums going to another town nearby, so he instructed the driver to show me the way. I met up with Jock Gardner on the quay at Felixstowe, as we waited to drive onto the Sunday afternoon ferry to Zeebrugge. Jock was in his late 40s, with about ten years; experience of Middle-Eastern and Commie-bloc work. He knew just about all there was to know about the job and had worked for nearly every East Anglian company doing continental haulage. However, Jock made it clear that it was my responsibility to keep up with him. If I was at the borders with him, then he would show me what to do – otherwise I was on my own.

I got little encouragement from Jock's attitude, as he was driving a brand new Scania 112 and I was still with an old Mercedes. It turned out that keeping up with Jock was not a problem as he was not in a hurry and his main priority was to make sure he found somewhere to have a drink in the evening. Jock knew every truck stop on the route; he even stopped to buy supplies at a village shop in Bavaria. The exceptional thing about it was that it was 10.00 o'clock at night and the shop was well and truly closed. The old lady seemed to know Jock well. She opened up and put all the lights on; Jock encouraged me to buy something, saying that I never knew when I might want to shop there again.

The next morning, when we crossed into Czechoslovakia, I found out about Jock's other great passion, besides drink: women. It seemed that Jock's ideal trip was to get drunk every night and have a woman in each country, on the way through. Jock knew every watering hole in every country, but I do not think Archie wanted him to stop at them all, when he asked the Scotsman to show me the way. We went from the Motorest at Pilzen, to the Motel Rokycany, and then to the services at Brno. At each place Jock showed me how to change Deutsche Marks on the black market, how to buy diesel fuel for Marks and where to find the best looking women.

After Prague, the motorway to Bratislava made our journey easier and we were soon in Hungary. Once again, we stopped at the places traditionally frequented by British drivers. These included the Hotel Wein in Budapest and the Windmill, a restaurant in the countryside, south of the capital. The old Mill had been converted into a smart eatery: it was not only popular for its good food, but also for the shower block built in the truck park. Jock thought there was a better class of girl at the Windmill, too. He recommended Erica, who he reckoned was every British driver's favourite Commie-block whore. Sadly, she was having a night off when we were there.

First thing next morning we crossed into Rumania, where Jock certainly knew all about the paperwork. It took half a day, but Jock managed to clear Customs, get the TIR carnets stamped and buy our visas with 200 Marlboro, a jar of Nescafe and some Wrigley's chewing gum - it was the normal procedure when delivering in Rumania, which allowed us to go straight to our destinations without dealing with further bureaucracy.

It was also Jock's birthday, and to celebrate it, he wanted a woman. When we left the border, it soon became clear how he was going to get one: Jock stopped at every bus stop, in every town and village, to ask any waiting females if they wanted a ride. As he did not seem to be having much luck, I soon got fed up pulling up behind him every few minutes. Eventually, I pulled round him and made steady progress on my own. But on leaving the next town, there was a girl hitchhiker. This was the very thing Jock was looking for, so I stopped to pick her up. She was tall and slim with long black hair to go with her olive-brown complexion. If it were not for her brown teeth, you would have said she was a 'ten'. The teenage Romanian was bubbly and full of life. As we went along, she tried on my sunglasses and went through my cassette collection, pleading with me to let her keep one of my Dire Straits' tapes.

I drove on for a few miles, before stopping in a picnic area for coffee and to wait for Jock. Minutes later, he swung into the car park and pulled up with his driver's door next to mine.

"Where the fuck did you get her from?" raged Jock, as he peered across at my passenger.

"Two towns back. Had any luck?" I asked, although I could see he was alone.

"No, I haven't. You jammy git," replied Jock.

"She's yours then – my birthday present to you. Take her," I offered.

"No. No, you found her. You can have her," shouted Jock, as he slammed the Scania into gear and roared out onto the road, showering everywhere with gravel.

We made love on the bottom bunk of the Mercedes, as the afternoon sunshine shone warmly through the gaps in the hurriedly drawn curtains.  I soon saw what a perfect body my passenger had, once she had taken off the shapeless nylon tracksuit that all Romanians seemed to wear.  My good looking lover was also good between the sheets, where she took control in an unexpected performance that belied her youthful appearance. Afterwards, she told me her name was Paula and she gave me her address in Arad, telling me in sign language to call on my way back..  I dropped Paula off in the next town, but not before she climbed across the cab for one last kiss.

"Marks, you give me marks?" asked Paula, as she ran her hands across my pockets, feeling for my wallet.

"Ten out of ten, very good," I could not resist saying, but Paula did not understand why I was laughing – although she was well pleased with the ten Mark note that I gave her.

By this time, the daylight was fading;  also, I had no idea where Jock planned to stop for the night.  It was not that I needed his expertise anymore, I just wanted to be sociable.  Jock had warned me of the dangers of night driving in Romania, with the common hazard of unlit horse and carts, so I took it slowly, driving defensively. I avoided the horses with their dozing drivers, while keeping half an eye out for Jock's Scania.  I found him – parked in a big lay-by on the outskirts of Carensebes.

Jock had not found a woman to share his birthday celebrations, so he had drowned his sorrows by drinking his bottle of duty free Johnnie Walker. When I arrived, he was asleep at the wheel, with the whisky bottle lying smashed beside the cab.

At 5.00 o'clock the next morning, incredibly, Jock was banging on my cab door, raring to go. We motored down to Craiova, where Jock stopped outside my delivery address, where he had unloaded on a previous trip. My tutor gave me some final instructions on how to find out about a return load, before setting off for the town of Alexandria and a similar government store to the one in Craiova. The trailer was unloaded and I had the paperwork signed by midday.

The only way to telephone out of Rumania is by using the services of the international tourist hotels. These are very helpful places with plenty of English-speaking staff, but they are expensive. You not only pay for out-going telephone calls, but also have to pay to receive a call. Two calls of less than two minutes each cost over £20, but the quick chats with Archie in England did give me my re-load address. A load of knitwear for London, from a Romanian textile factory in Piatra Nment and a similar factory in Suceava: two towns in the north of Romania – a good day's worth of driving from Craiova.

Romania is a vast country, with no motorway system. The single carriageway roads were usually poorly surfaced, although relatively traffic free. The speed limit for TIR trucks was 50 kilometres per hour or 30 mph, which left the Mercedes pottering along with four unused high gears in the 12 speed gearbox. For fuel economy reasons, I wanted to run in to gear. This inevitably brought me trouble with the police, who pulled up foreign trucks as a matter of routine. The standard payment for speeding was 20 king-sized cigarettes; the favoured brand in Romania, for some unknown reason, was Kent – practically unheard of elsewhere. Marlboro would get you out of any trouble anywhere else in Eastern Europe, but it was Kent in Romania. I was thankful for Jock's recommendation to buy 400 at the border duty free shop. Hardly a day went by without a speeding fine.

At Piatra Nment, I arrived, 60 cigarettes lighter, but could not find the textile factory anywhere. A helpful receptionist at the tourist hotel telephoned the head office in Bucharest, to find out the name of the factory for me. The girl wanted me to take a room as well, but I told her I could not afford one, after paying the exorbitant cost of the telephone call. With her directions, I found the factory with ease, but was told that my goods were not ready for loading. I was advised to come back in two days.

I went to a parking area on the shore of a lake that I had noticed when driving into town. It was a quiet place to park, so I rested all the next day, but was surprised when the manager of the knitwear factory turned up in the evening and told me my load was ready to load first

133

thing in the morning.  I had not told anyone where I was going to park, plus, you could not see the truck from the road:  but somehow, they knew where I was.

The workers hand-balled the cartons of knitwear onto the trailer in the morning and, armed with a hand-drawn map of where to find the Suceava factory, I headed north.  This time, the exports were ready.  I was loaded, with the paperwork done, by early afternoon.  Suceava is in the province of Moldova and, on looking at the map of Romania, my best route back to Hungary seemed to be due west – through Transylvania.  What seemed to be a major transit route on the map, turned out to be a poorly surfaced road – the equivalent of a British 'B' road.  It was also mountainous country and, although it was very picturesque, it was slow-going for the Mercedes, even with a comparatively light load.  The Romanian sign posting also left a lot to be desired, with several occasions when it was left to my sense of direction.

I was well into the second day of a long, hard slog across Romania, when I reached the border, at Oradea. This was my first border crossing in Eastern Europe without the assistance of Jock Gardner.  My old tactic of watching what everyone else was doing did not have any relevance this time – I was the only person wishing to cross at this remote frontier outpost.  However, I need not have worried;  the atmosphere at Oradea was completely different from the tension and frantic activity at the main crossing point at Nadlac.  Everyone was friendly, even pleased to see me – especially when I donated a jar of

Nescafe to the Customs' staff canteen. The lady in the Romtrans bureau wanted to practice her English, so it took ages to type out the TIR carnet, but it was all very relaxed and pleasant.

My good day was complete when I got a really good deal on a tank-full of black market diesel fuel. I bought enough to get me all the way back to England, but I had to risk getting caught with too much fuel when I crossed into West Germany. There was a 200 litre limit on imported fuel --any more than that and you had to pay duty. At the German border, the officials seemed more interested in asking me about any Czech army movements I may have seen, rather than checking my fuel tank, so I got away with it. Halfway through Germany, I saw Jock Gardner going the other way, with another load of fruit tree spray. When I got back to Ipswich, I found that all Romanian loads had gone, but there were two loads of Perkins diesel engines waiting to go to Turkey.

## Chapter Twelve

Rob Bulmer was in the office when I went to collect my expenses for the Romanian trip.

"Do you two want to do these Turkish loads?" asked Archie, without giving us time to reply, he added, "I know neither of you have done Turkey before, but it doesn't matter because you won't be running together anyway."

Rob and I were still trying to work out the logic of the statement when Archie continued:

"I've got one set of permits for Czech-Hungary and one set for Austria-Yugo.   Who wants what?" asked Archie, while handing out the papers before getting an answer.

My set of permits was for Germany, Austria, Yugoslavia and Turkey:  permits were not needed for Belgium or Bulgaria.   I left my passport to be couriered up to London for a Bulgarian visa, while Rob needed visas for Czechoslovakia, Hungary and Bulgaria.

We left Felixstowe on the Wednesday afternoon. Rob and I ran together as far a Nurnburg on the Thursday night.   On Friday morning we split up, as Rob headed east for the Czech border, while I continued south-eastwards, passing Munich and following signposts for Salzburg in Austria.   It was the first time I had crossed into Austria and Rob Bulmer had warned me about the complicated road tax system inflicted on foreign trucks. He recommended that I find an agent at the border and pay him to do all the paperwork. Rob had done regular Austrian work before coming to drive for Archie Fredericks. He reckoned it took him at least half a dozen trips to get the hang of the forms.

On my way over to the agent's office block, I was approached by another British driver who was also driving his maiden voyage to the Middle East. His name was Chris Wood and he was delighted to see me, as he thought I could help him with his papers. Chris was disappointed to find that it was my first time, too, but we agreed to tackle it together. It took us a long time to get through, but I am sure two heads were better than one, and it could have taken a long longer. The Austrian Customs were a nightmare, even with our forms filled in by the agent. There were rows of frosted glass sliding windows where you had to push your papers under the glass. If it was the wrong papers to the wrong window, then they were rejected without explanation. All the signs were written in German: we only conquered the system by using the process of elimination. It got to the stage when both of us could only see the funny side of the situation. At the end of our ordeal, the Austrian Customs officials must have wondered just what sort of people British truck drivers were – Chris and I went from window to window, laughing helplessly.

We left the crossing point together and drove through

Austria, reaching the border with Yugoslavia just after nightfall. Neither Chris no I could face the prospect of another disastrous Customs encounter on the same day, so we decided to leave it until the morning. On Saturday, however, our decision turned out to be the wrong one, as the border was closed for the weekend. We were stuck until midnight Sunday, but every cloud has a silver lining and two more British trucks had arrived during the night. It seemed that the drivers knew they would not be going anywhere for a couple of days as neither occupant surfaced from his bunk before midday. When they did get up, we all had lunch together in the restaurant, overlooking the crossing. The late arrivals introduced themselves as John Bruce, who drove for Astrans, and Gavin Benson, working for Sampsons. John was en route for Oman, while Gavin was just going to Istanbul – the same as Chris Wood and myself. We told John and Gavin that we were first-timers and John said he would show us the way, as long as we kept up. John was particular who he ran with, but said he owed it to the driver who had taken him under his wing when he was on his first trip. The idea was that we should help anybody in a similar situation to us in the future.

Gavin was an old friend of John's, who went back a long way; his casual attitude contrasted greatly with John's seriousness. I thought Chris and I were fortunate to get the chance to run with two such experienced drivers who would virtually guarantee our safe arrival in Istanbul – it certainly eased my mind. Gavin had a saying, a motto that applied to about 50% of British drivers doing the Middle East work – it was: "The job's fucked: let's go on the piss". He would say this line every time he raised his hand to order four more beers, which the waiter duly brought over to our table. The four of us spent the whole of Saturday drinking in the restaurant, as we looked down on the comings and goings at the border. After a long lie-in on Sunday, we spent the rest of the day doing exactly the same as Saturday, at exactly the same table.

One of the differences between Middle East drivers and drivers to other European countries was that Middle East drivers never made early starts. Sometimes, possibly because of the drinking during the previous night, but mainly because they knew that they were not going to reach their destination that day however early they started. On the Monday, we all had a leisurely breakfast, before John shepherded Chris and me through the maze of Austrian and Yugo Customs' procedures. This involved paying even more road tax to use Yugoslavian roads, even though we would have to pay motorway tolls en route.

The road through Yugoslavia from Maribor in the north, to the Bulgarian border in the east was called "Death Road" and for a very good reason: it was a single carriageway for much of its length and was used by both farm traffic and vehicles wanting to cross continents, which led to many fatal accidents. The cause of which was nearly always due to the vast difference in vehicles' speeds that necessitated frequent overtaking. The deaths in the crashes were marked by roadside shrines of flowers and crosses. I had lost count of how many we had passed by the time we reached Belgrade. With the right-hand drive Mercedes, it was difficult to overtake. Gavin was up ahead, where he tried to help by signalling to me about the on-coming traffic, but with only 260 horsepower, it was never easy. Every time I overtook one of the slow, over-loaded local trucks, it was a close shave. The most common on-coming danger was the endless stream of old German-registered Mercedes cars, full of Turkish families making their way back to Germany, after visiting relatives in their homeland.

John and Gavin wanted to stop for the night at the National Hotel on the northern outskirts of Belgrade, but it was packed out with trucks of every nation when we arrived in the late evening. John managed to have a chat with a couple of homeward-bound British drivers before we moved on to park for the night at a service station, south of the capital. The news that it was taking three days to queue up to cross the border from Bulgaria into Turkey prompted John and Gavin to change our route so we avoided the trouble-spot. We carried on driving east, before turning south, in order to go through Greece. You did not need a permit to transit Greece, but John figured we might have problems if we did not make it to the border in one day. To stop overnight in southern Yugoslavia was asking for trouble from the notorious gangs of gypsies who preyed on unwary foreigners. Gavin illustrated John's warning with a couple of lurid tales of misadventure. He had stories to tell on most aspects of Middle East driving, but the one about the gypsy girl sitting on the driver's face, while her sister searched the cab for his wallet, was most disturbing. It was a good job for me that they did not know that trick in Rumania.

Chris Wood and myself had no qualms about the change of plan, as we continued to tag along behind the other two. We made it into the Greek truck-stop at Evzoni just after midnight. There had been a problem about paying extra road tax, due to our re-routing, but John Bruce knew how to handle it and made it look simple. I just hoped I could remember all this avalanche of information, after John had taken so much time and trouble in explaining everything. Gavin was happy to be in Greece, so he brought out another of his sayings to celebrate the successful traversing of Yugoslavia: "Good job well done, let's go on the piss." He was still drinking steadily when I went to bed at 3.30.

The next day's run was planned by Gavin over breakfast at Evzoni. Our destination was Kavala, via Thessalonika: Gavin would lead the way, as only he knew the short-cut through Thessalonika. John added a warning about the steep hill down into Kavala and off we went. All was well, until Gavin did a sharp left turn across the traffic, as we came into Thessalonika. I was last of the four and by the time I did my turn into the narrow road between two blocks of flats, the dust kicked up by the other three was worse than any fog. I blindly followed along on what turned into a rough track with raised manhole covers and half-made kerbs. At the top of the track, where the housing finished, I was confronted by Gavin's DAF coming towards me, with a line of laundry draped over the front of the trailer. Gavin made hand motions, indicating that I should turn round in the field behind him, before we all made our way back down to the main road. We had to endure a stream of verbal abuse from dozens of irate Greek housewives, who had just seen a morning's washing ruined by four inconsiderate Britons. It turned out that we wanted the next left, just 100 yards further down the road.

Even with the detour, we still made it to Kavala by early afternoon. It was a medium sized port, with ferries and fishing vessels, but the important thing about Kavala, after you had negotiated the long, twisting descent down to sea level, was the truck park on the beach. A long, narrow parking area, shaded by trees and serviced by cheap, friendly restaurants, serving ice cold beer. What more could a driver wish for? It was said that many weary souls on their way back from the further eastern destinations, spent as long as a week at Kavala, re-charging their batteries, before returning to the UK. We were only going to spend one night on the beach, so Gavin wasted no time in getting his folding chair, in order to sit on the sand with a cold bottle of Lowenbrau in his hand.

John warned Chris and me to take it easy on the beer as the next day was one of the few days on which an early start would be beneficial. The Turkish Customs at the border only made two clearances each day: one at midday and one at midnight. You had to get into the

Turkish Customs' compound before 9.00 o'clock in the morning to have any chance of leaving before noon. The Ipsala crossing was not a busy frontier, as Greece and Turkey were not the best of friends, having fallen out over Cyprus. The Bulgarians and the Turks were not very friendly towards each other either, but due to necessity they crossed the border into each other's country. No Greeks or Turks crossed the border at Ipsala – it was only used by foreigners to both countries.

We all used the services of the Customs' agent called Youngturk, who handled all the paperwork. The four of us retired to the restaurant for a cup of chi, the sweet tea, drunk without milk. The only other travellers crossing into Turkey that morning were Dutch and German tourists in camper vans: three going east and two vans returning west. The outer near-side tyre of the drive axle had picked up a bolt on the early morning run to the border and had slowly deflated. It would have saved time to change the wheel while we waited for the Customs' all clear, but John reckoned that messing about under the noses of the border officials might make them unnecessarily suspicious, so we decided to leave it until we got up the road. The first thing I did on Turkish soil was to change a wheel, although Chris Wood did most of the work, while swearing at Gavin, who did absolutely nothing.

Gavin was more interested in the contents of a Dutch registered coach that was sharing our lay-by. The passengers were all young Australians and New

Zealanders, mostly girls, who were doing the European Grand Tour, so popular with antipodean twenty-somethings. The coach party had stopped for lunch and sat eating cheese salad sandwiches on the grassy slopes above the road. Gavin referred to the vehicle as a 'slut-bus', an unflattering term used by all Middle Eastern drivers, which did not accurately reflect the contents of the coach. It was more of a label given, because of the constant failure of the drivers to get anywhere with the girls.

We left the lay-by with instructions to look out for the long descent into Tekirdag and not to forget to stop at the police checkpoint at Silivri. It was not a steep hill down into Tekirdag, but it was long and twisted, down a narrow valley, so that you would not see the end; a low gear was needed to get you safely to the bottom. The road went straight through the town and it was easy to envisage runaway trucks careering down the hill, with their brakes on fire. After catching up the others at the police checkpoint, it was just an hour's drive into the Londra Camp, situated on the western outskirts of Istanbul, near the airport. It was an old campsite, originally for camper vans and back-packers, but it had widened its entrance gates to accommodate trucks. The Londra was the Number One rendezvous point for everyone going across the Bosphorus.

Rob Bulmer had arrived the previous evening and was parked in the section of the truck park that British trucks reserved for themselves. It was the shadiest corner, nearest the showers and the bar, but furthest away from the noisy road. Rob had been to see our agent in Istanbul that morning. He had told Rob that we were clearing Customs at Izmit. The agent left instructions with Rob that if I arrived during the day, I was to follow Rob to Izmit where, hopefully, we would be unloaded in the afternoon.

Izmit was on the eastern side of the Bosphorus, about two hours' drive from the Londra Camp, but on Friday morning, we could not leave until 10.00 o'clock. This was because of the rush hour restrictions on the Bosphorus bridge, where the toll doubled before 10.00 in the morning. This was not much of a deterrent for a car, but for a four axle truck, it was an extra £90.00. It was good for me that Rob had arrived a day earlier, as it was normal to loose a day while you went to tell your agent to arrange for Customs' clearance: as it was Friday, I would not have tipped until the Monday. We were both back at the Londra Camp before dark, after having unloaded the diesel engines at a truck building plant, right beside the main Istanbul-to-Ankara highway. As I sat waiting at the Customs at Izmit, I saw John Bruce go by, on his way to Muscat. I don't think he knew how much easier had had made my job: I could not thank him enough. Gavin and Chris Wood were still at the Londra Camp when Rob and I returned. They had been to see their agents and would tip on Monday.

"You got a result there alright! A good job well done: let's go on the piss," said Gavin as soon as we got back.

In the restaurant bar at the campsite, Gavin recommended the chicken – it was the only thing he recognised.

"That other stuff probably won't do you any harm, but if you found out what it was – the you would be ill," suggested Gavin.

Everybody drank Efes Pilsen, the local strong lager. Rob and I sat with Gavin and Chris at a table in the middle of the dining room, soon to be joined by other British drivers. A new Zealand couple also came to sit with us and listen to Gavin recount some of his road stories. The New Zealanders were studying music and the guy had with him a soprano saxophone. We cajoled him to play something and when his girlfriend brought out a small bongo drum, to beat a steady rhythm, the Kiwi blew an amazing set of ethnic Turkish tunes.

A lot of the drivers there that night were Kurds from eastern Turkey, Iran and Iraq; they began chanting, dancing and clapping – they appreciated the New Zealander's talent even more than we did. A whole stream of Efes bottles were sent over to our table and shared amongst us all.

We sat drinking away into the night and I was just thinking what a great job it was when Gavin came out with a chilling statement that stunned us all:

"We've got big trouble. Nobody leave the table.

Stay exactly where you are," he said soberly.

"What on earth do you mean?" we all chorused.

"Don't look now, but we are surrounded:  there's one Turk at every table;  earlier they were all drinking together – now they're waiting for us," continued Gavin.

Gavin was right.  We were the only table of drinkers left in the room:  there were two waiters standing behind the bar, waiting to close up, and the only other people present were the seven Turks, each one seated at a different table.

"What do they want with us?" asked Chris Wood, "nobody has upset them, have they?"

"I don't think so.  The way I see it, they see five men with one women, laughing, joking, having a good time. They reckon those five blokes are going to take turns with that woman and if they can take that woman away from those men – then they can take turns with her," stated Gavin.

"Oh, thanks a lot, Gavin," said the New Zealand girl, "that says a lot for me."

"Well, it's a different culture out here," went on Gavin, "you just don't see Turkish girls out for a drink with the lads.  Most Turks only see western women on

TV, in films or in magazines. It's all glamour and sex. They think they're easy."

"Are you sure about this, Gavin? What are we going to do?" asked Rob Bulmer.

"Not 100% sure, no; but I bet at least half of them are carrying knives. I, for one, am not going to do anything, and I don't want any of you to do anything either. We're out numbered and pissed and I don't fancy a-beating. We'll sit it out," suggested Gavin.

"What if they make a move?" I asked, looking round for a suitable weapon.

"No. They won't start anything in here. It'll be outside, or in the bogs. If you want a leak, you'll just have to piss yourselves," concluded Gavin.

The stand-off lasted till dawn, when the Turks finally gave up and trooped out to their cars. The waiters looked as relieved as we all were. All in all, I thought Gavin had got it right. It was a valuable lesson about getting drunk and dropping your guard in a foreign country. Rob Bulmer and I decided to have a rest day on the Saturday, in order to catch up on our sleep, after sitting up all night.

While we were sleeping, a telex arrived with out re-load details. Two loads of marble floor tiles for the new Waitrose supermarket in Harpenden, to be collected from Mezdra in Bulgaria. It was a shame Rob and I would not be able to run back to the UK together, but at least we could help each other find the pick-up point. After making sure we were not the last customers left in the bar on Saturday night, we left the Londra Camp early on Sunday morning.

The road heading west through Edirne and on to the Turkish-Bulgarian border, which was practically deserted of traffic. There was a charge for crossing on a Sunday, which put most people off. Rob and I debated the pros and cons of paying the surcharge versus the probable Monday morning rush. We thought it would be easier to go through on a peaceful Sunday. The fact that we were empty also helped and we were soon on our way across Bulgaria.

Mezdra was in the north-west of the country. It looked like the best way to get there, would be to head for Sofia and then, just before the capital, leave the main east-west transit track, in order to head north. It all went to plan, until the turn-off to Mezdra: from there, the signposts were only written in Cyrillic script, and with no road numbers to follow, we were helpless. To make matters worse, it was pouring down with rain, which meant there was no one around to ask directions. Suddenly I remembered the old AA Road Book of Europe that my Father had given me when I first passed my HGV test. It was not new then, and I never used it, as the small scale on small pages made it difficult to use as a route planner. However, the book did have a section in the front with facts about each country. Luckily, under Bulgaria, there was a chart showing the Cyrillic alphabet, along side the Roman letters.   Rob and I had a cup of tea, as we worked out the names of the towns in the area.   Afterwards, I stuck up a sheet of paper on the dashboard, with the translation of Mezdra written on it in large letters, before we carried on in the unrelenting rain.

Mezdra was in mountainous country, as you would expect for a marble quarrying area.   The road twisted alongside a swollen river, in a steep, wooded valley. Narrow tunnels and even narrower bridges made us think that, maybe, we were going the wrong way, but with no where to turn round, we had no option but to carry on.   Eventually, we came to Mezdra, at around midnight. It was still raining, so with nobody about, we parked in a lay-by at the edge of town.  In the morning, Rob and I were delighted to find that we were parked in the holding area for trucks waiting to load at the marble factory.

Rob loaded first, in a factory where women seemed to have equal status to men. The wooden crates of marble tiles were swung onto the trailer by a female crane driver, who handled her machinery as well as any man.   After the load was complete, the forewoman asked us to join her for lunch in the works canteen.  For starters, there was a pink soup that tasted awful, although the bread roll was okay;  the main course was mashed potato, greens and a boiled pig's trotter that had no meat on it. Rob and I did not want to appear ungrateful, but here was no way we could eat our meat. The locals devoured their trotters with relish. If asked, we agreed to plead 'vegetarian', but managed to slip away unnoticed before dessert. Back at the trucks, we opened some tins and had a proper meal, before Rob set off, back to England.

The carpenters at the factory were still making the crates for my marble tiles, so I had to wait until the next day to be loaded. I left, just before lunchtime on the Tuesday, so I did not have to decline an invitation to dine. When I got going, I found the marble was much heavier than the load of diesels I had brought down across Europe. The Mercedes V8 struggled all the way back to Zeebrugge. The engine started first time, every time, never missed a beat and was ultra reliable – it just did not have enough horsepower. The 12 speed gearbox had a cog for every occasion – the only problem was that my gears were a lot lower than all the other trucks. It was Sunday morning before I arrived in Dover, where I spent most of the day waiting at the Eastern Docks for Customs' clearance. I ran up to Harpenden in the evening, ready to deliver the tiles at the supermarket on the Monday. Rob Borgman turned up with his load, just as I was leaving. He had come through Dover on the Saturday morning and had gone home for the weekend.

I did a couple of Italian trips after the Turkey trip, but as the weather began to warm up, my thoughts turned to the south of France and the beach. At the end of May, I handed in my notice and told Archie I was going away for a few months. He said he would take me on again in the autumn, if he had an opening.

## Chapter Thirteen

Rupert had kept in touch during the winter, which again had seen him working at the smaller end of the road transport industry. We agreed to run the VWs in convoy down to the south of France. Two days after leaving home, the vans rolled into the car park behind the beach at Ramatuelle. It was on the next day, when Rupert and I were returning to the beach after spending the morning in the village that we saw Davy Breitner. He was standing outside an isolated farm building, about half a mile from the sea. We pulled the vans over onto the verge and Davy asked Rupert and myself to come in for a drink.

Veronique, Davy's long-time girlfriend, was there, along with Carolyn Bailey and the contents of the Cannibale snack bar. Over a beer, Davy and the girls told of the plans that they had for the barn. They had rented the place for the whole summer and using the equipment from the Cannibale, they were going to have their own snack bar, called "The Poney Express". The building had a water supply and was connected to the electricity. All it needed was cleaning out and the kitchen setting up. Davy offered Rupert and me the construction work, which included building a bamboo roofed canopy at the rear of the barn, using the old timbers from the Cannibale. Carolyn, who was financing the project, could not pay us, but agreed that Rupert and I could have half-priced food and drink for the whole summer. We shook hands on the deal and started work straight away.

Within four days, the work was finished and the place was ready to open for business. The old woodwork was bolted together, to form a lean-to at the back of the barn, then covered with bamboo that grew in the nearby hedgerows. The bar was placed in front of the kitchen door, the tables and chairs arranged in the shade of the canopy at the edge of the vineyard; the main interior area, where everything had been kept during the winter, was left empty for dancing, except for a small bar and a couple of tables. The other room was the kitchen. In it, Davy and Veronique had their bed, along with two chest-freezers, a fridge, a cooker, a deep fat fryer and a sink. The place did lack toilet facilities, but if anybody asked, Davy just waved his hand in the general direction of the vines.

While us men had busied ourselves with the construction, the women, Carolyn and Veronique, had dealt with other things. They had organised supplies of fresh and frozen food, applied for a drinks' licence that allowed for the sale of beer and wine, as well as arranging for the delivery of the booze and soft drinks. Carolyn bought the loudest stereo cassette player that she could afford, while Veronique painted a big sign saying "Poney Express Snack Bar" which Rupert and I nailed onto a post, at the side of the road.

On the opening night, Alain, the proprietor of "Chez Tony" – a Bar in Ramatuelle, brought down a gang of his friends to try the fare. The Frenchman had been a great help with his advice on what to do, where to go and who to see; also, his donation of two boxes of beer and wine glasses was very generous. The eight French diners occupied on long table, while Rupert and I were joined at ours by George, an old Englishman, Ray Brennan and Marlene, who had just arrived from Holland, plus Claire and Louise, two French girls who happened to stop, while looking for somewhere to eat. Carolyn was the cook, Davy waited at table and Vero served behind the bar. The food was excellent and no portion control. The meal finished with strawberries and ice cream, after which we all toasted to the success of "The Poney Express" with champagne.

Rupert sat next to Louise during the meal, where he knew enough French to strike up a conversation. They seemed to get on well, although I did not take much notice, unlike Ray Brennan.

" Rupert's in there, betcha he's pulled," whispered Ray, giving me a nudge.

Later, I came back from a visit to the vines, to find Ray was right. Rupert and Louise were kissing passionately, beside the French girls' 2CV, while Claire waited patiently behind the steering wheel. The driver did not look too happy, but that might have been because she had sat next to George all night.

"We're going out as a foursome tomorrow," said Rupert, after finally letting Louise go back to her campsite. "I've promised the girls that we'll take them to a deserted beach, with crystal clear water and golden sand – just like paradise."

"Where's that then?  Who's paying for the Lear Jet?" I asked sarcastically.  "That place you're always on about - round the rocks from L'Escalet.  I thought we could take a picnic," suggested Rupert.

"I've only ever been there on a motorbike.  It's a hell of a rough track.  I don't know if the van could handle it," I said negatively.

"Let's give it a go.  We'll take your van, it's got better tires.  Hey, I think that Claire fancies you, y'know," said Rupert positively.

Next morning, Carolyn made us some salad rolls; there was just enough room to fit them in the ice box, on top of the Kronenbourg.  The girls arrived on time and left their Citroen at the Poney Express, as we all set off, in the van, to the Bastide Blanche.  The track to the beach was worse than I remembered;  it was three kilometres of twists and turns, with loose rocks on steep drops. The surface had deteriorated, due to the increased use of four wheel drive vehicles, which scrapped at the stones and dirt with their wide tyres.  It was downhill all the way to the shoreline:  the problems would come on the return journey.

The track led to the peninsular, called "Cap Cartaya". This is a 200 foot high, rocky outcrop, joined to the mainland by a thin sand bar. The Cape was the location for the start and finish scenes in the film "Chitty, Chitty, Bang, Bang". It is a beautiful place, but on the day of our visit, its splendour was marred by a lot of seaweed that had been washed ashore. The four of us took all we thought we would need and left the van, in order to scramble round the rocks to the beach called "Bastide Blanche". The sun was shining, the sea was calm, there was no seaweed and also no people. We had nobody within 100 yards of us, as we dumped down the gear and all went for a swim. The only other people about were those who had come ashore from the four boats, moored in the bay.

We stayed all day. Claire and Louise were going home the next day, so they wanted the best tans they could get. The girls loved the place: they were reluctant to leave, even when I said I did not want to tackle the dirt track in the dark. The van, with its rear engine and rear wheel drive, coped well with the rough gravel. The only causalities were a couple of wine glasses in the cupboard. We finished up, back at the Poney Express, just as the lighthouse on Cap Camarat started its night's work.

After a meal, we walked down to the beach, in the late evening warmth. I sat at the water's edge, while Rupert and Louise disappeared, arm in arm, into the darkness. Claire came and sat down beside me, real close. I was surprised when she sat so close. The young Sarah Kennedy look-alike had not spoken to me all day.

For a few minutes, I thought about the situation, and then decided to make a move on her. I reached over and put my arm round her shoulders. Claire immediately gave a little yelp, so I quickly pulled away. The poor girl had over-done the sunbathing and was badly burned. Sitting beside her, I could feel the heat radiating out of her body. From then on, we sat in silence, until the lovebirds returned, but Claire did thank me for a wonderful day and for showing her the paradise beach.

The rest of the month of June and July, was spent either on the beach, or at the Poney Express. Rupert and I played a lot of cards, mostly crib, and drunk a lot of Kronenbourg. The Poney Express soon became the 'in' place, as it became popular with the beach-sellers who, although they never spent much money, made the snack bar look busy and thereby attracted even more people. Before he went up to the Dordogne to do some work for Marianne on her farm, Rupert found himself another girlfriend who was a tiny little thing called Mandy. One night, when there was a lot of us drinking wine down on the beach, Rupert asked to borrow the van so he could run Mandy, her friend Sue and Sue's boyfriend, Bob, back to their campsite. Not for the first time Rupert was having trouble finding petrol for his van's fuel tank. I gave him the keys and off he went. Rupert came back soon enough, but with some bad news.

"I had an accident on the way back. I've dented the front corner and lost the indicator," he said, sheepishly.
"What did you hit?" I asked.

"A Citroen. I was driving on the wrong side of the road. I swerved to miss it, but just clipped the front corner," said Rupert.

"What did they say? Did you exchange details?" I enquired.

"No. I didn't stop. I think I've had too much to drink – I'm over the limit. I didn't know if I was insured or not," explained Rupert.

I went over to have a look at the van, which still bore the scars of the previous summer's crash. It did not look too bad as the headlight was still in tact. What was I to do? Hide the van or make a run for it? Rupert and I were sitting on the beach, discussing the situation when we saw the single headlight of a battered Citroen coming towards us, accompanied by the sound of metal scraping on rubber. Four men got out and came over, asking who owned the van. I told them I was the owner, but not the driver. Rupert did the honourable thing and admitted he was driving, but I do not know how we escaped a beating. The Frenchmen seemed satisfied with the insurance details; they did not want the police involved, because I think they had also been drinking. I was shaking like a leaf when I wrote out the information from the Green Card.

A few days after the crash, Rupert went to the Dordogne to start work on the farm. On his last night, Carolyn took him out for a meal at one of the restaurants in Ramatuelle village. Carolyn said she wanted to show her appreciation for all he hard work Rupert had put in when building the Poney Express. The lucky sod ended up staying the night in her tent on Les Tournels Campsite. In the morning Rupert told me what a good night it had been. I could not wait for Carolyn to show the same appreciation to me.

Without my regular cards and drinking partner, I found myself drinking with Badger most of the time. His real name was Ben Robson, but because of the two grey streaks in his hair, everyone called him 'Badger'. The Geordie from Peterlee was in his late twenties and had been 'drifting' since his career as a professional footballer at Leeds United had been cut short because of a knee injury. During the previous summer, Badger had formed a firm friendship with Davy Breitner, so when he found his old mate was running a bar, Badger moved in and started sleeping on the floor of the barn. Davy gave Badger the same half-price deal as myself. We usually just sat and drank the night away, while everyone came and went at the snack bar. English was the language of the Poney Express: Dutch, Germans, Danish, Belgians and French, all spoke to each other in English. Many international friendships started that summer. I never tried too hard, but still did alright. There were even one night stands when I didn't get to ask the girl's name. Vero, the beekeeper, returned for another summer holiday and we continued our affair in the same manner as the two previous years. Anka, from Amsterdam, moved into the van for two weeks, which was not something she intended to do when she left Holland. The athletic Dutch girl was not looking for social contact, after the finish of a long-term affair, but I caught her on the rebound. The romantic atmosphere of St Tropez always made love affairs seem the natural thing to do.

The beach sellers' party had been talked about for over a week before it happened. L'Escalet was chosen as the site, while anyone with a vehicle was invited, in the hope that the driver would take some poor sellers to the isolated beach. Sellers of ice cream, donuts, cold drinks and toffee covered peanuts from all the beaches in the St Tropez area descended onto L'Escalet, a small rocky beach. I went with Anka and took a van full that included Davy Breitner, who thought he would come along as the Poney Express looked like it would have a slack night.

Ray Brennan and Marlene packed in four party-goers across the back seat of their Simca, before we all set off, along the back lanes to the party. There was no village at L'Escalet, just a few villas dotted about on the high ground surrounding the bay with its beach and slip way. The only road in or out dropped sharply down to sea level, where there was a big car park and two mobile snack bars that were closed for the night. The car park was nearly full when the Poney Express convoy arrived and, as we all made our way down the narrow path to the rock beach, I could see hundreds of people partying in the light of numerous camp fires. There were more people on the sand then than ever was during the day, even in the height of summer.   As I wandered around with Anka, listening to the competing ghettoblasters, I was amazed by the number of people that I knew.

Unfortunately, the party did not last long.  Somebody, somewhere, telephoned the police.  Only one police van arrived, but the two gendarmes had no hesitation in lobbing half a dozen CS gas canisters down onto the beach.   In the ensuing panic, I made my way up the path to the car park, only to be met by the police coming down.   Each officer had a baton in one hand and a CS spray in the other. I got the same treatment that everyone on the path in front of me received – that was a spray of CS gas in the face and then a push into the thorn bushes at the side of the path.   I struggled to my feet, in order to grope my way back to the van with my eyes streaming.  To get rid of the spray, I ducked my head in a bowl of cold water, but it did not do any good.  When all my passengers returned, I started off back to the Poney Express, but the only way I could keep my eyes open was by sticking my head out of the window as I drove along. My tears ran back into my ears. When all the vehicles had limped back to the Poney Express, everyone had their own horror story to tell.   I counted myself lucky not to have been hit over the head with a baton.   Some people wanted revenge and were disgusted that a couple of cops with a case of tear gas could break up a trouble-free party and get the better of over 200 people.

"I think its best if we all just let it go.  Put it down to experience," suggested Davy Breitner.

"It was probably you who tipped off the cops, so that everyone would come back and drink at your bar," Ray Brennan said to Davy, unfairly.

I just wished I had not got a beard – it was days before I got rid of the CS gas on my face.

Anka's holiday finished with a trip to the Gorge du Verdun. Ray and Marlene came along in their car and, once again, the prospect of finding gold had everyone in an excited, buoyant mood. We arrived at the Lac de Ste. Croix, with the Dutch-registered Simca making ominous knocking noises. It turned out that a front wheel bearing was breaking up. Luckily, Richie Bishop, a bus mechanic from Gloucester, was with us and he soon stripped down the hub. Ray, Richie and I then went off in the van to find the nearest Simca garage at Aups, which fortunately had the part in stock. The car was back on the road by mid-afternoon. Although we did do some exploring, along with a little panning for gold, once again, the hot weather, with a complete lack of sea breeze, made it thirsty work. It was the same old story: too much thirst-quenching alcohol equals no more endeavour. The routine of the beach was now being broken by the routine of the Gorge.

Badger broke his routine by going to Holland with Anka's group, when they returned to Amsterdam. Pat and Maggie O'Malley had come for another long holiday in their old ambulance, although I did not see as much of them in the evenings as Pat's budget did not allow him to drink at the Poney Express.  The beach car park was full of camper vans every night.  The largest of the vehicles, by a long way, was the home of a Scottish couple, Angus and Donna.  The converted removal van carried everything anyone could possibly need, whilst touring Europe.  Angus made a living by performing Punch and Judy shows on beaches and in town squares. The talented Scotsman could do the voices in French, Spanish and Italian; also he gave late evening fire-eating demonstrations, which added up to quite a good, tax-free income.  Angus and Donna had a comfortable lifestyle in their well-equipped truck.  They seemed to have everything they needed and protected it by keeping Alsatian dogs tied to the front bumper when parked.

## Chapter Fourteen

Regine and Pascaline, from Nancy, were back on the Les Tournels campsite and split their day three ways: afternoons on the rocks at L'Escalet; evenings at the Poney Express, and mornings in Ramatuelle village where the girls held court at the Bar Tabac, in the Place de 'Ormeaux. Every morning, an international following of Dutch, German, English and French occupied most of the tables on the terrace, eating croissants and drinking coffee as they discussed the projects for the day, before going off to various beaches for the afternoon.

The public section of Pampellone beach, between L'Esquinade and the Cabine Bamboo, was still my regular spot for the afternoon. Most people seemed to have regular habits, as I found myself sitting amongst the same faces most afternoons. Along with swimming, the windsurfer was my main source of exercise. The chess set exercised my brain. Richie Bishop and Irish Danny were regular opponents and we all won as many as we lost, except when Eric, from Amsterdam, came for a game – he never lost. The chessboard proved to be a magnet. Quite often, complete strangers would come to sit and watch the matches. Many finished up by playing, obviously encouraged by the poor standard demonstrated by everyone, except Eric. After observing a summer of chess under my parasol, I came to the conclusion that most people hated losing at chess because they thought it showed they were somehow mentally inferior to the winner. Personally, I overcame this by playing in a carefree, detached way, while trying to see a defeat as a way of making someone else happy. My matches tended to be short, win or lose, but I did make a lot of friends.

Many of the strangers who came to watch the chess also partook in the other afternoon ritual: a cup of tea at 4.00 o'clock. This daily event was a great source of amusement to the non-English on the beach, as they could not see the point of a hot drink at the hottest time of the day. The whole thing was seen as a typical English eccentricity, but out of the dozen people usually assembled under the parasol at 4.00 in the afternoon, less than half were from England. Richie and Danny nearly always did the preparations by boiling the water in the van and then bringing everything onto the beach. Often, somebody would bring along a packet of biscuits. Only the amount of cups kept in the van limited proceedings, although some regulars started bringing their own crockery.

One of the best evenings of the summer was the O'Malley annual barbecue, when Pat invited all his friends, and most of the unattached females on the beach, for a cook-out in the car park. The Kronenbourg-drinking Irishman enjoyed entertaining young girls of all nationalities, but it did make a lot of work for Maggie. On this occasion, Pat had booked Angus to give a Punch and Judy show, which turned out to be a risqué adult version, plus some fire eating after it got dark. It was after Maggie's excellent barbecued chicken and before

Angus' fire show that I found myself with my arm round Ulrike, as we sat on the ground in the car park. Ulrike had arrived a few days earlier with Ingrid, who was one of the Regensburg girls who had come to Ramatuelle in the big green Mercedes van two years before. This time, Ingrid had come in her Fiat Panda, which she and Ulrike were using as if it was a camping car. At the end of the night, Ulrike and I finished up in each other's arms and she quite happily came back to the van. We made love all night and I made coffee in the morning. It was only when Ingrid joined us for breakfast that I realised there was something wrong. The two German girls spoke sharply to each other in their native tongue before Ingrid turned to me.

"Do you know how old Ulrike is?" she asked, in a matter of fact tone.

"She's the same age as you, isn't she?" I replied, thinking they were at college together.

"No. She is 15," said Ingrid, before going off in a huff to sit in her car.

"I am 16 in one month's time," said Ulrike. "Ingrid is jealous. She has no lover yet."

Ulrike slept every night after that in the van, until the end of her holiday. The young girl certainly did not look, or act, like a 15 year old, but I never told anyone her age. A girl of 15, going on holiday with her friend was not unusual, nor was someone of that age sunbathing topless on the beach;   maybe for Ulrike to be living in a van with a man nearly twice her age was not normal, but I do not think it did her any harm.  Ulrike was thankful for the comfortable bed, plus the lack of mosquitoes:  they had made her nights a misery when she slept in the Panda.

As the season was drawing to a close, Badger returned from Amsterdam with a Scottish girl, called Jeanne.  They had met when Jeanne was working in a topless hairdressing salon and Badger had gone in for a trim.  By all accounts, it was a really sleazy place, where the question: "Is there anything else, sir?" did not just mean buying a condom, but also wearing it while you were given a blow job - there in the barber's chair. Jeanne had been promised a job in his friend's bar, so it did not take much to persuade the hairdresser to return with Badger to the south of France.

Jeanne was soon put to work, but not at the Poney Express as she expected.  Badger had her giving head down on the beach, at a 100 francs a time.  In the early evening, Badger would take his woman down to the car park, where he would approach some of the local Arab farm-workers who were always wandering around at that time of the day.  There was no shortage of clients, as the word soon got around on what was on offer.   Whilst Jeanne was taking her punters off into the bamboo thickets, Badger would often come on to the beach for a chat.  The likeable Geordie had changed a lot since he went to Amsterdam:  he was now a businessman who talked seriously about his new venture. Badger told of how he was looking after all the money and how it was necessary to give Jeanne a slap, once in a while. He also showed me the knife that he now carried, in case a customer was reluctant to pay.

One afternoon, when the weather looked like rain, Badger asked if it might be possible to use the van for Jeanne's entertaining; he even offered to pay, but I made hasty excuses about not wanting the upholstery messed up and not wanting people knocking on my door all night, expecting to find Jeanne inside. Davy Breitner had this problem at the Poney Express, where he had to forbid Jeanne to sit in any place where she could be seen from the road. Badger had taken to living off immoral earnings so well, it was easy to think he had done it before. It was such a nice little earner, he reckoned there was no way he was going to be picking grapes again that year.

Francis Boi, at the Domaine de St Genevive, had agreed to take back the same pickers as the year before, so everyone was waiting for the second week of September, when the work would begin. Ray Brennan and Marlene had earned enough by selling cold drinks not to be obliged to stay for the harvest. They were forced to dump their old Simca when the gearbox jammed, but it had done well for them – providing transport, lodgings and dry storage for their gear.

It was at this time that I first noticed a particularly gorgeous girl. There had been a lot of good looking females on the beach over the years, but most of them, I had considered, to be out of my class and I thought that I did not stand a chance with them. I had looked at them, but never wanted them. However, this was different, maybe because this beauty kept looking at me and giving a little smile every now and again. After keeping watch for several days, I was able to build up a pattern of her time on the beach. Olivia would be dropped off with her sister just after lunch by an older man who I took to be her father. The pair always took up a position on the sand five metres to my right, neither in front nor behind. They swam, sunbathed and read paperbacks or magazines until collected by the father, now accompanied by his wife. The couple would often sit with the girls until they were some of the last people to leave the beach.

The object of my desires had a perfect body, but the most striking thing about her was the way she walked: Olivia had the most tremendous wiggle. I had never seen anything like that – it was so natural. After deliberately following her along the wave line, just to watch her bum, I found out how Olivia did it: her footmarks in the sand looked as if the left foot was on the right leg and the right foot was on the left – the feet did not cross by much, but just enough to give the rear end a nice little twist at every step.

Besides walking, swimming was another thing Olivia did well. Often I would be windsurfing at around 200 metres offshore and Olivia would be there – not swimming hard or going anywhere, but casually floating around and doing surface dives. My mermaid started giving little waves as I sailed by and I started waving back. Sure, I went out on the windsufer after I saw Olivia roll up the top of her one piece swimsuit, before going for a dip; but there were just as many occasions when she followed me into the water. More and more of my time was spent in trying to think of a way I could engage the girl in conversation and ask her for a date – presuming she spoke English.

My big chance came late one afternoon, when I saw Olivia looking for her purse before going to buy an apple doughnut. I grabbed my wallet, jumped up and reached the doughnut man just ahead of my quarry. I knew the seller quite well, as he had drunk tea under the parasol on many occasions. He would not take my money for the doughnut and as he went on to serve Olivia, I asked him if he wanted a cuppa. The seller declined my offer, as he was just about finished and wanted to get off home, but when I asked the same question to Olivia, my heart skipped a beat when she said 'yes'. We walked over to the van, to brew up, and I found Olivia spoke good English. When her parents arrived to collect Olivia and her sister, we were still at the van, talking. I just had time to arrange a rendezvous for later that evening: 10.00 o'clock under the plane trees at the Place des Lices in St Tropez.

At 9.00 o'clock, I was watching the games of boules being played in the square. Olivia did not show up until way past ten, but she looked stunning, in a simple white shirt and faded blue demins. We went off for a coffee at the Café des Sports, which Carolyn had told me was the least expensive of the trendy, sit-outside bars. Then Olivia and I walked through the town and along the quay, admiring the portrait painters at work, with the multi-million pound yachts tied up behind them. At the end of the harbour wall, we had our first kiss and kissed again at the stone monument that marked the spot where the American liberation troops had landed during the Second World War. The Yankee soldiers must have come ashore thinking about meeting French girls just like Olivia, but I doubt if any found one as passionate as my date that night.

"I want you," I whispered, when our tongues momentarily went back into their own mouths.

"Me too" murmured Olivia, as she pulled me hard against her body.

The heaving mass of people that congregated every evening on the St Tropez water front had thinned out as we made our way to the van at a fast walking pace. The apartment at which Olivia was staying was situated in the old part of town, behind the port. The most convenient parking spot was on the hill above the town, next to the old fort. I found a space and straight away, we climbed through into the back of the van. Under her jeans and shirt, Olivia was wearing the most beautiful white silk underwear. Her well tanned body against the pure white looked amazing in the light of an overhead sodium street lamp that shone though the open roof vent.   I had seen girls in nice expensive lingerie before, but it had always been worn under party dresses and posh frocks:  to see it come from beneath a plain top and faded 501s was a real turn on.  It made me wonder if Olivia always wore such good gear, or if she had put in on especially for me.  We were in bed together on our first date, after speaking for the first time only hours before hand.  After spending all those days just thinking about Olivia, the situation was now blowing my mind.

That night, we did not speak at all – mainly because our mouths were otherwise occupied.  Something kept telling me it must all be a dream, but my body knew what it wanted.  It did not let me down, as we made love with a mixture of tenderness and passion that rose to a crescendo of force and brutality as we climaxed together.   I had never known it could be that good.  Afterward, as we lay together, we did it again, in a slow loving way:  caressing each other's bodies with light strokes of the hand – such a contrast to the scratching and biting that happened an hour earlier.  Before Olivia left in the morning, we made love for a third time:  more tender than the first, but more energetic than the second.  It was the perfect way to start the day and with such a beautiful person laying beside you when you woke up – it was only natural.  I promised Olivia I would teach her to windsurf when I saw her on the beach that afternoon.  She hurried off home, hoping to get into bed before her parents got up and realised she had been out all night.

During the following week, before Olivia went home and I started work at Vidauban, we met every night at the Place des Lices; always at 10.00 o'clock and always Olivia was late. After a couple of nights, I went to Olivia's apartment, where I hid round the corner. When she came out and went off towards our rendezvous in the square, I followed. It was great to watch her walk down the street with that amazing wiggle and, from the amount of heads that Olivia turned, I was not the only one that thought so.

Every night, after coffee, our evening stroll in St Tropez got shorter and shorter, as neither of us could hide the true reason for our meeting. Olivia seemed to have a never-ending supply of sexy lingerie: it was always jeans and a plain blouse, but underneath, the styles and colours varied every time. The perfume that Olivia wore was another great thing. Her body was always sweet smelling and freshly showered: it made a change to go to bed with a girl who did not have sand between her toes and taste of salt. I am not saying that the other girls had hygiene problems, but when you are living out of a rucksack, or the boot of a car, conditions are not ideal.

Taking a shower was not a problem for me, as I had found that by putting a twenty litre water container in the front window of the van at lunchtime, by evening, it would be hot enough for a shower. The container had a short length of hose and a spray nozzle from a watering can fitted to its tap; when the water was placed on top of the windsurfer, which was on the van's roof rack, it gave an adequate supply of hot water, under which I took my shower. If anybody was staying with me, I just put two containers in the window to catch the sun.

## Chapter Fifteen

Finally, it was time to leave the beach and make my way up to the Domaine de Ste Genevive. Over the weekend, all the old picking crew began to arrive - Billy Carroll was in charge, as usual. This year, there were two extra weeks of work, as Francis Boi had contracted to pick a neighbour's grapes after we had finished those at St Genevive. Marianne was back again, with her brother, Pierre. Speedy and Gerry Turner, who came down from the Dordogne in the same car. The two fractured skull merchants had been at the sheep farm for a fortnight before Speedy picked up his serious injury of the year. This time, it was a fractured wrist, obtained when Speedy was trying to start one of the farm's tractors with the starting handle. The engine had backfired, but because he wrapped his thumb around the handle, instead of having it on the same side as his fingers, the kick had broken Speedy's wrist. The invalid's right arm was encased in plaster of Paris up to the elbow, but he was adamant it would not hinder his grape picking capability - although Speedy was sure he could not do any washing up.

The same local Arab farm workers were still there, along with Bridget and Celine, Francis' two eldest daughters. The tractors and trailers were the same, so was the work and the weather – hot and sunny. After a few days, my aches and pains eased, as I became accustomed to carrying the buckets of grapes, but it was not the same for Marianne who, I noticed, was feeling her back.

"Is the work too hard for your back?" I asked.

"No, it not the work, it's the ground that is too hard. I'm not used to sleeping in a tent," Marianne replied, leaning back and rubbing her lower back with both hands.

"Why don't you move into the van? I have plenty of room. It's a big bed and you'll be more comfortable," I suggested, while swapping Marianne's full bucket for an empty one.

"Thank you," she said, as I wandered through the vines, back to the tractor and trailer.

Was it a "thanks, but no thanks" or a "thanks, I accept your offer" – I could not tell. Marianne and I had known each other since she worked with Kate in the supermarket at Les Tournels. At the cheese counter, Marianne would always cut and weigh a small piece of cheese before wrapping up a big bit and sticking on the small price ticket. We were friends, but I had never had a conversation with her longer than when I had offered her my bed. When I went back to the van that night, Marianne was already there – lying in her sleeping bag.

Out of all the girls that stayed in the van over the

years, Marianne was the only one who was not on holiday. Maybe it was because we were working, but there was not much time spent together during the week. Even on our days off, we rarely talked to each other, even though Marianne spoke good English. The silences were long, but never strained – it was just that we only ever said what was necessary. At the weekends, we went off in the van: to the Gorge one week, to the beach the next; Marianne loved the time away from the farm, indulging in her passion for seeking out regional specialities in local shops. The country girl bought meats, cheeses and jars of things I would never have tried. There was also a whole array of other goods that we just sampled at the producer's expense. Being a farmer's daughter, all the traditions of rural France were important to her, as well as an enjoyable education for me.

In bed, nothing happened between Marianne and me for quite a few nights. I knew Rupert had spent a lot of time at the sheep farm and from what Speedy had said, it was clear Marianne was Rupert's girl. On the other hand, taking into account what the other grape pickers were saying, it was as if we were already lovers. One night I decided to try a casual sort of cuddle, to see what the reaction was and take it from there. As Marianne lay on her side, with her back to me, I gently stroked the top of her bare arm with my hand. These light touches were as if I had given my sleeping partner a signal she had been waiting for. Marianne turned round in one movement, pushed me onto my back and sent her tongue darting down my throat before my head had hardly hit the pillow.

Marianne then unzipped my sleeping bag, before going down on me. We made love, with me still on my back, as the quiet, hard-working country girl showed a hitherto unseen appetite for sex.

We made love most nights after that, usually in a more relaxed way, as our bodies became accustomed to each other. Marianne showed a lot of affection after the first night when, although we had been sleeping together, we had never had any physical contact. If I had not made the first move, I do not think Marianne would have – which would have been a shame, because we both enjoyed the cuddling and falling asleep in each other's arms.

Pierre, Marianne's younger brother, only spoke English when he was drunk. After a heavy drinking session one night, we had our first and only conversation.

"Chris, after the vendange has finished, you must come to Rupelon and live with my sister on the farm," said Pierre.

"But Rupert is already there," I replied.

"Yes, but you are a better worker," concluded Pierre.

Marianne did want me to visit the farm, where her lifestyle in the old fashioned farming tradition sounded very attractive. I felt it was an opportunity not to be missed. As Danny Rudd had been there a couple of times, I asked him for his opinion of the place. He was not enchanted by the farm at all. His account was of meadows and woods in the middle of nowhere, making him bored stiff, and of old dilapidated buildings being unfit for human habitation. To me, it sounded like an ideal place to live, while the renovation of the two cottages was an exciting challenge.

With the extra vineyards that Francis had agreed to harvest, the work lasted for six weeks. For most people, this was too much. Many never wanted to see a grape again, once we had finished. Billy and Vicky said it was their last year, as did a lot of the others who had now done grape picking for four years. The novelty of free wine and getting wrecked every night had worn off. It was also difficult to fit in six weeks work in France with a steady job in England or Ireland – sadly it was the end of an era. There was a farewell lunch in the garden, when all the grapes had been picked. Francis cooked the food and his five daughters waited at table. Then we all said our sad goodbyes and went our separate ways: Marianne and Pierre went to visit some relations, before going back to the farm; while I had some unfinished business concerning the insurance claim that was still unpaid. We agreed to rendezvous in two weeks' time, at the farm in the Dordogne. There were no explanations from either Marianne or I on how we felt about our relationship. Conversation was sparse but I did have an invitation to visit. I was sure Rupert would be cool about Marianne staying in the van.

It was over a year since the crash in the van. My correspondence with the French insurance company had got me nowhere, so I had decided to visit them at their Marseilles office. Since Danny Rudd had been with me on that fateful day, I asked him if he would come with me and act as an interpreter. He spoke good enough French and I did not think he had anything planned. During the six weeks' work, Danny had become friendly with three Italians who had started picking during the second week: Luigi, the oldest, was an out-of-work chef who had cooked some great pasta meals which made him very popular; the second man was Luigi's cousin, who I do not think had spoken a word to anyone all the time he was at the farm; the third Italian was a 19 year old girl, called Gina, with whom Danny had become romantically involved – much to the disgust of the silent cousin.

Gina's father owned a campsite in the town of Ventemiglia, just over the Franco-Italian border. Everyone was invited to go camping in Italy after the grape harvest had finished. Danny Rudd was definitely going, as was Irish Danny, who had been joined by his Belgian girlfriend, Ariane. Luigi had told the Irish chef it would be good experience for Danny to work in Italian kitchens, although the chance of a job seemed remote, considering he was unemployed himself.

Danny Rudd and I had a long discussion where we came up with a plan that suited us both. I would take him to Camping Roma at Ventemiglia; we would catch the train to Marseilles, do the business at the insurance company and then return to Ventemiglia. Danny had a chance to be with Gina and I could leave the van somewhere safe. I did not want to take it to Marseilles as it was supposed to have been rebuilt. It would have been just my luck to have been seen with it still dented and scratched. Four of us went to the Camping Roma from Vidauban: the two Dannys, Ariane and myself. The campsite was quite small, but was in the built-up area of Ventemiglia and close to the beach. It had a mixture of sited caravans, chalets and pitches for tents or tourers; all were well shaded by mature trees, with vines trained along high wires, giving extra protection from the sun. There was a small shop on site, plus a combined restaurant and bar, where we all dined on our first night. As it was out of season, we four, plus Gina, were the only customers, but with plenty of cash from the grape picking, we ate and drank well. Gina's father cooked the meal and afterwards he joined us at our table, bringing with him a large bottle of liqueur. The patron spoke French, but no English. Irish Danny translated that Gina's father had made the spirit himself and would like our opinion on its strength and taste.

The eau de vie was crystal clear, with the viscosity of cooking oil. The distiller poured each of us a large glass and one for himself, but not for his daughter or Ariane. I took one sip and my immediate reaction was that it was nail varnish remover. Although, never having tasted nail varnish remover, that thought was probably unfair to nail varnish remover. The two Dannys emptied their glasses in one gulp, said it was good stuff and were each given a refill. I had another sip and another shudder. Gina's father and the Dannys were on their fourth, when I thought I might be seen as unsociable, so I downed the rest of my glass in one. The burning sensation went from my mouth to my throat and down into my stomach. When my eyes focussed again, I saw my glass had been refilled. A second bottle of fire water was empty by the time I had the courage to gulp down my second glass. After that, I made some excuses and went to bed. I left them to it, but if the Italian campsite owner thought he was going to drink the Englishman and Irishman under the table, he had another think coming: the two Dannys had just finished six weeks of high alcohol in-take at the Domaine de Ste Genevive.

The next day, nobody was about until after lunch. It was mid-afternoon before Danny Rudd and I went down to the station to check on the train times to Marseilles. We talked through what we were going to do and say at the insurance office. I reckoned that the next day, which was a Friday, would be our best opportunity to go for it. It would probably be our only chance of success, therefore we went over every situation we thought we would encounter.

We planned: a good cop, bad cop scenario; rehearsed our use of body language; decided on our reaction if they just said no, and agreed on a time limit, if we had to sit it out. Danny was 100 % behind me and I rated our chances better than 50:50.

We had just finished drinking our cappuccinos at a sea front bar and were walking back to the campsite when an ambulance and fire engine came flying passed, with lights flashing and sirens wailing. Quite soon afterwards, we found out that their destination was also Camping Roma. The restaurant kitchen was on fire and there had been an explosion. Gina's father was badly injured in the blast. The paramedics were just stretchering him into the ambulance as we arrived. Gina went with him to the hospital. Danny and Ariane came back from a fruitless search for hotel work as everybody mulled around, while the firemen finished damping down the ruined building. It soon became apparent what had caused the explosion. In the store cupboard, behind the kitchen, Gina's father had kept a still for making illegal liquor; he had been working on the still when something had gone wrong – there had been an almighty bang, and the fireman thought the guy was lucky to be alive.

"This is all your fault" I said to the Dannys. "If you hadn't drunk all the poor chap's stock last night, he wouldn't have been in there, trying to step up production."

## Chapter Sixteen

Despite the disaster, the trip to Marseilles was still on. It started in a light hearted way, when I bought my ticket at the station.

"Marseilles s'il vous plaît," I said in French, even though we were in Italy.

"Ventimiglia," replied the ticket clerk.

"Oui. Marseilles, retour à Ventimiglia," I stated, thinking of where else I would return to, if not Ventimiglia.

"Ventimiglia," re-stated the clerk, in the same nonchalant way.

"Ventimiglia, Marseilles, Ventimiglia," I said, this time with my right arm swinging back and forth to help me get my point across.

"Ventimiglia," said the clerk, for the third time.

"I think he is trying to tell you the ticket price is venti mila, 20,000 lira," chipped in Danny, who could see I was quickly becoming irate.

"Oh! Right, I see," I said, handing over two 10,000 lira notes, before joining Danny and the clerk in a little chuckle.

What a strange name for a town: 20,000 or "XX miglia" as the locals wrote it. Our little verbal exchange must have been the ticket clerk's revenge for the old "return" "where to?" "back here of course" routine. It reminded me of the story that Helen told about West Ham Mick, when he first went to visit her in Holland. Mick was going by train to Helen's home in the town of Helloo.

"A single to Helloo," said Mick to the ticket clerk.

"Hello," said the clerk.

"Hello. A ticket to Helloo, please," said Mick.

"Hello," said the clerk

"Yes. I want a single ticket to Helloo, please," said Mick

"Helloo," said the clerk.

Getting nowhere, Mick went off to look at the timetable, where he found the name of the next station down the line.

"A single ticket to Alkmaar," please said Mick

"Certainly sir," said the clerk.

From then on, West Ham Mick always bought tickets

to Alkmaar, even though Helen told him that the ticket clerk played the same game with everybody. Our Italian friend was doing the same, although it would never have happened if Danny Rudd had let me buy his ticket. He insisted on buying his own, saying I could reimburse him, only if our scam was a success.

To put us in the right frame of mind for our forthcoming encounter, we had a flaming row with the ticket inspector on the train. He started it, by insinuating that Danny and I would stay on the train until Paris, when we should get off at Marseilles. We countered this by indicating that we had bought return tickets and would not have wasted our money, if we planned to do as he thought. The inspector then pointed out that we were English and said that he knew what the English were like. We backed our claim that we only intended to go to Marseilles by showing that we carried no luggage. When this argument did not change the inspector's attitude, Danny and I went onto the offensive. We questioned his parentage and followed up by asking that, given his obvious north African heritage, if he had the legal right to live and work in France. The Arab then became aware of his numerical disadvantage and moved on quickly, as the atmosphere became increasingly hostile.

The train arrived on time and we were delighted to be able to give the ticket inspector a single finger hand signal, as we strode off down the platform. The insurance company offices where quickly found, so it was not long before we were at the front of the queue of people waiting to be seen.   The two of us were shown into one of the booths where things started well when the girl taking down our details went and found a colleague who spoke English.   However, all the two junior employees could say was that the problem could not be sorted out there and then.   Danny then made our position clear, stating that I had been waiting for a settlement for over a year; that we had come all the way from England to get the matter sorted out and that we would not be leaving until I had my money.  A more senior official then came along in order to ask us to wait at the back of the queue.  I told Danny that we would give them an hour and if nothing was done, we would start stirring things up.

During the next hour, Danny had plenty of time to teach me all the relevant French words that described our situation.   As the clock ticked round to the hour, we sprang into action and began to tell all the waiting customers, as well as the ones in the booths, what a disreputable company they were dealing with.   The senior official soon re-appeared and threatened to call the police.   Danny called his bluff by agreeing that the police should be called as it was quite plain to see who was the victim and who was the villain.  He also added that the media might be interested in the story of an English tourist getting ripped off by a big insurance company. Danny and I were then shown into an unoccupied office where they hoped we could not annoy anyone.

Things seemed to be going pretty much as I thought they would.  It was not going to be easy, so I went over the plans with Danny one more time.   Once again we sat quietly for an hour, before showing our restlessness by pacing angrily up and down the glass sided office. We were like a couple of caged animals, throwing in the odd thump on the filing cabinet and a few kicks to the door.  Our presence must have been quite disconcerting for staff and customers alike. Two bearded foreigners in scruffy clothes and with unnaturally dark sun tans would have been scary almost anywhere, but when you know that they are angry and liable to explode at any moment, you would hope that your bosses dealt with the problem quickly.

The fact that we were not going to go away must have eventually got through to those in charge because, after about ten minutes walking, we were ushered into the office of the top man.   He tried to soften us up with friendly handshakes and cups of coffee, but then came out with some awkward questions.

"Where is the vehicle now?"

"It was sold at auction, to pay for the cost of the repairs."

"Why was the work done before any payment was made?"

"Because the insurance company admitted liability."

"Why weren't the repairs done in France?"

"Because I had to get all my things back to England."

"Why did it cost so much?"

"The body shell of the vehicle was twisted and it needed re-building."

The office manager then made an offer of 39,000 francs, that worked out at roughly £3,500 – which was about 700 quid short of what I had billed them for. The top man was watching us intently, as I leaned towards Danny for a whispered discussion.

"What do you think?"  Shall we settle for 39,000?" asked Danny.

"It's more than I thought they'd offer, but I think the big man smells a rat.  I'm not going to jump at it," I said cautiously.

"Shall I try bargaining with him?  See if I can get it up a bit?" offered Danny.

"No.  I'll make out I'm not happy and you make out that you're trying to persuade me to accept the offer.  Act as if you're fed up being here and just want me to settle up, so we can get going.."

"I am fed up being here," said Danny, looking at his watch and gesticulating towards the door.

"Right, start talking me into it," I said, shaking my head, before lowering it into my hands.

Danny went on, in lowered tones, about where we were going to eat that night and speculated if the Camping Roma restaurant would be open again. I let him continue until I thought our little act had got the desired effect. Reluctantly, I signed an agreement for 39,000 francs and was told the cheque would be sent from the company's head office in Paris to my home address that night. We left the office with Danny still telling me I was doing the right thing, while I still looked terribly unhappy.

Back on the train to Ventemiglia, it was all smiles and laughter. We had pulled it off! Two English lads against the might of one of France's biggest insurance companies. For £900 worth of damage, we had come away with three and a half grand. All I had spent on repairs was 120 quid on a new windscreen and a door mirror.

Irish Danny and Ariane had helped Gina clear up the bar while we were in Marseilles. It was drinks all round as we celebrated. Gina's father was still in hospital, but she said the doctors thought he would be okay and out in a couple of weeks.

"Are you going straight up to Rupelon now?" asked Danny Rudd, as we waited for the pizzas that Gina had ordered by 'phone.
"No. I'll give it a week. I think I'll tour round the

south-west before I go and see Marianne," I replied.

"Is it alright if I come with you?" asked Danny surprisingly.

"Sure. But I thought you were alright here. Two weeks with Gina's old man out of the way and all these empty chalets."

"I know what you mean, but er, well, your know what I mean?" stammered Danny.

"No. I don't know what you mean, but you're welcome to a lift. You can show me where the farm is," I said, baffled as to why Danny wanted to get away from the frizzy haired little Italian girl who would do anything for him.

Gina was as baffled as I was regarding Danny's departure. Tears flowed, as they said their goodbyes, before we set off, back into France. Irish Danny and Ariane stayed behind to help Gina straighten out the mess caused by the fire.

I got on well with the easy-going Danny Rudd during our week of cruising around. We never argued or had any problems – which was mainly due to the fact that he agreed with all my suggestions. Danny had studied Russian at college, but had dropped out, even though he had a talent for languages and spoke fluent French. Many of his jobs had not lasted long either: these had included everything from working in a burger bar, to being a Club 18/30 rep in Ibiza. Danny's one and only passion was his guitar. From when we first met, I had noticed a vast improvement in his playing: the strummer with a couple of chords had turned into an accomplished jazz guitarist. He could always be found lounging about with his axe, as he called it, on his lap, picking a tune.

The ports of call on our tour included: Arles - an old town on the river Rhone, south of Avignon; Cap d'Agde - a concrete tourist trap with no character, and Carcassonne – a fine old walled city with many historical military connections. Some years before, I had read "The Holy Blood and the Holy Grail" which was a book that centred a lot of its action in the south-west of France. I was particularly fascinated by the stories about the Cathars, who were a fanatical religious people who were completely wiped out because of their beliefs. In the hills around Carcasonne, Danny and I toured the ruins of the many old Cathar castles. The medieval fortresses were all built on high, sheer faced cliffs that seemed to be impregnable positions, but they had all succumbed to the sieges laid by the Roman Catholic armies. A policy of 'no surrender' had meant that every last Cathar had perished, taking with them the secret location details of the legendary Cathar treasure which still has not been found.

Leaving the last stronghold of the proud Cathars behind, Danny and I headed west, to the principality of Andorra. Much of the architecture of the Pyrenean mountain state had a lot in common with Cap d'Agde. The shopping arcades, selling beach toys and postcards were now stocked with duty free alcohol and tobacco. Danny took the chance to stock up with Samson, his favourite Dutch hand-rolling tobacco; while I could not resist the genuine Mexican Tequilla that was on special offer, if you bought a case. We both passed up the chance of paying 100 francs for a three litre plastic drum of five year old Scotch whisky. Our Andorran stay only lasted a couple of hours when, I think, we saw everything there was to see, before filling up the VW with cheap petrol and returning down into France.

Down from the mountains, our route followed the banks of the Canal du Midi, the 17th century waterway that joins the Atlantic Ocean to the Mediterranean Sea. North of Toulouse, we diverted to the town of Lourdes, attracted more by curiosity than by religious or medicinal reasons. Neither Danny nor I knew what to expect from a place we had both heard about, but knew little. Our first impressions were ones of dismay, as we came to a multitude of tacky souvenirs displayed outside very shop. This, however, contrasted greatly with the atmosphere of peace and calm that started as soon as we entered the holy site. There were people from all over the world: the healthy, as well as the sick and disabled. As we watched them come in through the gates, they all seemed to have a look of hope on their faces.

Danny and I wandered around the grounds, looking at people as much as things like the cave with its spring and row of redundant crutches, hanging on wires. At the visitors centre, a young Vietnamese girl asked us if we would like to see a slide show telling the story of Lourdes and its miracles. She was a bit disappointed when she found out there was only two of us in our party but, nevertheless, Danny and I were taken into a small cinema and told the moving story, by pictures, with an English language sound track.

A day's drive later, we reached Marianne's farm at Rupelon, near the village of La Coquille. The property lay about five kilometres west of the Paris to Perigeaux road, in the heart of the Dordogne. Two country lanes ran from the national route, passing the farmland to the north and to the south; a single tracked lane ran through Rupelon, joining the lanes, but was practically traffic-free. The 500 acres were split equally between woodland and the ten fields which surrounded the farm buildings. Two small lakes lay behind the farmhouse and were fed by spring water that surfaced in the highest field. Marianne's mother and brother, Pierre, lived in the big old farmhouse which had been built between two older looking stone barns. Marianne's home was a single storey dwelling that was situated on the other side of the lane, opposite the main farm entrance. It was a traditional longère, with one-third barn and two-thirds living quarters that had housed farm workers and their families since the middle ages. Inside, an Inglenooke fireplace dominated one end of the large living area, while two doors led into two bedrooms at the other end.

In the fields, which were all set to grass, grazed 100

ewes, three rams and what was left of that year's 169 offspring. A derelict long house, similar to Marianne's home, was hidden in the surrounding woods and along with the walnut tree grove, this was a typical, small French farm that had not yet dragged itself into the 20th century. Marianne had taken on the running of the farm after her parents had split up. She had the seemingly impossible task of making a living from the old-fashioned, low intensive style of farming prevalent in the Dordogne area. On land that had been owned by the family for over 500 years, Marianne intended to keep on with the traditional methods of French sheep farming, preserving her heritage was much more important than monetary gain for a farmer's daughter. With no mod cons like a washing machine or television set, the furnishings in the long house also reflected a desire to preserve the lifestyle from her grandparents' generation.

Danny and I had a warm welcome from Marianne and Rupert when we arrived, with a fine evening meal at the long table, in front of the log fire. Afterwards, we opened a bottle of tequila, sliced up a lemon and passed around the salt. The bottle was finished by midnight, but we all sat and talked for hours afterwards. Marianne saw an opportunity to get some much needed improvements made to the long house.

The shy, retiring girl who rarely spoke more than two sentences an hour, could see that three men with time on their hands could do more in a month than she could in a year. With an unprecedented exhibition of her command of the English language, Marianne told of her plans for the farm and hoped that three of us could make her dreams come true.

The living area needed quarry tiling; the second bedroom had been earmarked for conversion into a bathroom, a cesspit and soak-away had to be installed before a flush toilet could be put in. To stop heat loss in winter, the loft needed insulating, some grassland could be cleared, so that a vegetable garden could start to make the farm more self-sufficient. The list was endless. This was all in addition to the daily running of the farm which included mending fences cutting logs from the dead trees in the woodland and working the sheep with the two Border Collies: Matt and Rick.

Danny Rudd stayed for a few days before going back to England on the train. The musician did not help with any of the work, but made himself scarce during the day – usually going off to sit on the straw in one of the barns and play his guitar. Drinking a bottle of Tequilla every night after dinner became a regular event and I do not think it was a coincidence that Danny left the farm the morning after we had finished the last bottle.

The days of hard work turned into weeks of hard graft, but progress was good and gradually things came together. All the new work blended in well with the old world feel of the long house. The fact that our workmanship was far from perfect seemed to help, as it was sometimes impossible to tell what was old and what had been recently constructed. Marianne was pleased with results and busied herself with the day-to-day farm work, leaving Rupert and me to work with the minimum of interruption. After buying the materials, Marianne had no money to pay us a wage, but showed her appreciation with endless quantities of food, wine and affection. Rupert and I would discuss endlessly such subjects as the best way to grout quarry tiles without getting the cement on the surface of the tile, but we never spoke about the way Marianne distributed her love.

On a night-to-night basis, her rota system was fair, although I could see the whole set up had no long term future. It was a satisfying situation to be in. I am sure Rupert felt the same way, even with no monetary reward.

Things changed when Marianne's savings were exhausted. All the work was practically complete but, as winter set in, something had to give. The catalyst to the break up of the workforce was Marianne's father who, when he found out about his favourite daughter's two lovers, insisted that she choose between one or the other. This was rather hypocritical of the man, as he had recently left his wife, the mother of his five grown up children, and set up home with his mistress, who was younger than Marianne.

But a choice had to be made sooner or later, so nobody was to blame for making Marianne relinquish half of her love life. Marianne's decision on who to choose and who to discard was not, however, as easy as she would have liked. The farmer's daughter could not make up her mind.

"Rupert, Chris, my father says that only one man can live here with me. I am asking you to decide who will stay and who will go. This is, if you both do not want to leave," said Marianne, before going over to the big farmhouse across the road.

"Shall we toss a coin?" suggested Rupert, "Winner gets a 500 acre sheep farm and the love of a good woman: looser drives away into the sunset."

"That's a bit too much to have riding on the flip of a coin. Why not play cards for it all! One game of crib, twice round the board, winner takes all?" I said constructively.

"No way. You're far too good at crib to let luck play a part. What about poker? One hand, five cards each, best poker hand is the winner?" replied Rupert.

"Okay. I'll go with that. I'll shuffle, you cut, I deal," I said.

"You're on. Winner takes all," said Rupert, as he leaned back to reach for the cards on a shelf beside the fireplace.

It was getting dark at 4.00 o'clock on a damp winter's

evening, as I dealt out ten cards, face down, on the long table, in front of a blazing log fire.  Rupert and I turned our five cards over, one at a time.

Ten of hearts beats four of clubs – Rupert leads.
Six of diamonds for Rupert, eight of clubs for Chris – Rupert sill leads.

King of spades for Rupert, four of spades for Chris – Chris leads with a pair.

Jack of clubs for Rupert, Jack of hearts for Chris – still Chris leads.

Last cards:  ten of diamonds for Rupert, three of hearts for Chris – Rupert wins:  pair of tens beats a pair of fours.

"You win Rupert – it's all yours," I said, offering my hand across the table.

"Yeah, right man," gulped Rupert, as we shook on it and realised that maybe the previous five minutes had shaped both our lives for years to come.

I was outside the barn, putting my tools in the van when Marianne came back from talking with her mother.

"I'm leaving in the morning," I said.

We hugged each other, but Marianne said nothing. Not much was said during the evening, but that was not unusual. Marianne had just about achieved all she planned in the way of restoration and decoration. The long house looked old and weathered from the outside, but it was warm and homely: it was filled with traditional, country paraphernalia – pots, pans and wicker baskets hung from the ceiling, jars of jam, cookbooks, jugs and bottles crowded onto all the shelves. The place looked like very woman's magazine's idea of what a French country cottage should look like.

I had the consolation of going home to the cheque from the insurance company, but that money would have gone such a long way on the farm. As I left in the morning, Rupert insisted that I should drop in any time I was passing. I told him I would, and drove back to England in two days.

## Part 2

## Chapter Seventeen

It was mid-December when I went to see Archie Fredericks over at Ipswich. He sat behind his desk in a high-backed swivel chair; he was leaning back, scratching his balls and still wearing the same dirty Mercedes Trucks driving jacket.

"Hello boy, do you want a turkey for Christmas?" he asked before I said a word. Before I could conjure up an imaginative reply about poultry, he continued,

"There's a trailer load of second-hand tractors for Istanbul standing in the yard."

"Yeah, why not," I replied casually.

Archie reached up behind him and pulled a bunch of keys off a hook; he threw them on the desk.

"Scania one-eleven, JPV 357V, diesel up and then get under trailer 303. I'll sort out the paperwork and get you booked on tonight's boat," Archie added as we both gave a self-satisfied grin.

Getting a job had never been easier. Either Archie held my talent as a driver in very high esteem, or there was a severe driver shortage. Probably the latter, who in their right mind would go away knowing that they would be spending Christmas sleeping in a truck, somewhere in the Balkans?   I raided Sainsburys for tins of this, that and the other;  transferred all my gear from the van into the Scania and 'phoned home to say that I would not be in for Christmas.   Two days after, I caught the ferry to Dover, I was crossing back to mainland Europe, en route for Zeebrugge.

The Scania III was everybody's favourite motor for doing Middle-East.   It was strong and reliable, did not mind the cold, had plenty of room inside and carried 200 gallons of fuel in huge twin diesel tanks.  I would be half way across Hungary before I needed to re-fuel.  At 280 horse power, the one-eleven was not as powerful as its vee-eight engined brother, the one-four-one, but with its roof rack, ladders and Asia-Europe written across the front, the Scania sure looked the part.

A break down is one of the worse things that can happen on a long Continental journey;   reliability is everything and you have to take care of the vehicle.  It is no good thrashing your way through country after country, sooner or later, something breaks.  As I had no hope of getting back to England much before the New Year, I took it easy.  The permits that Archie gave me were for Germany, Czechoslovakia, Hungary, Rumania, Bulgaria and Turkey;  I knew the way as far as Bucharest, but expected Bulgaria to be a problem.  I did have a transit visa in my passport, but the amount of freight traffic would govern my progress at the borders.

The weather was cold, but I did not see any snow. After Germany, the tachograph laws did not apply, so I was able to make good headway on the better quality roads of Czechoslovakia and Hungary. At the Windmill, another Archie Fredericks truck was parked up for the night. The driver was on his way back to England, after having tipped in Istanbul and re-loaded with car tyres in Rumania. As we dined together, he warned of the queue at the Turkish-Bulgarian border; but as I had no permit for Yugoslavia, there was no way I could avoid it. We had a chat about Erica, but once again it seemed to be her night off.

The next morning, I was up early and down to the Rumania border before sunrise, in an attempt to beat the rush. Traffic was light at Nadlac as I soon remembered what Jock Gardner had shown me, earlier that year. I crossed out of Hungary and into Rumania in less than an hour, at a border where the two countries share the same Customs building. Armed, with 400 Kent cigarettes from the duty-free shop. I set out on the long haul across to Bucharest.

I had bought enough diesel on the black market in Hungary to get me through to Istanbul, so my only problem was the question of where to stop for the night. It was only breakfast time, but already my thoughts were concentrated on how I could get a trouble-free night. On the main transit route across Rumania, all sorts of things were liable to go missing when you stopped to sleep. Wheels, lights, mirrors, batteries and diesel fuel were all vulnerable, not to mention the six tractors in the trailer. There were three main options to combat the problem: one was to hide up in the middle of nowhere and hope that anybody who is out thieving does not find you; another was to park in the middle of a town and give the local police patrol some cigarettes so that they will hang around to protect you; the last alternative was to drive across the country in one day and park with the other trucks waiting to cross into Bulgaria, hoping that there was safety in numbers. None of the choices was foolproof and during the long day of driving, I changed my mind many times as to what I was going to do.

That day I had also been trying out the "salute" method of speeding fine avoidance. This technique involved saluting the police officer as he stood in the road, trying to wave you down. With his ingrained military training, the policeman's response to seeing someone salute him was to stand to attention and return the gesture, hopefully standing aside as he did so. By the time the truck had passed, it was too late for the officer to pull his revolver and do any damage. Rumanian police rarely gave chase as they usually only had enough petrol in the car to get them back to the station.

During the day, this routine had worked 100%, but on the third occasion, I came unstuck. It was late, I was tired, he was quick and I was slow. My speed had dropped as darkness had fallen, I was still speeding, but when I saluted, the engine was in the wrong gear. I tried a quick down change, but missed it. The policeman did not see my hurried touch of my head as a salute; when he did not see me slowing down, he went for his gun. I anchored up just as he pulled the automatic from its holster. All this happened about 20 kilometres before Bucharest,at the start of the only piece of dual carriageway in Rumania. There was a parking area, with a kiosk set back in a pine wood; it was crowded with trucks, but I just managed to squeeze into a space at the far end. Before I had taken the cellophane off the carton of Kent, the policeman was knocking on the door.

Knowing that most officials do not like it if you lean out of the window to talk to them, I opened the door. I was not going to get out and give up my superior elevated position, but I did not mind showing that I had nothing to hide. The officer did not seem angry, but went on to give me a long lecture in Rumanian, which I did not understand at all. Presumably it was about speeding. However, as he spoke no English, I was wasting my time arguing with him. In the end I gave the traffic cop twenty Kent king-size; at least this made him put his gun back in its holster as he needed two hands to put the cigarettes in his jacket's breast pocket.

The cigarettes did not stop the policeman rambling on in his native tongue; he only quietened down when the girl with the longest hair I had ever seen came along and started speaking to him. The good looking female then pulled herself up the steps of the Scania, climbed across my lap and plonked herself down in the passenger seat. Her black hair was plated into a ponytail, but was still long enough to sit on.   The copper was still hanging around, so I gave him another packet of cigarettes and as he walked away, I shouted a parting shot:

"And make sure my spare wheel is still there in the morning."

Coffee was the only thing that was going to help me;  so I made a flask full using a paper filter and proper coffee.  Martina was not in a hurry and we chatted, as we drank two cups each.  The girl told me she was 20, lived in Bucharest, supported Steaua Bucharest, hoped to get into the Rumanian Olympic rowing team and never slept with Turkish truck drivers.  I was well knacked so it was sod's law that such a willing young lady should come my way at such a time.  As we drew the curtains and got undressed, I could see she was something special. Martina reminded me of the page three model, Stephanie Marianne, with her small pert, upturned tits.  Even a badly chipped front tooth only made her look cute when she smiled.  The perfectly built Rumanian knew she had a good shape too.  When naked, she knelt on the passenger seat and rubbed her hands all over her body.

"You like?  You want?  You like?" smiled Martina.

Thankfully she recognised how tired I was and when we made love, Martina insisted on going on top; probably worried I would fall asleep on top of her if the positions were reversed.

"You give me dollars?" asked Martina, as she got dressed.

It saved her from my marks out of ten line, but on that night's performance I would have given her an eleven. For myself, I scored a poor two out of ten, although Martina saw it differently.

"Very good, very sexy, very good," she said with her cheeky smile when I handed over a ten Deutsche mark note.

"Very kind," I replied.

"My address, you visit?" said Martina as she wrote it out in the back of my diary.

"Yeah, sure, no problem," I said finding it hard to stay awake.

"We go disco in Buch. Meet Nadia Comaneci. She is my friend," said Martina when she climbed out of the cab and blew me a kiss.

After her gymnastics on the bunk, I did not doubt Nadia was Martina's friend, but I just pulled the door shut and collapsed back into my sleeping bag. Sleep came immediately which saved me from worrying about where I was parked and if everything would be alright in the morning.

The 40 king-size must have done the trick; everything was intact and in place when I awoke. After skirting round the south-west of Bucharest on the ring road, I reached Georgui in a couple of hours and found the border crossing devoid of any traffic. The Rumanian police and Customs house was at the northern end of a combined road-rail bridge that crossed the river Danube. This bridge was the single rigid crossing point across the river between Rumania and Bulgaria. It was an old iron girder bridge, with the roadway running above the rail track; similar in style to the bridge over the Mersey and Manchester ship canal at Runcorn, but on a larger scale and not so well looked after.

Soon I was up on the bridge, crossing into Bulgaria. The soldiers of both countries patrolled the bridge from their side to the middle; everyone of the guards put his hand to his mouth to mime cigarette smoking as I trundled passed. An hour later, I pulled out of the checkpoint at Russe and headed up the pass known as Cobblestone Mountain. Luckily the road was dry and not a problem but why this section did not have tarmac like all the rest, I do not know. Coming down from the highlands, I continued south until I came to the main east-west transit route between Turkey and Yugoslavia. Turning eastwards at the T-junction, I carried on until I came to the back of the line waiting to get into Turkey.

On the first day of waiting in line, I spent some time cleaning the cab windows and sweeping out the inside. The line of trucks moved twice, about one kilometre each time. Nobody pushed passed and I made friends with my neighbours by standing around their campfire while looking suitably pissed off. There were four Turks immediately ahead of me, two in Dutch registered vehicles and three Yugoslavs right behind, warming up at our brazier. Most of the other trucks were the same, with a few Rumanians, plus a couple of big American rigs with Irani number plates. I could not see another British truck ahead or behind me in a queue that went from one horizon across to the other. One good thing was that when things moved, you did move a long way in one go; at least you did not have to sit with the engine running and your foot on the clutch.

Day two had three moves; on the last one I came to rest beside a sign that read: Kapitan Andreevo 7 Km. I figured it was another eight kilometres to the border. My little section of queue inherited some more campfires and kept them going by pouring on diesel fuel, which was siphoned off from our tanks By now, we were all on first name terms with everyone except me having pulled a family photograph from their wallet; I had never had to refuse so many offers of cigarettes in my life.

Another three moves on the third day made me think the end must be coming soon and this was confirmed when two British trucks coming out of Turkey stopped to say it was about two kilometres to the border. I thought it was nice of them to pull over and make a cup of coffee, but the real reason that they stopped was to sell me all their surplus Turkish lira. Two more Brits stopped on my

209

fourth day, although only one wanted to change money. The drivers had not seen any British trucks ahead of me in the line; it seemed everyone was leaving it until after the New Year. By mid-afternoon, I was at the front of the line and with the help of my Turkish and Yugo mates, made an easy crossing into Turkey.

It was then that I was shocked to find I had no Turkish permit; the piece of paper issued by the British Department of Transport that gave permission for a truck to enter Turkey - without it I was going nowhere. I searched the cab high and low, with no success. I wondered if anyone could have stolen it, but it was the only thing missing. Did it blow away in the wind? Did I hand it in at some other Customs bureau and they kept it? Did I bring one with me in the first place? I could not remember. Youngturk, the agent, could not help; a bottle of whisky would work miracles for small problems, but not for a major disaster like not having a permit. I went to bed thinking of what I could do to save myself the hassle of asking Archie Fredericks to send down the piece of paper by DHL.

My luck changed in the morning when two British trucks came through from Bulgaria. John Mansfield in his Volvo 88 and George Young in a V reg Foden parked right next to me. The owner drivers from Humberside had also queued for four days and were pleased to see they were not alone. Amazingly, George had a spare Turkish permit with him. John insisted that he gave it to me. The Foden driver was reluctant to part with the priceless piece of paper because it had his name on it and any mis-use could be directly traced to him, but I said a bottle of Johnnie Walker would take care of minor details like that. The Yorkshireman let me have it in the end, but then refused to take anything for it. I told him I owed one.

John had a load of Perkins diesel engines that were going to the same place I had delivered to earlier that year. George had six second-hand tractors which, when we compared the paperwork, we found were going to the same place as mine. The three of us did the border formalities together; then ran in convoy to the Londra Camp, arriving just after sunset on the shortest day.

It was unwise to take the truck into town to visit your agent; also it was better to take a taxi, rather than a bus. Jimmy was the man who controlled the cars used by all the truck drivers when they wanted to go down town in Istanbul. Having lived in London for a few years, he spoke good English and knew the location of all the agents' offices. First thing after breakfast, we found Jimmy in the campsite reception where he soon organised two cars and drivers: one for John and the other for George and me, who had the same Customs clearance agent.

The rush hour trip into Istanbul was like the Wacky Races, with no one showing any lane discipline whatsoever. I am glad I was not driving. The white knuckle ride was hairy, but we arrived at the agent's office block in one piece. The driver told us he would wait outside, in order to take George and me back to the Londra Camp when we had finished.  He had a long wait;  for the agent wanted to practice his English.  After a cup of chi, Naci, the agent, opened the fridge in his office and we all started on  his stock of Tuborg lager.  Naci talked about anything and everything. In George, he found someone more than willing to join him in endless conversation. By the time we left, all the beer had been drunk but our driver was still patiently waiting.

"Did you have a problem with your agent" asked John, who had returned to the Londra Camp hours before us.

"Yes," said George, "his fridge was too small."

While we were in town, another British truck had arrived at the camp.  It was a low loader carrying a 360 degree tracked digger;  the driver had the same agent as George and myself.  Our paths had crossed in the taxis. The next morning, while John went off to Izmit with his engines, Naci came to the Londra Camp, from where he led his three charges to a vehicle compound somewhere in the suburbs of Istanbul. The site was littered with imported tractors, other farm machinery and plant.  At a wide concrete ramp, George and I started to unload our Massey Fergusons.  Most would not start, so we had to help each other by pulling them off with a chain, attached to one of the few tractors that would run.  To get six tractors on one trailer, it was necessary to take off one of the front wheels and half of the front axle.  That way, when the tractors faced each other lengthways in the trailer, it was possible to slide the two engines passed one another and save a lot of space. It was a tight fit, but at least it meant that nothing could move around en route. It was tricky coming down the ramp on only three wheels, but George and I could not be bothered to re-fit the other bits, which we left in a pile beside the tractors. Mervyn unloaded his digger in less than half the time it took to do our tractors. The only serious snag of the morning came when Naci locked his keys in his car. The agent was so impressed with my skill with a wire coat hanger that he insisted the three of us went back to his office for drinks after we had taken the trucks back to the Londra Camp. As we were now four, the re-stocked fridge full of beer did not last as long, which meant the taxi driver did not have such a lengthy wait. George and now Mervyn were quite happy to talk all afternoon about the difference between Green label and Red label Tuborg. In the end, I think Naci was genuinely sorry to see us go even though we had drunk all his beer.

A reply to my earlier telex came while I was down town, it had instructions of a re-load at Radauti, a town in Rumania, right up in the north of the country, near the Russian border. John came back from tipping his diesel engines at Izmit to find he and George where re-loading at Iasi (pronounced Yash), also in northern Rumania. We decided to run together; leaving early the next morning. George was not keen on going back through the Bulgarian border at the town called Kapitan Andreevo so he persuaded John to take us through a small crossing point north of Edirne, called Maliko Tarnovo. We all filled up with as much fuel as we could carry; John led the way, George was in the middle and I brought up the rear.

After leaving the main road from Istanbul, we headed north into the hills, where we were soon tackling sharp hairpin bends on steep narrow roads. With dry conditions and empty trailers the gradient was not a problem, but the tarmac surface carried many scars from when drivers had attempted this desolate route in wintry conditions. At the highest point over the range of hills, we came to the Bulgarian-Turkish border, which was deserted, except for the bare minimum of guards and officials. John had been through this way several times before, so he soon showed us the ropes.

In fact, John seemed to specialise in going through out of the way border posts and visiting remote areas of foreign countries. The intelligent owner driver with a university education seemed to give priority to exploring, rather than to economics. Apart from that, John was very business-like but given the chance, he would always put a little adventure in his life. George, on the other hand, was a more traditional truck driver, as well as being a typical Yorkshireman. He had become an owner driver after being laid off by his long time employer. With his redundancy money, George had bought the Foden and, after several years' work in Great Britain, was now trying to make his fortune in Europe. The taciturn northerner let John do all the talking and make the decisions, but could come out with some notable quotes that rivalled those of Gavin.  For instance:  when asked why he drove an old Foden and not a more popular European Marque, George came out with a classic observation:

"A good truck is like a good woman, it's not how old she is or what she looks like, it's the amount of money she earns that matters."

Yet again, I had struck lucky when it came to finding good people to run with;  as I followed the other two down to the Black Sea coast, once more I did not even have to navigate the route.  When we came to the sea, it was dark, while the temperature was much colder as we battled into a strong headwind that slowed our progress along the coast road to Burgas.  On the southern edge of the city, John selected a big parking area on which to stop for the night.  There was no shelter from the biting wind at the edge of the beach, so to get some protection, George and I parked close to the lee-ward side of John's trailer.

"Don't worry about your leader, I'll survive.  I'm tough.  You take all the shelter you can get," said John sarcastically, as we piled into his cab for our evening meal.

"What do you want us to do, put the wagons in a circle?  Why do we have to stop here anyway?" replied George, who disliked being ridiculed when not at fault.

In the absence of any café, bar or restaurant, British

truck drivers, when running together, always ate the same thing: camion stew. Each member of the convoy was required to provide at least three tins of food for the meal. One of which should always have been a tin of meat, such as steak and kidney pie filling or meat balls in gravy. The other two being vegetables or something like spaghetti hoops. Tinned new potatoes and baked beans were always well received, while mushy peas were usually rejected. The chef was the man with the biggest saucepan, into which all the tins were emptied. The pot was then heated until it bubbled furiously for at least ten minutes. The more experienced drivers came equipped with a large soup bowl, rather than a plate, as the end result of all the culinary preparation with the can opener was usually a broth. John even had a ladle and the camion stew that he cooked that night was one of the best, although I had never had one that did not taste great.

As we sat, peering out into the darkness, listening to the wind howl and the sound of the waves pounding on the beach, John told us of a previous visit to his favourite Bulgarian car park. He had been loaded with 18 tonnes of putty, bound for Baghdad when he stopped to pick up two hitchhikers, a few miles south of Prague. They were two East German girls, who had set off with their backpacks, hoping to spend August on the shores of the Black Sea. John turned out to be the last lift they needed. All three became such good friends on the journey that our chef stayed with the girls for the first five days after their arrival. Parked in the same carpark, the sun was shining, the nights were warm and they went swimming in the sea. A hell of a contrast to the conditions we had on the day before Christmas eve.

The wind seemed to have grown stronger in the morning, as we turned inland towards the bridge across the Danube at Russe; a fine snow blew against the side of our vehicles. Bulgarian Customs' formalities were quickly completed before the three trucks gingerly climbed up the curving ramp above the railway line that led onto the bridge over to Rumania. The sea going vessels on the Danube needed plenty of headroom so the bridge was high and exposed. At altitude, the wind was even stronger; ice was forming on the windward side of the metal beams.

Halfway across, George stopped, forcing me to pull up behind him at the place in the middle of the bridge where a white line ran across the road, marking the boundary between the two countries. The truck cab was in Rumania and my trailer was in Bulgaria. When I got out to see what was the matter, unbelievably there was a line of trucks stretching from the Customs' post at the Rumanian end of the bridge, right up to the centre and I was last in the queue. It was midday, mighty cold and howling a gale. John told George and me to keep as close together as possible; also to keep the motors running. Our leader rightly thought the wind chill would freeze up the fuel lines if we switched off the engines. It was so cold that even the soldiers preferred to stay in their sentry boxes rather than come out and cadge cigarettes. For the rest of the day, progress was painfully slow. As daylight faded, it got markedly colder. It was gone midnight when I received a stamp in my passport for the 25th December, and finally entered Rumania. The last 500 metres had taken 12 hours; I pulled up in the shelter of some Russian trucks and went straight to bed.

On Christmas morning, I was laying awake, wondering how long I could last before having to get up and go for a leak when there was a crash of metal on metal as the cab rocked violently. I jumped up, pulled the curtains and found that a Russian truck had driven into the offside of my cab. The driver was trying to back away, but was only spinning his wheels on the ice, as the two vehicles rubbed together. Because of the cold, I had been sleeping with my clothes on, so after puling on my boots and grabbing my jacket, I climbed out of the passenger door to inspect the damage. As I went round the front, the Russian driver finally found some grip and the two truck cabs parted company. The Scania had a broken indicator, a cracked mirror lens and the mirror arm, which seemed to have taken the blunt of the impact and was badly bent. The Russian Kaz had similar damage; the driver was tall, young and not in the least bit apologetic.

I rubbed my thumb and forefinger together to indicate to the Russian that I wanted some money for the damage he had done. The Kaz driver scoffed at my demands and started gesticulating that it was all my fault because if I had not parked so close to his truck he would not have hit my cab.  It was then that I elected to hit him; deciding to use my head and nut the Russian.  He had shown no remorse or respect, which made me angry.   I had pulled my head back, ready to thrust it forwards into his face, when I realised I was standing on a sheet of ice. The small movement had transferred too much weight to the rear of my body, causing my feet to shoot out from underneath me.  As I fell to the ground, I inadvertently drop kicked the Russian in the shins;  he came down on top of me, with his nose colliding painfully with my knee.

All this was witnessed by the two other Russian drivers, who had been drinking coffee in their cabs.  The first time I noticed them was when they got out of their trucks and slammed the doors.  A quick glance at the registration plates made me think I was in big trouble but, luckily, they failed to recognise my rearward head movement as an act of aggression. The Russians just came over to help us back onto our feet, even seeing the funny side of the situation.   After making a cup of coffee for me and the guy with the nosebleed, the Russians advised him to give me some money.  The Kaz driver came out with 200 Rumanian Lei and we shook hands on it.

John and George got up about an hour later, by which time all three Russians had gone off in the direction of Bulgaria.
"What have you done to your mirror arm?" inquired George.

"Is that blood on the snow down there?" asked John, as we sat in my cab, drinking coffee.

"Where were you two when I needed you?" I said, continuing the interrogation line of conversation.

"Christmas is supposed to be a time of peace and goodwill to all men," quoted George.

"Boxing Day is tomorrow," quipped John, before I told them of my early morning encounter.

The thick, freezing fog of that morning was like no fog I had ever seen before;   instead of being a calm, still day, the wind was blowing at gale force.  As the trucks headed north into the blast, they became encrusted, all over, in ice more than an inch thick.  With my heater fans on full and all the air directed at the windscreen, it just about remained free from ice.

Up ahead, John's Volvo was struggling with an oil leak in the air compressor, which meant that the engine had to be run at high revs to stop the brakes from coming on.  However, George in the Foden was in real trouble: his heater and fan lost the battle against the ice.  The only two areas of clear windscreen on the Foden were two half circles, the size of a dinner plate, at the bottom of the glass, close to the air vents.  To cope with this problem we all had to stop and chip away at the ice every few miles.  I was a bit too heavy handed with the scraper for George's liking.

"Break that screen and you'll be having your first drive in a Foden, a freezing cold Foden."

By mid-afternoon, we had only covered a 150 kilometres which had brought us onto the wide open plain north of Bucharest. As the relentless onslaught of the freezing fog showed no sign of easing, John was anxious that we should find some shelter before nightfall and the inevitable fall in temperature. In the limited visibility, all we could see were the big flat fields of the communal farms. The only cover that we came across was a group of haystacks in one of the fields. John took a chance by driving onto the frozen dirt, but after he managed to get some shelter from the wind, George and I followed.

It was the first time I had ever worked on Christmas day, for the distance travelled and the trouble we had it was hardly worth it, especially as Boxing Day turned out clear and bright. Just after the town of Roman, we stopped at a lay-by in order to fill our water containers from a nearby well that John had discovered on a previous trip. As the turn off for Iasi was only a couple of miles up the road, I said goodbye to John and George and carried on alone, hoping to reach Radauti that night.

Running on the hard packed snow and ice was not a problem for the Scania. In the flat countryside, the only problem I had was when I encountered a low bridge, just before reaching my destination. Normally, low bridges were only a couple of inches lower than the front of the trailer, but this one only came up to the bottom of my windscreen. It was a wide, flat road, with several car tracks in the snow. I could not understand why the bridge had been built so low or what it carried over the road. When I got out to have a look, I soon figured out what was going on: it was a road bridge over a river and I was driving on top of the frozen water. When I reversed back along the river in the dark, it was not easy, but I did not dare try a U-turn as I would have surely lost too much traction. All the water must have been frozen solid as I did not hear any cracking in the still night air. In the limited light of my hazard warning flashers, I retraced my tyre tracks to the slight slope where I had left the road, before charging off the ice covered riverbed and back onto ice covered tarmac. The local traffic must have used the river as a short cut to somewhere as the tyre tracks showed an equal amount using road and ice.

In Radauti, by chance, I came across my collection address without having to ask for directions and the night-watchman helped see me back into the factory yard. It was no surprise when the factory manager came along the next morning and told me the load would not be ready for a couple of days. Optimistically, I thought the delay might give the weather a chance to warm up – but it did not. The goods I was taking to Britain were barbecues – the cheap, circular tin type that only last for one summer if you leave them out in the rain. The old metal work factory made other things as well, there was even a blacksmith department for shoeing horses, but all production seemed to be directed towards my barbecues and was held up by the spray shop where the cold weather refused to let the spray paint dry.

Half way through my first morning, one of the factory girls came up and asked for a cigarette. I offered her a packet of 20 if she would go off and get me some bread. It was a job to make her understand English, so I tried "brot" and "pain" before she got the message – the Rumanian for bread sounded like "ping". As the boiler-suited worker went down the road with a pack of Kent king sized, I wondered if I would see her again; but I need not have worried, for she soon re-appeared with six large loaves. Her name was Marina, she looked about 17 and was shorter and chunkier than the average Rumanian girl. I told her to keep half of the bread, because I would never have eaten all of it before it went mouldy. We chatted away, using sign language with some German words. I asked Marina to dine with me that evening at the Scania Cab Motel. The message must have got across pretty well because she turned up at just after 7.00.

Marina had a great sense of occasion which showed by the amount of effort she had put into her appearance. Under her long black Crombie-style overcoat and silver fox fur hat she wore what seemed to be the Rumanian national costume. Elegant, lace-up black leather ankle boots, embroidery trimmed, calf length black skirt over a slight longer lace trimmed petticoat; frilly long sleeved white blouse, done up at the neck with a blue, red and yellow choker; a black satin waistcoat, trimmed with the same national flag colours and a matching headband pulling back her long black, wavy hair. Whether her mother had told Marina to get dressed up, or whether her get-up was standard eveningwear for Rumanian girls dining out with foreigners, I do not know. Maybe it was worn as an excuse to get out of doing the washing up. Whatever it was, Marina looked great. After seeing her in army boots and dark blue overalls, I thought she looked alright. Now seeing her in all the old fashioned gear, I fancied Marina like made.

With such fine company, I should have done better than camion stew. The meatballs, new potatoes and baked beans were well received, also the pineapple rings for dessert were a new taste for Marina, but all through dinner, I was thinking I should have been serving roast beef and Yorkshire pudding. To finish the meal, I made some proper coffee. As we sat back to relax, Marina sorted through my tape collection. She selected Dire Straits, "Brothers in Arms" which came on just at the start of the title track. Somehow, it complimented the moment perfectly. At the end of the evening, I caught Marina's eye and glanced at the bunk, tapping my hand on the sleeping bag as her eyes followed mine. But, as they say in the Sunday papers, she made her excuses and left. Later, as I lay alone in my bed, I reflected that it was good to know that not every Rumanian girl was available for a few marks, a packet of smokes or a jar of coffee.

The barbecues came in kit form, that were boxed in cardboard that was about the same quality as a wasp's nest; but once the loading did start, the trailer was quickly filled from floor to roof with over 1300 of the things. It was a fairly light load, so when I started for home, late the following afternoon, I made good progress, with the cold north wind now behind me. The direct route across Transylvania and the Carpathian mountains was a daunting prospect in winter, so I opted for the longer option of returning south to Bucharest, before turning east towards Hungary. Also, I had a chance of meeting up again with John and George, which would have made things more enjoyable.

As it was, our paths never crossed; so I spent New Year's eve alone, on the motorway services, south of Prague. The Scania gamely plodded on through the constant sub-zero temperatures; always starting first time, although I rarely switched the engine off. In order to keep warm, I ran the motor all night, every night, which seemed to be the policy of most East-European truck drivers as well.

## Chapter Eighteen

Back at Ipswich, I dropped the trailer in the yard and took the unit round to the workshops for a steam clean and a service. A load of diesel engines for Izmit stood ready to go to Turkey so, after a couple of days at home, I left, once more, for Istanbul.

With the prospect of another four-day delay at KapitanAndreevo in Bulgaria, I managed to persuade Archie Fredericks to give me a permit for Yugoslavia. He felt it was too expensive to pay the Austrian transit tax, so I still had to go via Czechoslovakia and Hungary, also the boss assured me that my re-load would be out of Rumania again. Of all the trips I ever did to Turkey, this one went the smoothest. I now knew the route, the Customs' procedures and the delivery address; even the pick-up in Rumania was on the outskirts of Bucharest, which saved a lot of time and trouble. The low point of the journey came when I bumped into the New Zealand couple that I had met the year before. They gave me the sad news that Gavin Benson had died in a truck smash on the road down from the Mont Blanc tunnel in France.

From winter into spring, it was back to back trips to Istanbul. On my next trip I ran with another Fredericks' driver, called John Lyons. The north Londoner had been with the firm for three years and from the way he talked you would have thought he had done Middle East work all his life; but from the way he stuck to my back bumper bar, I soon began to think he had never been further than Munich. Things started to go wrong for us in Hungary, where the police had cracked down on black-market diesel sales. Most of the familiar faces at the filling stations had been arrested; the ones that had not, quickly waved us off their forecourts. In the end, John Lyons and I had to go to the tourist office to buy some legal fuel vouchers which were very expensive. We bought just enough to get us down to the Greek border, after crossing Yugoslavia.

Half way between Belgrade and Nis, John Lyons met an old north London mate, on his way to Baghdad. He, too, was having trouble getting enough fuel; even so, I was astounded when John Lyons let his friend siphon off a load of diesel from his tanks.

"What are you letting him do that for? We've hardly got enough for ourselves," I said indignantly.

"He's a mate, he'll pay me back when we get to Istanbul," replied John Lyons.

"Get the money now, we might not see him again," I advised.

"Yeah, but he's only got mickey twenties – I'd rather have the diesel back," muttered John Lyons, as if he did not want to grass on a mate.

It was one thing to work for a firm that expected you

227

to buy fuel on the black market, but to be expected to buy it with forged bank notes was something else. Eventually, John Lyons' fuel tanks ran dry, before we got to Greece, so I had to go back to him and give him some out of mine. Then I ran out, so he had to give some back. We coasted into the Shell station at Evzoni with the engines running on fumes. All the hassle should have been unnecessary; it was always me who tipped the cabs and bled the air from the filters while John Lyons stood around all clean and tidy in his flares and his Scania driving jacket.

Everything went OK after that, until we reached the Londra Camp. I turned into the entrance, expecting John Lyons to be right behind me, but in the darkness and early evening traffic, he had dropped back. I just caught a glimpse of him as he missed the turn and sailed passed. It was impossible for me to get back on the busy road to go after him. I just hoped that he knew that he had overshot and could turn round; although were he would be able to do a U-turn with a fifteen metre rig on a six lane highway in the rush hour, I did not know.

Two hours later, after I had showered and been over to the restaurant for a meal, John Lyons turned up. His attempt to retrace his steps had not been easy; when turning in a side road, he had bumped a car. It took 300 Deutschmarks of his running money to placate the Turkish driver – the cash stopped the man calling the police, which was not a bad deal when it was all John Lyons' fault and things could have got awkward. But it was money he could ill afford to give away after our fuel problems on the way down.

We delivered the diesel engines to Izmit two days later and returned to the Londra Camp where John Lyons' friend who owed him the diesel still had not shown up. As our resources were low and with not much prospect of cheap diesel fuel on the way home, we decided to telex England for some money. John Lyons needed £250; I reckoned an extra £150 would get me home. Youngturk, the agent, came to the Londra Camp the next morning with £500 worth of Turkish lira, which was just as well, because the re-loads were from the Radauti barbecue factory in Northern Rumania. It was no good taking Turkish currency out of the country as nobody in the Commie Block would take it; so we spent it all on diesel. When the running tanks were brim full, we put the rest in the belly tank, under John Lyons' trailer. There was now more than enough to get us both back to England. A British driver, on his way to Doha, who saw us fill up, said he would tell the Arabs to step up oil production.

The snow and ice of winter had now all melted; the run through Bulgaria and up through Rumania was done on dry roads, in warm spring sunshine. Even the bridge over the Danube was traffic-free. As we waited at the Customs, the Sofia to Moscow Express trundled slowly off the bridge into Rumania. In the old elegant carriages, I could see the passengers gazing out of the dirt streaked windows, as the interior glowed golden in the evening twilight. Stern-faced businessmen in suits, immaculately dressed, middle-aged women in fur trimmed coats, families with perfectly controlled children looking up from their books, not a smile amongst any of them; just

229

a few mouths moving, reading the name on the truck cab door: "A Fredericks, Ipswich, England" and if my lip reading was correct, the pronunciation of Ipswich was giving everybody trouble. One of the great train journeys of the world was just passing by.

Before we reached Radauti, I made a point of looking for the place where I had driven on to the ice, during my last visit. When I came to the spot, it was easy to see how I had made the mistake. The shallow river ran close to the road and a man in rubber boots was standing in the middle, throwing buckets of water over his Dacia; in spring, summer and autumn, my ice rink was the local car wash.

At the metalwork factory, John Lyons and I had just found out that our loads were not quite ready, when Marina came wandering along.

"I would," hissed John Lyons.

"I have," I lied, before I exchanged kisses on the cheek with the smiling little Rumanian.

"You dirty bastard, she's only a kid," retorted John Lyons.

"What? You hypocrite. You just said you would," I exclaimed, adding, "go and get twenty Kent and she'll pop down the shop and get us some bread."

Marina came back with only four loaves, which showed a fifty per cent increase in the cost of bread since the winter, when a packet of king-size bought six. I performed the eating mime of alternately raising my hands to my mouth while chewing, but Marina shook her head and skipped off, back to work. So that night, for the umpteenth time, I had camion stew with John Lyons.

"Why do you reckon that little Rumo gal didn't want to eat with us then?" asked John Lyons.

"Marina probably thought she would have to sleep with both of us if she did," I proffered.

"Well, nothing wrong in that," said John Lyons.

"Obviously she doesn't fancy you, and because of that I'm missing out as well," I said, trying to make him feel guilty.

Marina stayed as friendly as ever when she came to chat during her lunch breaks. I thought about dropping the trailer, so that I could take her out for a drive after work, but the barbecues were ready sooner than I anticipated. John was loaded first and I gave him the chance to get going on his own, but he wanted us to stick together. Before we left, we stocked up with bread; I gave Marina a tin of pineapple rings, as well as 20 Kent, in exchange for the loaves. When we set off across northern Rumania, John Lyons stayed so close behind, you would have thought there was a tow bar between us.   By the time we reached Germany, I was fed up with having my mirrors constantly full of his Scania's cab, so I made an excuse about going into Regensburg to see Ulrike.

I told John Lyons I would catch up with him at the Wally stop, in Belgium.  Ulrike was in, when I telephoned. She lived with her older sister, Belinda, above a florists, just a short walk from the city centre.  When I arrived, they had just finished tidying up the flat.  Ulrike had already telephoned Ingrid, so when she arrived, we went out for a McDonalds and then on to a bar for a drink. I spent most of the night in conversation with Belinda, which rather upset her younger sister.  After we left the bar, I went back to my cab alone, thinking I had made things awkward for when I called again.  Which I never did.

Back in the UK, with the barbecues safely delivered, Archie Fredericks swapped my Scania III for a six-wheel Mercedes 2028.  It was the only left hand drive vehicle on the fleet and was Archie's pride and joy;  although he had bought quite a few new Scania 112s since the Merc had first come home.  Coupled to a tri-axle trailer, I went off to Wolverhampton to load up for Istanbul.  The cargo was 18 tonnes of re-conditioned drive axles;  big, heavy ones for trucks and buses.  With instructions to leave six foot of clear floor space at the back of the trailer, I started back to base.  Either the axles weighed a lot more than 18 tonnes, or the Mercedes was severely under-powered, because it just did not want to get going and died at the sight of a hill. A big wooden crate, containing a crankshaft for a power station turbine, filled up the trailer back at Ipswich, where I also filled the trailers' belly tank with 1200 litres of red diesel.

I resigned myself to a very slow journey. Archie knew it was going to be a heavy load, too, or why else would he have made sure I was running on six axles, when I normally had four? It was embarrassing to be overtaken by the old Rumanian M.A.N trucks on the German autobahns, but at least I never got stopped by the police and taken away for a weight check. I expected problems in Hungary, which was the keenest of all European countries when it came to heavy loads and weighed every truck as it came across its borders. There was a ten tonne axle limit so, theoretically, I would have been alright up to 60 tonnes, but I did not take any chances and went into the weighbridge office armed with a bottle of Johnnie Walker Black Label. The operator shook her head as I went in, but when she saw the whisky she printed out two tickets for the next truck onto the scales and gave one to me. I tried to ask how much my rig did weigh, but the operator just waved her down-turned palms above her head and laughed.

It was slow going; the hills were long, rather than steep, so I knew I would be able to get up them, even if it took an eternity in crawler gear. The Commie Block was used to slow trucks; also, I avoided speeding fines and I thought that once I had dropped off the crankshaft in

Bucharest, the going would get easier. It did help a bit, but in Bulgaria, I had to tackle Cobblestone Mountain. Going up, it was first gear all the way, which seemed to take forever. Then coming down the other side, the whole thing just wanted to run away. I had selected second gear and had my heel on the exhaust brake the whole time. I tried to dab at the foot brake, hoping to slow up, as I entered the bends, but the engine was revving fit to burst, which meant I soon had to use the brakes all the time. At the lay-by, half way down, I thought I would stop, to let things cool down a bit, but as soon as I pulled into the parking area, I knew I could not stop and went straight out, back onto the road. Smoke was now coming from both sides of the trailer axles. I was mighty relieved when the road flattened out at the bottom. The problem with the over-revving engine blowing up had passed, but to have stopped straight away would have probably seen a fire break out in one or more of the wheel hubs. My only option, in the absence of a handily placed fire station, was to coast along, hoping the cool air against the brake drums would lower their temperature.

The first stop I made was in the border town of Kapitan Andreevo. The wheels were still too hot to touch and smelt terrible, but at least they had stopped smoking. The queue to cross into Turkey was only a few hundred metres long, unlike the ten kilometres-plus that I endured at Christmas, so I was out of Bulgaria by midnight. The Turkish police and Customs were supposed to be working, but nobody was processing anything, so nothing was moving. I hoped I would get through during the night when there was a good chance I might not be weighed. The weighbridge at Kapikule was always breaking down and out of action for most of the time. I went to bed knowing that if the scales read anything over 38 tonnes, I was in for a morning full of trouble.

Plan A was to lighten the load on the scales by manoeuvring the steering axle off the front of the weighbridge; but this failed miserably when the little Turkish operator came running out in order to direct me to reverse back on. Plan B was to offer the operator a 100 Deutschmark note in exchange for some other truck's weighbridge ticket that was for less than 38 tonnes. The second plan failed because the angry little Turk did not like the way I tried to con him with my first scheme. My ticket was for 42.5 tonnes and I had to change 700 Deutschmarks into Turkish lira in order to pay the fine.

With most of my running money gone, it looked like I would have to telex England for more funds, but I could not face the wrath of Archie Fredericks for the second consecutive trip. So, after I had tipped the axles, I withdrew a whole rake of Turkish lira on my Barclaycard, which bought me enough diesel to get home. Once again, the re-load was Rumanian barbecues from Radauti, up near the Russian border. Marina was there again to run my errands down to the bakers. This time 20 king-sized bought three loaves of bread. I did not ask her to come to dinner, as I did not think she would accept the invitation. I did not think I was going to get anywhere with Marina anyway.

It was a bit of a shock when, at 7.00 o'clock, the little Rumanian girl came back round to the factory. What was even more surprising was that she was pushing a pram. I climbed down from my cab so that I could be introduced to Dimitri, aged about 15 months. The little lad came out of his pram and toddled about rather unsteadily, as I tried to get out of Marina if it was her boy, a younger brother, or if she was just baby-sitting. Amidst the anxiety of watching and waiting for Dimitri to fall over, I never got an answer, but somehow I got the impression Marina was being deliberately vague. I felt obliged to give them something, like when a new mother brings her baby to her old workplace to show her former colleagues. A pound coin for his moneybox would not have done little Dimitri much good, so I opened a tin of sliced peaches. With my one bowl and spoon, each of us ate a slice in turn, before Marina slurped down the syrup when all the fruit had gone. As the sun was setting on a mild April evening, Marina and I exchanged our usual pecks on the cheek and she took Dimitri home to bed.

The Mercedes pulled much better with just a load of barbecues on board; it was a trouble-free run back to the UK.

Now the days were longer and the weather was warmer, once more my thoughts turned to the beach. I reckoned on one more trip, before I quit for the summer. The load was made up of large packing cases of agricultural machine spare parts, bound for Basrah in Southern Iraq. I was to take them to Istanbul, where they were to be transhipped onto a Turkish truck for the rest of the journey.

After making the frequent trips through the countries of Eastern Europe, my passport had amassed a fine collection of stamps and visas. Because most countries liked to use a fresh page each time, it had become full and, although it still had several years to run, it needed renewing. British passport offices were notoriously slow in dealing with replacement requests, so Archie Fredericks recommended that I try and get one at a British Embassy on the way down to Turkey. Brussels was en route, but I thought parking might be a problem, so I decided Bonn might be a better bet.

Bright and early on the morning after I left England, I turned up at the Embassy in Bonn, only to find that they could not help be because the passport department was at the British Consulate in Dusseldorf. When I got there, the office was closed for lunch, but they came back at 2.00 o'clock and at a quarter to three, I walked out with a brand new 94-page passport. The 45-minute turnaround included filling out all the forms and having a chat with a British squaddie, who was having his new born baby put on his passport. It helped by having my old passport with me, but I did not need my birth certificate or any signatures from people who knew me. Probably the quickest passport office in the world.

It looked like being a quick trip. I made such good progress, I treated myself to a whole day off at Kavala.

My truck was the only vehicle parked on the beach in the warm May sunshine. It made me think that my next visit to the seaside would be in the south of France. My instructions on reaching Istanbul were that I should go to the TIR parking at Hyderpasa, on the eastern side of the Bosphorus and telephone my agent from the nearby Harem Hotel. The agent would arrange for the transfer of the load, under Customs' supervision. On no account was I to stop at the Londra Camp as normal.

After the usual morning at Ipsala, I arrived at the Londra Camp in the early evening. There was no way I was going to go past the chance of a good shower and a decent meal. I stayed a couple of hours, after which I found the TIR parking quite easily by following the comprehensive directions given by a table full of British drivers. When I telephoned the Customs' agent from the hotel on the Wednesday morning, he came down to the park immediately, but brought with him the news that because of the upsurge in fighting in the war between Iran and Iraq, it was proving difficult to find anybody willing to take my goods on to Basrah. The man left, saying he would return at the same time tomorrow, hopefully with better news.

There were no other British trucks on the park, which was mostly full of Turkish, Polish and Hungarian trucks, with a few Dutch-registered units that were driven by Turks. I managed to make friends with the Turkish drivers by helping out one of the locals. The guy from Adana had dropped his heavily loaded trailer, so that he could go off in the unit and get some repairs done. When he returned, he found the unit would not go back under the trailer, due to the decompression of the unit's rear suspension. The fifth wheel turntable was way too high to go under the trailer. As it was not normal for Turkish tractor units to have sloping ramps behind the fifth wheel, the driver had a big problem which none of his mates could help him with.

However, one of the more senior Turkish drivers, parked nearby, knew that British units had these run-ups ramps. Soon the driver and his advisors came trooping over to peer under the front of my trailer. I knew what the problem was, even though I did not understand the language. The Turks asked nicely. They even wound down my trailer legs while I uncoupled the airlines. With the aid of the ramps and by lowering the air suspension, I managed to get under the Turkish trailer quite easily; then, by inflating the air-bags, the trailer went up to the exact height of the Turkish unit's turntable. The legs on the trailer were then wound down to take the weight and I pulled my unit away. The Turk then backed under the trailer with no difficulty, but had a hard job winding up the legs before the unit took the weight.

The agent came, as he said he would, on the Thursday, but he had no news of any truck being found to take over my cargo. This left me with the rest of the day to myself, so I thought a little tourist exploration might be in order. On all my visits to Istanbul, I had only ever been to the Londra Camp, the Customs' agent's offices and across the bridge. The truck park was by the waterside, on the eastern bank of the Bosphorus, within walking distance of the ferry to the west.

The ferry looked very similar to the ones that cross the river Thames at Woolwich, but the river traffic was far heavier than east London. From the ferry, I could see the cathedral of St Sophia and the Blue Mosque. Once on the west bank, I walked the short distance to these impressive buildings. With my fair hair and beard, I stood out as a stranger in a foreign land; every taxi driver tooted his horn at me, hoping to get a fare. All the English-speaking guides outside the cathedral and mosque also enquired if I needed their services. They took no for an answer only when I told them I was not a tourist but a poor truck driver with time on his hands. Although a guided tour would have been worthwhile, because I knew nothing about the history of these hugely impressive buildings. On the way back to the ferry, I passed the Topkapi Palace and the Harem. If I do not get unloaded tomorrow, I thought to myself, I will come over to visit those places. When the agent came the next morning with the bad news that there would be nothing done before Monday, I had enough time for the palace, the harem and the bazaar. I bought nothing from anyone, but was sorely tempted to get a made-to-measure leather jacket that would have been ready in two hours.

On the Saturday morning, I went off to the local bakery and green grocers stall to get some food for the weekend. I was a regular customer now and served with

240

great courtesy and patience. One loaf and a bag full of mini pizzas was my standing order at the bakers, while at the fruit and veg man, I ordered a bag of tomatoes, but was given onions, peppers, courgettes and a couple of lemons, along with the tomatoes. Why? I do not know. Maybe the greengrocer was just giving me what he thought I needed for a balanced diet. Back at the truck park, two British trucks had turned up, after spending the Friday night at the Londra Camp. They, too, had loads for Iraq that were to be transhipped onto willing Turkish vehicles. When I told the British drivers I had been waiting since Wednesday, they were not impressed, but they liked the mini pizzas.

When Dave Telford and Roy Johnson came through the border from Greece, they met up with two Australian girls hitch hiking to Istanbul. The four had spent the night at the Londra Camp and made arrangements to meet up again at the Pudding Shop in Istanbul city centre. Dave and Roy asked me if I would like to tag along. The Pudding Shop was the bar-restaurant used by all English speaking ex-pats passing through Turkey; it was within walking distance of the ferry, in the square called Sultan Ahmet. After having a strip wash and digging out my best clothes, we all set off for an Istanbul Saturday night. Vicky and Nikki came round from one of the cheap back-packer hotels and everybody got stuck into the Efes Pilsen. It was a good night; the girls were lively company, while Dave Telford had a never-ending repertoire of amusing road stories. Also, there were plenty of other Australians and New Zealanders who came to chat at our table. By the time we left at closing time, all of us were drunk and we had missed the last ferry back to the truck park. The only way to get across the Bosphorous was by the bridge; so we hailed a taxi and said goodbye to Vicky and Nikki. On the way round, Roy decided he was hungry and ordered the driver to take us to a restaurant. We joked about the taxi driver having a brother or a cousin who owned a restaurant, but sure enough, we went miles out into the Istanbul suburbs, before being delivered to the front door of an eating house at the bottom of a block of flats. Roy tried to get Dave and me to be enthusiastic about eating traditional Turkish food in a place probably never before visited by westerners; but we did the traditional English Saturday night thing by ordering two kebabs and two bottles of lager. While Roy devoured some unidentified, unpronounceable local delicacy, we ridiculed him about the authentic Turkish cuisine. Dave and I had our kebabs served up in half a baguette. Roy got even more stick when we got back to the trucks: the late night meal and taxi fare cost more than we had spent, drinking all night in the Pudding Shop.

Sunday was spent lazing around in the sunshine with a visit to the Harem Hotel in the evening. When Monday brought no news of any unloading, the rest of the day took the same pattern. However, after our evening Ef-es at the Harem, we returned to find two more British trucks on the park. Now we were five, all with the same agent, the same load and the same problem. The new arrivals: Ron and Mickey, were very much from the "Job's fucked, let's go on the piss" school of truck driving. So, after Mr

Suliman, the agent, came with no news of our unloading, we all went for a beer. From the Harem Hotel, we then went across the Bosphorus to the Pudding Shop and sat, drinking Ef-es all afternoon. Eventually the topic of conversation turned to women and Turkish women in particular.

"Pigale is the place to go for a Turkish girl," said Micky.

"Is that Pigale or Pig Alley?" asked Dave.

"Pigale, Pig Alley, it's all the same, a load of old dogs, the lot of them," slurred Mickey.

"So you've been and had a look then?" questioned Roy.

"Yeah, course I have. It doesn't cost anything to get in. There's a whole street of houses, all with dozens of girls in the windows. You just take your pick," tempted Micky.

"A bit like the Red Light district in Amsterdam?" asked Dave.

"No, nothing like it," replied Micky.

"So you've been there too," taunted Roy.

"Let's get a taxi and go over there. Then you can see

for yourselves. It's somewhere to go. It's boring in here," suggested Ron.

All five of us squeezed into a taxi which then sped off across Istanbul in the fading light of the evening. Fumes from the traffic hung in the warm, still air as our cab spun its front wheels furiously attempting the steep slope to our destination. With six of us in the four-door saloon, the weight was too much for the incline. We offered to get out and walk the final 50 yards, but he driver would not let gravity beat him; he screamed the engine and smoked the tyres on the cobbles as we inched slowly uphill. Our driver finally gave up when Ron and Micky got out and walked ahead, while the speedo was reading 25 kph.

Pig Alley was different from any other street in Istanbul in so far as it had an eight-foot high corrugated metal fence across both ends. A narrow doorway through the barrier was guarded by two policemen and was the only public entrance or exit. At the time of our visit, the place was crowded with loads of women in the shops and plenty of men on the roadway, although there seemed to be little business taking place. Very few of the men were Europeans, while not many seemed to be Turks. Many were from Iran, Iraq and other Gulf states, with a few Pakistanis, stopping off while travelling overland to and from western European. The women came in all sizes and ages, but most wore black, mini-skirts and white blouses. There were plenty to look at, as we five drivers discussed what would be our choice.

244

There was an atmosphere similar to what you would find when a load of kids visit a chocolate factory. Personally, I had drunk far too much strong lager to protest when one of the girls pulled me out of the crowd and led me into her house of disrepute.

The fair haired Turk was quite short, but with a good figure. She was one of the youngest and definitely one of the prettiest. We went upstairs to a room at the back, where she asked for the money first. Halfway through the blow job, Ron stuck his head round the door.

"Everything alright then?" he asked.

"Yeah, great," I said instinctively, and he disappeared.

When I came out, the others were all grinning.

"Was she any good then?" asked Ron.

"Not bad, what was yours like?" I asked.

"No, I didn't have one," replied Ron.

"What was you doing up in my room then?" I enquired.

"Oh, I saw her running around at the back and thought you were in trouble," said Ron.

"No trouble, she had just gone to get my change. I only had a 10,000 lira note," I said sharply.

"Heh Ron, if you want a watch, you should go to a jeweller's", quipped Dave Telford.

None of the other drivers did any business at Pigale. They day finished with us all back at the Harem Hotel, still drinking steadily, with no prospect of our situation changing.

"What's it like to pay cash for sex then, Chris?" asked Dave.

"She was pretty. I could've been chosen by a lot worse. 4,000 lira, that's about eight quid. You would spend more than that taking a bird out for a meal and still not be guaranteed a jump. Paying for sex? We do it all the time," I said, under the influence of alcohol.

Ef-es pilsen was a pleasant beer to drink when it was chilled; it would quench any thirst a hot and smoggy Istanbul could give you. The downside of using a strong lager as the body's sole source of liquid was that, in the morning, you became completely dehydrated – your mouth was like the bottom of the proverbial budgie's cage. My solution to this problem and the lack of drinkable tap water, was to go back to the Harem Hotel and drink more Ef-es, telling myself that the hair of the dog would do me good. It was only after I had been resident on the TIR park for over a week that I made an effort to break the circle and went to the local grocery store for five litres of mineral water.

Dave Telford was the most cultured of my British neighbours; he enjoyed his extended stay in Istanbul more than the others did. The charmer became friendly with the receptionist at the Harem Hotel and, through her, organised a trip on one of the passenger boats that ran up and down the Bosphorus. Sunday lunch was included in a cruise that lasted all day. Semra, the receptionist agreed to come along and act as our guide. But quite unexpectedly, we were all unloaded on the Friday afternoon. Mr Suliman, the agent, came in the morning with the news that five Turkish trucks from Adana were in Istanbul, looking for re-loads. The transfer of the goods took place in the dockyards, just along from the truck park. Under Customs; supervision, the trucks lined up in two rows of five. On a deserted quayside, a fork lift truck, with double length forks, scuttled across between the open-sided trailers until all the crates had been transhipped. After ten days' waiting, it took less than an hour and a half to tip.

I was in a dilemma whether or not I should now stay for the boat trip, but with over a week of inactivity, I thought I had better get going. At the Londra Camp, a telex was waiting for me with details of a collection at Brasov, in central Rumania. So, after a badly needed shower, I left Istanbul with Roy, who was going back to Germany for his re-load.

The road through Bulgaria and up to Rumania was becoming familiar to me now, which helped me make good time up to the furniture factory at Brasov. But even so, I was not quick enough to make up for the lost time in Istanbul and my load had been collected during the previous week by another British truck. All the office staff could do was to give me the address of another Romanian timber export factory at Carensebes.

It was a full day's drive across to the new pick-up point, but I do not know why I hurried, because when I got there the reproduction table tops were not ready. The trailer was backed up to the loading bay for two days, as the large, thin cardboard boxes were put in the back, as they came off the production line. It was only when I was loaded and underway that I realised what a problem load these pieces of wood were going to be. At every bend, the cardboard boxes slid from side to side, which soon began to damage the trailer. The forty foot TIR tilt, as it was called, was built to the specifications laid out by international Customs agreements. A metal framework was covered by a close-fitting canvas canopy, with metal drop-sides along the bottom. A series of metal loops on the sides and back aligned with eyelets in the canvas which allowed a long, plastic covered steel cord to encircle the trailer, making it impossible to enter without breaking the seal joining the two ends of the cable.

The constant banging of the boxes onto the frame of the trailer made it bend out, halfway along the top edges, while the welds holding the upright posts to the trailer floor had started to crack. I had no means of securing the load, so I had to take it steady - praying that the whole thing stayed glued together. On the motorway in Czechoslovakia, I tried to make up time, but was stopped for speeding. I later calculated in my diary, for the twenty-seventh time in six months. With no Marlborough or Kent king-sized cigarettes to pay the fine and a severe shortage of Deutschmarks, due to heavy beer consumption in Istanbul, I paid the traffic cop with a box of Vesta Beef Risotto, which had, by then, done all of the journeys that winter without being consumed.

At Dover, I telephoned Archie to tell him to send down some straps, so that I could try and keep the table tops still. Half a dozen, two inch wide webbing straps helped hold the load down but, by now, the trailer frame work was swaying about by itself. At Dudley, in the West Midlands, the furniture was delivered, in tact, but I was glad it was my last load for a while. What with the messing about after a passport, the ten day wait to get tipped, going up to Brasov for nothing and then having the nightmare of the sliding tables – I needed a few months on the beach to recover.

# Chapter Nineteen

It was the last week in May, when I set off again for the south of France. The Volkswagen van had stood idle for most of the winter, but ran as good as ever; even though the scrapes along the driver's side were now rusting badly. For the first time in all my trips, up and down France, there was not a single hitchhiker thumbing for lifts. Also, when I arrived, I found no one sleeping on the beach. Was St Tropez loosing its appeal to the young economy-minded adventurers?

The season seemed to be starting slowly everywhere, as there was only one other camper van on the beach car park that first night. It was a high top Mercedes 208 Westfalia conversion and by the registration plates I could tell it came from Karlsruhe. With a company name and telephone number on the door, I guessed it was part of a hire fleet. This fact was confirmed by the driver when she came over for a chat, just after I had showered and eaten my evening meal. The mother and daughter were only staying at the beach for a few days during the school's half term break. The pair had rented the camper for a week, but half of that time would be taken up by driving between Germany and the Mediterranean.

Anna, the mother's main reason for speaking to me, was to ascertain if the car park was a safe place for an overnight stay. I told her that for the previous two summers, I had not had any trouble. Anna also asked what there was to do in the evening. I recommended a trip into St Tropez, but they had already done that, so I invited the mother and daughter to share my duty free bottle of vodka with Tarzan when we had our traditional start of season drink, that night.. My first reaction when I saw my two German neighbours with their short spiky hair and close rapport was to think they were lesbians. It was also Tarzan's first word to me, when I told him I had taken the liberty of inviting the two guests. However, when he found out that they were mother and daughter, Tarzan warmed to the idea of them sharing our evening. Although, if I had brought along a couple of blokes, he would have cancelled the whole thing altogether.

Tarzan greeted the women in German, but then, as a mark of politeness to me, everybody spoke English for the rest of the night. I opened the Blue Label Smirnoff and poured, while Tarzan brought out a jug of fresh orange juice and a bowl of ice cubes. The four of us sat on our bar stools and sipped the screwdrivers, as the waves gently lapped on the shore, while the white beam from the Cap Camarat lighthouse circled through the warm night air. It was a situation I had come to take for granted, but it had a profound effect on Anna, as she put her hand on my knee and thanked me for giving her such a magical moment. We talked about our contrasting lifestyles, while Tarzan and Eva chatted away to each other at the opposite end of the bar.

The vodka and orange, in long tall glasses, with plenty of ice, was easy to drink. Soon the alcohol gave me a mellow, relaxed feeling; but to Anna, who rarely drank more than two glasses of wine, the spirit was more effective. The mother now recognised the situation as threatening: two male strangers, a foreign country, isolated, intoxicated.

"You have brought me here and got me drunk," said Anna, pointing an unsteady finger.

"Yes, that is true," I agreed.

"Do not try anything or it will be the end of you," she threatened.

"I wouldn't dream of trying anything. Half an hour ago you were thanking me for putting you in this situation. Nothing's changed, relax, take it easy. Let's go and sit on the sand," I suggested, as Anna's bar stool now seemed an unstable perch.

As we sat at the water's edge, I continued to placate Anna with calm, reasoning. I assured her there was nothing sinister going on and that she should continue to enjoy the evening. Anna lay back quietly on the sand, with her eyes closed. I thought I would give her some space, so I went back to the bar to finish my drink.

"Is my mother OK?" asked Eva

"I dunno, maybe she's had a little too much to drink," I replied.

"It is always the same. She is not used to it. She gets very happy and then gets very sad," said Eva, matter of factly.

This was the first time I had spoken to the daughter; after Tarzan went down onto the sand to sit next to Anna, Eva turned to talk to me, as I sat on the bar stool beside her. Eva was a big built girl, who made her mother seem small. She was neither fat nor thin, just a big size, exactly the same height as me, six foot one inch. At 17, Eva easily passed for 21. She was very self-confident, with an attitude that bordered on arrogance, but Eva was willing to listen to what you had to say and fixed you with an eye-to-eye, clear blue stare.

Eva was still drinking the vodka and orange at the same rate that I was, with seemingly no ill effects. We sat talking until way after midnight, as our legs slowly became entwined. Our hands first stroked each other's knees, before pulling our bodies together, as we kissed passionately. When Eva and I finally broke the embrace and gulped for air, we turned to see Eva's mother watching us from the bottom of the steps that led to the beach.

"Good night, I am going to bed now" said Anna, as Tarzan stood by, ready to walk the still unsteady mother back to her camper.

Tarzan returned shortly afterwards, to continue the main purpose of the evening: to finish the bottle of vodka. The Smirnoff made little impression on Eva, but at 100 proof, I could detect a distinct sway in my walk as Eva and I returned to the van, after leaving Tarzan at the bar with the empty bottle. Coffee was suggested, but never made, as lust was left to battle tiredness on its own. Stripped naked on the bed, I could not believe I was about to make love to a schoolgirl with the body of an Olympic athlete, whose mother lay sleeping a few yards away. In a few hours, my thoughts had gone from branding the pair as gay, to thinking I had a chance with the mother and finally to bedding the daughter. But it did not happen; Eva asked about contraception. As I had no condoms with me and Eva was not on the pill, we did not do it. I had to make do with Eva giving me head, but she refused to let me put my head between her legs as she found the tickling of my beard totally intolerable on her inner thighs.

In the morning, Eva had gone before I woke up; her mother and the Mercedes were also nowhere to be seen. I tried to remember if this was the day they intended to set off back to Germany, but having gone up to Ramatuelle village for groceries and coffee, I returned to find the pair back in the car park, after doing their shopping at Les Tournels campsite supermarket.

It was to be their last day at the beach and the three of us spent it on the sand together. I brought the windsurfer down off the roof of the van and Anna showed herself to be a very capable sailor. Eva was not so good, but when it came to swimming, I had never seen a girl who could swim faster. Mother and daughter were both very athletic and competitive, even with games like chess which we played under the parasol when the sun was at its hottest.

"Chris, I would like to come and visit you during my summer holiday. Would you like that?" said Eva, while we were playing chess and her mother had windsurfed far out to sea.

"Yes, it's OK with me, if it's OK with your mother," I replied, without giving the matter any thought.

After Anna returned from somewhere close to North Africa, the mother and daughter spoke about the proposal at great length in German.

Eventually, when Eva went for a swim, Anna grilled me on my plans for her daughter.

"So you think it would be good for my daughter to spend her summer here with you on this beach?"

"Yeah, it's a good life here, sun, sea and sand – what more could anybody ask for?" I said, realising quickly what a stupid question I had just asked and hoping that Anna's English was not good enough to come back with the cliché answer: "sex".

"Yes, OK, if you think you can put up with Eva for six weeks, it will be a great help to me. The long summer break from school is always a problem for me," said Anna, in a tone that led me to believe that Eva had inferred that her return to the beach was my idea.

With her full size and body of a grown up, Eva had made me forget she was still at school. I had envisaged a two or maybe three week visit, but now it looked like it would be six. Suddenly I could foresee difficulties with a headstrong and demanding female who had just manipulated an awkward situation to her own advantage with no trouble at all. On the plus side, I need not go chasing any more girls, and a young, fit competitive girl would keep me on my toes.

That evening, Anna cooked a meal in the Mercedes. Tarzan had a previous engagement, so he could not make it. The three of us discussed plans for the summer, over spaghetti bolognese and a salad. Eva would write to me at Poste Restante, Ramatuelle, with her arrival date and time. I would confirm these by telephone, before meeting the train at St Raphael, hopefully during the third week in July. Meanwhile, Eva would go on the pill and I would not go with other women. Anna thought it sounded alright to her and hoped the expense of keeping her daughter would not be too much for me.

Eva had everything a guy could wish for, except a sense of humour. It nearly ruined our whole relationship before it started, when she questioned me about whether I had ever been married. I spun Eva the old yarn about having had two wives, but unfortunately they had both died: the first had eaten some mushrooms that turned out to be poisonous, she went into a coma and passed away some weeks later; the second wife, to whom I had only been married ten weeks, died from a fractured skull. In first class double act fashion, Eva asked how wife number two came to get the fractured skull. But when I told her it was because she would not eat the mushrooms, Eva went and told her mother that I was a mass murderer. Thankfully, Anna had heard the joke before.

Mother and daughter headed back to Karlsruhe, first thing Saturday morning, while I headed up to Ramatuelle to do some shopping and have a drink at Chez Tony. While I was in the bar, George, the old Englishman, came in and joined me at my table. It was the first time I had seen him since the year before, when he was a regular at the Poney Express. George was the caretaker of a villa owned by a rich London-based South African businessman, he lived on the property in a small cottage in the grounds and buzzed around on a moped that went with the job. His care-taking duties were light, mostly pool cleaning, gardening and grass cutting. George organised a maid to do the housework for the weeks when the owners or clients were in residence. The villa was occupied for less than 12 weeks in a year, so the major part of George's time was spent as a security guard – which he accomplished by just being there.

During the previous summer, George had tried to cultivate an air of mystery and intrigue around himself, with unfinished stories of a dark, dangerous past. But regulars at the Poney Express soon began to notice large discrepancies in his tales as he re-told them, time and again, to any new arrivals who would listen. The general consensus was that George had been out in the sun too long without a hat; also, when his constant promises of a barbecue and swim in the pool, up at the villa, failed to materialise, most people began to ignore him.

Accompanying the 60 year old George at Chez Tony was a pretty New Zealand girl, in her early twenties. She was a nanny to an English family renting a villa near St Tropez; she had met George that morning, at a bar near Gassin La Foux. It was the nanny's day off and George had offered to show her the sights of Ramatuelle. I think the New Zealander was grateful to get away from the children and relax with English speakers, while having a cold beer. The three of us sat around the table, drinking and chatting until I started to feel hostile vibrations coming from George; he thought I was trying to nick his bird. It was about time I was on the beach, so I paid my bill and left.

What happened next between George and the nanny was told to me by R W Lewis, who was the husband of Karen, the housemaid George employed to clean the villa. Late in the afternoon, George took the girl back to the villa to have a meal. After the food, George tried it on with the pretty nanny and would not take no for an answer. The girl was so terrified of the naked Englishman with an erection, that all she could do to get away was to run up the villa and seek help from the clients renting the place. They saved the nanny from molestation by taking

258

her back to St Tropez in their car;  but the clients were so worried by George's conduct that they telephoned the villa's owner in London to complain.   Within a couple of days, the South African businessman had flown down to Nice and fired George.  At the same time, the owner brought with him, a man from his local pizza delivery company, whom he installed as the new caretaker.

I became involved in the story again, when George came to the beach in order to ask me to tow his old caravan away from the villa.  When I went round to collect the caravan, I met Mr Harvey, the owner, and the new caretaker, who everyone called Chubs.  The atmosphere seemed calm, but George must have been devastated to loose such an ideal job, as well as a nice home.  Everything he owned was now bundled into a ten foot long caravan, which he had nowhere to site and nothing to pull it with.

After a lot of unpractical ideas from George, I decided the best place to take the caravan would be the old derelict villa, up by the lighthouse.  It was much as it had been when the grape-pickers had stayed there, two years previous, but with a lot more graffiti.   We unhitched the caravan in a small flat clearing, well away from the road.

"Look at the state of this in here," said a disgusted George, as he opened the door.

"You should have put all those glasses and plates

somewhere safe, before we set off," I suggested, as I surveyed the mess on the caravan floor.

"It's your crazy driving that's smashed up all my things. Now what am I going to do?" said George, angrily.

"Don't talk rubbish. If I was driving crazy why aren't the glasses in the van broken? Don't have a go at me, just because you lost your job and your cottage," I retorted, as George came out of the caravan, with two handfuls of broken glass, which he threw in the direction of my van.

"Fuck off," said George, as he shut himself in the caravan.

"If that's all the thanks I get for helping you out, you can get someone else to tow your caravan next time," I mumbled, as I tiptoed, barefoot, across to the van.

"If I get a puncture driving out of here, I'll come back and have you," I continued, when I drove away.

In the first weeks of the summer, very few of the familiar faces turned up on the beach. Only Richie Bishop, the bus mechanic from Gloucester, and Irish Danny joined me for afternoon tea. The three of us played a lot of chess, while Richie finally mastered the art of windsurfing. There was no Poney Express, so our evenings were spent on the sand. RW and Karen Lewis, with their two boys, Christopher and Paul, came to visit in the late afternoon, as part of their daily routine. The family was camping wild, down the dirt track to Cap Cartaya. Their pair of ridge tents were a permanent fixture amongst the collection of camping cars that took long stay holidays on that beautiful but inaccessible stretch of coastline. Karen's housemaid job at the villa took up most of the morning, while R'dub and the boys killed time up at Ramatuelle. Reunited at lunchtime, the family spent the afternoon on the beach, by their tents, only coming to Pampellone after the car park attendant had gone home. They had left England in a Ford Fiesta, at the beginning of May and intended to stay all summer. Now that George had lost his job, R'dub had his heart set on taking over the caretaking position at the end of the season.

I did not find out straight away, but Karen eventually told me why the Lewis' had come away to start a new life. Not for the first time, R'dub had started playing away and the woman's partner took exception to it. There was a showdown, where R'dub gave the guy a good hiding. When it went to court, the combatants were bound over to keep the peace for one year. R'dub and Karen figured the best way to keep out of trouble was to come to France, where they could also try and rebuild their marriage.

R'dub was an ex-boxer and very fit, although quite short at 5' 4", he had a more muscular body than even Tarzan. He was an excellent swimmer and could do over 50 metres underwater in one breath. The only thing that stopped R'dub being the perfect male was his receding hairline, which he tried to disguise with a comb over. R'dub had even developed a technique for pulling his hand sideways across the top of his head, as he surfaced after a dive. Once the lads on the beach had noticed this little habit, it never failed to bring a smile to everyone's face. For the rest of the summer, when R'dub was mentioned in conversation, there would be a chorus of R'dub as all those present swiped the top of their heads with the palm of their hands.

It was one evening after R'dub and his family had left, that four student nurses from TBB made their appearance on the beach. TBB pronounced "tay bay bay" was short for the really long named German town called Tauberbischofsheim; it was also the registration letters on the girls' VW Golf. Richie, Danny and myself were sitting round our small fire on the beach when the girls came over. We had sifted the sand for the buried remains of a recent barbecue and had re-lit the coals, so that we had some heat for popping some corn. Although frowned upon by the safety-conscious locals, a fire on the beach always proved to be magnetic to any north European tourist who, somehow, saw it as romantic. It was dangerous, with the close proximity of the bamboo groves, but I always kept my fires small and only lit one if the breeze was blowing out to sea.

Digging up the charcoal from old discarded barbies provided the best fuel. Popcorn was the cheapest and easiest food to cook. There was always a lot of debate over whether to add salt or sugar to the finished pan – I preferred salt, but had to admit that too much spoilt the popcorn, where as too much sugar was not a problem. As it was my saucepan, we were eating salted popcorn, when the nurses joined us.   Having left Germany, bright and early that morning, the girls were tired, but determined to make the most of their fortnight in the sun. A Campfire on the beach was just the sort of thing that they were looking for, on a pleasant summer's evening – being offered a hot snack was an unexpected bonus.

The talking between the seven of us went on long after the popcorn had finished with first Heidi and then Barbara, falling asleep on the sand.   Eventually, I went back to the van to make coffee for everyone who was still awake.  Rosetta came to help, but we somehow started kissing, as we waited for the kettle to boil;   then one thing led to another.  If there was anybody still awake on the sand who really wanted a coffee they did not come and get it.  By the time Rosetta and I had finished our cups, we were in bed together, so we did not take the coffee over to them either.

Rosetta only stayed for the one night.  I did not see anything of the four nurses over the next few days, as they explored various beaches and the night life of St Tropez.  When the girls did return, they were amazed to find Danny, Richie and myself still occupying the same piece of sand.

"Why chase off round the world when you can let the world go round you?" Irish Danny told them.

From then on, the Germans were regulars on the patch of sand between L'Esquinade and the Cabane Bamboo. More and more, I found myself being drawn towards Claudia, the shortest of the four who was the owner of Tao, a little terrier they had brought with them. With her diminutive stature and having a dog in tow, Claudia reminded me of Regine and Virgile. They also shared the same outrageously daring style of dress, plus, both had the ability to twist a man round their little fingers. I did not know it at the time, but Claudia had set her sights on me and there was nothing Rosetta would be able to do about it.

The windsurf lesson was her first positive move, where Claudia did quite well, before getting tired. Afterwards, I gave a demonstration of the basic skills, while Caludia lay on the back end of the board, as we sailed out to sea. At the 300 metre buoy, I looped the outpull rope around the floating plastic ball, which anchored us while we sat and chatted. I think Claudia expected me to make a pass at her, out there, at sea, but I could feel the motion of the waves bringing on a mild attack of sea sickness. This only ever happened while the board was stationary: when the mast was up and I was sailing, everything was always alright. It was the same with car travel: if I was at the wheel, it was fine, but if someone else drove and asked me to look at a map, I would be carsick. I put it down to the fact my father never drove and I never went anywhere when I was a kid. Later in the afternoon, when Claudia and I walked with Tao, the dog, along the coastal path towards the lighthouse. I knew she expected me to make a move then, because she told me so later, when Claudia left the other three nurses at the campsite and came to visit me in the evening.

The problem of how to be alone for the night with Claudia had been on my mind all day. Now it had been solved for me by someone who knew what they wanted and knew how to get it. We did not jump straight into bed and I was thankful of that because Rosetta turned up, just after I had poured out two large vodka and cokes. Claudia was sitting opposite me in the back of the van, Rosetta stood at the side door.

"Hi," I said, as tension gripped the air.

"Hi," said Rosetta, as Claudia looked straight ahead, saying nothing. A long silence followed, while Rosetta stood and drew circles in the dust with her big toe.

"Can I have one of those drinks, please?" asked Rosetta, at long last.

"Sure you can," I replied, thankful to have something to do with my hands.

"I am going to take this drink onto the beach," said Rosetta, without adding the next line, "Will you join me?"

Rosetta walked away onto the sand and sat down looking out to sea. Quite neatly, she had given me the choice of Claudia or her. I could take my drink onto the sand, or I could stay in the van. It was all too subtle for me. I did not see it until the next day. Half an hour later, Rosetta had tears in her eyes, when she brought back the empty glass. Like a prat, I asked her if she wanted a refill, but Rosetta just shook her head and walked back to the campsite. Claudia and I had another stiff vodka and coke, before I folded down the rear seat to make up the bed. The sex was as good as I expected it to be with the small, but beautifully proportioned nurse. Claudia said it was a long time since she had had it so good, but I cannot help feeling I would not have enjoyed it at all if I had known how much I had upset Rosetta.

Just before midnight, Claudia left and took the car back to the others. The next time I saw Claudia was when all four nurses came down to the beach car park in the morning. Heidi came over to tell me that by changing my affections from Rosetta to Claudia, I had caused a lot of argument. Because of it, the four girls were changing their holiday plans and going off to spend their second week at the Gorge du Verdun. It was a bit ironic that they should be going to somewhere that I had recommended, but it was all my fault. My 'notches on the bedpost' mentality was clearly to blame. Rosetta liked sugar with her popcorn, while Claudia preferred salt, but they were both nice girls and did not deserve to have their precious two week holiday ruined through arguments over a beach bum.

## Chapter Twenty

The next weekend saw the return to the beach of Vero, the beekeeper from Gap. She had come on her own for a couple of days and was driving the van she used for work. Vero seemed pleased to see me, but I could see something was wrong, as she rarely smiled and the sparkle in her eyes was missing. There was no eye contact like before, which had been important to two people who hardly ever spoke to each other. Her head was continually bowed. Vero only raised it to gulp down her vodka and lemons. Thinking that it was boyfriend trouble, I kept quiet. I did not assume Vero just wanted sex, as on other occasions. The only times Vero and I had ever laid down together for a cuddle was when we had both exhausted ourselves by shagging, but on this night the French girl had come to me for love and not sex. It was hard for me not to do it, when I thought of every other time we had been in bed together, it made it even harder. A couple of large vodkas helped, although having messed up Rosetta's holiday, only a few days earlier, I was determined to learn from my mistakes and control myself.

Our two vans spent the whole weekend parked side by side. Vero and I spent more time in each others company than ever before. Eventually I did make love to Vero, at day break, on the Sunday morning. I prefer to think she was still half asleep and not just laying back, letting me do it because she felt obliged to. Afterwards,

I moved round to lay beside her and we stayed in each others arms until the sun heated up the van so much that we had to get up.

Later in the day, Vero told me that her bees had caught a disease that made the honey taste peculiar. There was a threat of extermination hanging over the 120 hives in her care. This went some way to explaining Vero's depression, but I did not think it was the full story. The last time I ever saw the beekeeper was on the Tuesday, following our weekend together. Vero had returned to Gap on the Sunday afternoon, not saying anything about coming back for her usual three weeks in August, or if there would be more weekend breaks. When she turned up on the Tuesday evening, I was surprised and did not know what the story was. Did Vero fall in love with me during the weekend and now wanted to spend the rest of her life with me? Was it that she had finished work early and felt horny, so had driven down to the coast for a quickie? Or was she running away?

It was the latter. Ten minutes after Vero arrived, her boyfriend pulled up in a cloud of dust at the rear of our two vans. I did not think for a moment that he would get violent, but it was a situation I did not want to be in. Vero and her boyfriend had a strange relationship. He would go with other girls, she went with other boys; he even used Vero to make up threesomes. There was nothing that they had not tried. When Vero went with me, she would do anything, anywhere, at any time and never complained.

They spoke to each other in French, but it was too fast for me to catch anything. It looked like he was pleading with her to go back with him. From Vero's body language, plus her movements between the two men in her life, I reckoned she was in two minds. I seized the chance to get them back together. The only way I could do it was to be nasty to Vero. Something which, over the years, and with other girls, I had shown a prodigious talent. I told her that I did not want her, did not love her, that I only ever went with her for the sex. I added that my girlfriend was arriving in a few days, we had no future together and that I never wanted to see her again - all in very poor French. Then I took Vero's handbag from out of my van and handed it to her boyfriend. Finally, I locked myself in and did not come out until they had both driven away. I like to think the couple from Gap got back together again. I hope they went on to form a close lasting relationship. For me, it was the second time in a week that things had turned out far from satisfactorily.

People from previous years were now returning for their annual holidays. The campsites and car parks were filling up. Eric and Ingo from Amsterdam; Regine and Pascaline from Nancy; Mick and Helen from Helloo, not selling drinks for a change; Andre, the tall hotel manager from Bochun and Ingmar, with his brother, Carsten, from Darmstadt. All these were old friends, who also knew each other. Many had brought their friends with them. More people who had come to see for themselves, the ever increasing multi-national scene that was centred on the village of Ramatuelle. There were less independent

269

beach sellers than in previous years and not many of my old grape picking buddies - except Keith Connery, who took three weeks off from his care-taking in Worthing; while Irish Danny found himself a second chefs job in the Ramatuelle pizzeria; but there was a distinct lack of absolutely penniless Dubliners.

One of the most interesting characters of the beach scene was Ingmar, from Darmstadt in Germany. Enjoying his second summer at Ramatuelle. Once again, he had brought his big 308 Mercedes van which was covered with Berlin wall style graffiti, predominantly in blue, black and yellow. The vehicle, along with the punk dress code of the driver, made every decent law abiding holiday maker extremely wary. A totally incorrect impression of someone who was as friendly and charming as anyone you could ever wish to meet. With his athletic build and long blonde hair, the 6'2" bespectacled German had great success pulling the birds; his ability to have two or three trouble-free relationships on the go at the same time was not only testimony to Ingmar's charm, but also to his physical fitness. Like Eric from Amsterdam, Ingmar could seem arrogant at times, but in reality, he was only telling it like it was. Besides being a very well endowed sex machine, Ingmar was an expert windsurfer, a capable car mechanic, a gifted linguist, a talented spray paint artist and he did all these things whilst looking through glasses with lens the thickness of milk bottle bottoms.

One day, while I was preparing an evening meal in the van, Ingmar came over to suggest that the dents and scrapes on the driver's side needed painting before the bare metal rusted through. I agreed that something had to be done about it, but did not think our short verbal exchange had given him the go ahead to create a masterpiece similar to those on underground trains. The music from a John Martyn cassette tape, playing on the stereo masked the hissing of Ingmar's aerosols. The first I knew of it was when I was asked for my critical appraisal. I do not know what I would have done if I had not liked his artwork, but thankfully it looked good.

On the white background there was a huge black fist with splashes of blue and lightening bolts of yellow coming from an imaginary impact. The words "Zap" and "Pow" were written in the style of a Superman comic with black outlines to all the coloured areas. The mural took up the whole of the right hand side of the Volkswagen Transporter, but took less than 10 minutes to paint - although Ingmar had probably been planning it for days. Forever after, the van always drew attention to itself; most reaction was favourable. Generally people saw the design as the ultimate example of where a little dent in the bodywork is marked, in felt-nib with the word "ouch". In the car park that evening, everybody came over to have a closer look and to pass comment. The owners of two Dutch registered couch-built campers said I was misguided to give Ingmar the go-ahead for the painting. I countered this by saying I had not given my permission and that the German hippie had just done it while I was not looking, adding that Ingmar was now looking for something bigger to show off his talent. For

271

the next week, Ingmar was forever creeping up on the Dutch campers and going "pisst" through their open windows, showing that amongst all his other attributes, Ingmar had a wicked sense of humour.

When the letter from Eva arrived at the Poste Restante, I quickly telephoned confirmation of its safe arrival as she was due to set off for the south of France the very next day. It was not an easy trip for a young woman to make by train and involved over 24 hours of travelling. From Karlsruhe, Eva had to make her way across to Strasbourg in order to catch a train to Paris. At the Gare de Lyon, in the French capital, she had to book a couchette, to travel overnight, down to St Raphael, where we were due to rendezvous at 8.00 o'clock in the morning.

It all went off without a hitch; the train was on time and we drove straight back to Ramatuelle. On arrival at the top car park in the village, Eva and I climbed through into the back of the van and made love. This set a pattern for the next six weeks, as Eva regularly chose the Ramatuelle car park, in the middle of the morning, as one of the times she wanted sex. During her stay, I never failed to meet any of Eva's demands, but the unusual timings did not help to make our loving memorable or romantic. Eva was not the lovey-dovey type, it was all matter-of-fact, with very little kissing and cuddling or foreplay. I always thought of myself as a "once in the morning, twice at night" man, but with Eva it was mid-morning, mid-afternoon and mid-night, with me on top every time.

Apart from the timing of our love-life, Eva fitted in pretty well with things on the beach. My circle of friends had grown since her visit in June; now there was always people coming over for coffee in the morning, tea in the afternoon and drinks in the evening. Eva thought it was a bit much, and I was being put upon, but I told her it was better than being alone for the whole summer. Having other people around, who you could trust, also made it easier to go off and do things like swimming and windsurfing without worrying about all your stuff on the beach. Not that Eva had much stuff: her small sports bag was mostly filled by two towels. It was a good idea to travel with just a bag, rather than a rucksack, as the single female backpacker attracts a lot of attention from the opportunists who prey on young foreigners in France. The lack of clothes did not cause Eva any problems, as she spent most of her time on the beach where she was always completely naked. At other times she chose to wear my clothes, which fitted her as well as they did me. This let Eva go through her whole holiday without doing any laundry for she never wore underwear either.

Within a week of Eva's arrival, Pat and Maggie O'Malley came back to the beach in their old converted ambulance. They had set out, from London, the day after the kids had broken up from school and hoped to stay until just before the autumn term began. Eva soon became good friends with the O'Malleys, as well as the Lewis family; she was pleased to meet people, other than my beach-bum friends. George surfaced again at this time because he knew Pat and Maggie from the year before. He started hanging around the car park in the evenings, but never mentioned his broken glassware and acted as if nothing had happened. I tried not to speak to him, after what he had done to the New Zealand nanny, I did not want anything to do with him. But as I was still the only person with a tow bar equipped vehicle, it was inevitable George was going to ask me to tow his van again.

"Chris, can you tow my caravan to its new site when you have got the time?" asked George in front of everyone, knowing how difficult it would be for me to refuse.

"Yes, of course, George, whenever you want, as long as you pack up all your breakables this time," I replied, without hesitation, knowing that it was better not to have someone like George as an enemy as you never knew what they might do when your back was turned.

The new site for the caravan was on a farm just off the St Tropez-Ramatuelle road.

Half a dozen permanently sited mobile homes occupied a small grass area amongst the vineyards. George was put alongside a similar sized caravan to his own. The old Englishman seemed on very friendly terms with the occupant of the neighbouring van, who introduced herself as Saronge. It was only later, when I had returned to the beach that I remembered where I had seen her before; Saronge was one of the resident artists on the St Tropez quayside, who painted endless canvasses of the harbour scene. If she was George's new girlfriend, he had really stuck lucky.

This year, Pat O'Malley's Kronenbourg consumption was even more than ever, a litre bottle was rarely out of his hand, let alone out of reach. Lager for breakfast instead of black coffee, like everybody else, indicated the problem was serious, while Maggie constantly begged Pat to let her do the driving. The beer was to blame for Pat rowing with R'dub about something he said about Karen. The families fell out, R'dub and Karen stopped coming to the beach, which was a shame for both sets of children, as they got on well and there was not many other English speaking kids to play with.

Just how much the alcohol was affecting Pat was shown when he decided to have a late afternoon barbecue on the beach. The mosquitoes were always out in force at the usual barbecue time of dusk, so Pat wanted to avoid the relentless attacks on his children by cooking early. Pat collected enough driftwood for a fire, which he hoped would give him enough glowing embers that would cook his chicken. Unfortunately, before you can have glowing embers, you have to have flames and smoke. As it was a hot sunny afternoon, the beach was still crowded when Pat lit his fire. The sunbathing tourists did not like the smoke. The protests came in all languages and from all directions, especially downwind. Pat protested back, indicating that if anybody did not like his fire they should go somewhere else. Pat had his most heated debate with a nearby French family, but while his back was to the fire, the eldest daughter of the French couple sneaked off down to the sea to fetch a pail of water and triumphantly doused the flames.

Meanwhile, Eva had become so embarrassed that she had gone back to Maggie, who was preparing the food at the vans. With the fire out and the wood soaking wet, Pat stormed off into the car park, letting everybody think that it was the end of the matter. But no, five minutes later, Pat returned, still with his Kronenbourg in one hand, but with an eight inch long kitchen knife in the other. He was not holding the knife down by his side either. Pat held it out in front of him with the point angled, menacingly, upwards. The drunken Irishman demanded to know who had put his fire out. Everybody on the beach was looking at Pat, but no one said a word or moved a muscle. Mick and Helen, who had been invited to the barbecue, pretended they were not with Pat and sat with their heads in their hands.

"For fuck's sake, sit down, Pat, you'll get us all arrested," mumbled Mick.

It was a grim situation, Pat was wild-eyed; he was ready to take on the whole beach. He had gone past the point of no return – there seemed no way Pat was going to back down, let alone sit down. Pat was the only person standing up for a radius of about 100 metres, so I felt that if I was going to talk to him I would have to stand up as well. He was a good friend and basically a good bloke who I had seen help out a lot of people over the years. I had to do something, in case somebody had telephoned the police to say that there was a madman with a knife, terrorising the beach.

"Give it anther 20 minutes and this lot will all start going home. The wood will have dried out and we can start again. But they won't go while you stand there with that knife. They're waiting to see what happens next. Sit down, Pat, and they'll soon piss off," I pleaded, casually.

"No, Chris, I won't sit down. I want that bastard who put my fire out," said Pat, who was visibly shaking.

"She's just a kid, Pat, you'll have to let it go," I suggested.

"No way. I'm not letting anything go," raged Pat.

I went through the points of my argument again, trying to show to the threatened onlookers that I was trying to calm the situation. But somehow I got the impression that everybody thought I was backing Pat. Maybe it was because we were both standing up, which made it look like it was now two crazy Englishmen against the world. The stand-off lasted for ages, during which time I heard the tell tale clicks of camera shutters, capturing the unusual holiday moment on film. It was hard to think of what more I could say or do. Grappling with Pat for custody of the weapon was not an option, so I stood in silence, as the naked Irishman swigged his beer, while he turned slowly round, glaring at the seated onlookers. By this time, normally the beach would be practically deserted, but on this day, the sun-worshippers were hanging on for the outcome of the knifeman confrontation.

It was down to Pat's physical state, rather than his mental determination, that made the drunken barbecue chef eventually sit down. Pat's legs became so tired, it was a case of sit down or fall down. Meanwhile, Maggie had put the chicken pieces into the oven to cook. Soon, the beach had emptied; only Mick and Helen sat with Pat and myself, beside the pile of driftwood, until Eva returned with the news that dinner was ready. After the meal, Pat swore about the intolerant French, spoiling his evening, but he said nothing about how rash it had been to take a knife onto the beach. None of us condemned him, but Pat did not go onto the sand during the next day.

The old ambulance only re-appeared after sunset when Pat pulled into the beach car park and promptly fell asleep at the wheel; Maggie was in a most distressed state. The family had spent their afternoon and early evening up at the Moulins des Pallais, which were a collection of old ruined windmills on the hilltop above Ramatuelle. There were fine panoramic views out across the Mediterranean. The small parking area just off the back road that linked Ramatuelle to Gassin was a popular picnic venue. While Maggie and the kids had explored the ruins, Pat had drunk more than his usual quota of Kronenbourg. When it was time to return from the hill, Maggie insisted on driving, but Pat pushed his wife aside, grabbed the wheel and set off at breakneck speed. Luckily the single-track road was deserted, as the heavy, cumbersome ambulance lurched round the blind bends, with a sheer drop on one side of the road and the rock face on the other. Faster and faster Pat drove, while everything crashed about in the back as Maggie hugged the screaming children.

They all feared for their lives because Pat refused to use the brakes and the automatic transmission did nothing to retard the engine. If ever the ambulance needed its old blue flashing roof lights, it was when it steamed through the village of Ramatuelle which was miraculously traffic free. From the village to the beach, the road was just as steep, but thankfully it was a little wider, so on-coming vehicles had a chance to get out of the way.

After she had tidied up the camper and put the kids to bed, Maggie came over to Eva and me for a cup of tea. Eva was all in favour of having Pat interned in a lunatic asylum for the way he had behaved with the knife and how he had endangered the lives of his family. I thought it might be a good idea to get away from the beach for a few days, so I suggested that we could all go up to the Gorge du Verdun for a bit of gold prospecting.

In the morning, everyone was in favour of a Gorge trip, except Pat.

"My motor won't be able to cope with the mountains," protested Pat.

"There's nothing steeper than the climb up to the Moulins des Pallais," I countered.

"It'll cost a fortune in petrol, we'd be better off staying here," moaned Pat.

"Take some people with you and charge them petrol money. Your kids are looking forward to finding lots of gold nuggets. Anyway, a few days away and all that lot on the beach will have gone home," I said.

"OK, you've talked me into it," said Pat reluctantly.

Mick and Helen, plus Richie Bishop, went with the O'Malleys to the Gorge, while Chubs asked R'dub and Karen to look after the villa so that he could come with Eva and myself in the Volkswagen. The O'Malley motor home coped well with the hilly terrain, mainly because Pat had chosen to run off the 50 gallons of fresh water that he normally carried. The two vehicles installed themselves alongside all the other campers on the lakeside, where we were promptly enveloped in the smoke from our neighbours freshly lit barbecue. The offending Frenchman could not understand why we all fell about laughing, but felt sufficiently inspired by our non-confrontational attitude to insist that we used his hot coals to cook our sausages. Pat lightened up after this episode, although his Kronenbourg consumption still rivalled that of the whole

Foreign Legion.

Once again, there was no reward for the hours spent crouched beside the river, panning for gold with the hub caps. The midday sun seemed hotter than ever in the absence of a cooling sea breeze. We had three nights and four days at the Gorge, all without unpleasant incident, before returning to Ramatuelle. Eva seemed happy at the change of scenery, so much so that she proposed a tour of other river valleys in the south of France. I put forward Pat's argument of extra fuel costs, which was a bit unadventurous of me, but life was so easy on the beach, I could not bear to be away.

While everyone was in the mountains seeking their fortune, Danny Rudd had returned with his mate, Roger, in an old Mark 2 Cortina. The pair had been making their way slowly across France since the beginning of the summer; earning money by playing guitars in the streets of provincial towns.

Danny and Roger had started in the north-west at the oddly named town of Quimper and they had redefined "Quimper" to mean: the fear to commence busking. It gave rise to the previously unheard of phrase: stop quimpering about and let's get on with it. The musicians played a new town every day, with just a few days' break at the farm of Marianne and Rupert, as they worked their way south-east. Now they hoped to spend the rest of the season playing to the pavement cafes of St Tropez, not only because they could save on the cost of travelling, but also because the Cortina's gearbox was knackered.

One thing Danny and Roger did have going for them, though, was that they played excellent jazz on their acoustic guitars, with their portable 12 volt amplifiers.

"Will you take me to Archachon, Chris? It is on the Atlantic coast near Bordeaux," asked Eva, a few days after we had returned to the beach.

"Why do you want to go there?" I asked, suspecting the German girl was getting restless.

"Because I told my grandmother I would be visiting Archachon and she is expecting a postcard from me," stated Eva, as if it was something I had forgotten about.

"Well, send her a card from St Tropez and tell her you won't be going to Archachon," I said, having instantly decided that such a feeble reason did not warrant traipsing right across France.

"I have already sent her a postcard from St Tropez and on it I told her I would be going to Archachon. If you will not take me, I shall have to go alone," said Eva with a firmness that indicated she was not bluffing.

"Ok, if you gotta go, you gotta go. I'll take you to the station at Les Arcs and you can go by train. I'll still be here when you come back, if you come back. But if you ask me it's a long way to go just to send a postcard," I said.

"People go everywhere to send postcards," argued

Eva.

Next day, after lunch, we made our way over to the town of Les Arcs, near Vidauban. It was on the main line, but I had no idea about train times or connections. At the fork in the road where there is the turn off for Le Luc, we stopped beside the ruins of a picturesque stone bridge, in order to make love for one last time. It should have been an emotionally tender moment, but it was baking hot in the van, even with the door open. Everything was sticky, soaked in sweat and the flies irritated us to such an extent that it was a relief to get back on the road, where the fresh air through the open windows cooled us down.

I left Eva at the station , long before her train was due, but as I had promised Danny and Roger that I would take them into St Tropez, I could not hang about. As I drove back to the beach, I did briefly consider racing across to Bordeaux and surprising Eva when I met her at the station in the morning; but I dismissed the idea as too expensive. That night, the busking went well, with over 150 francs gathered from the diners of the half dozen restaurants entertained by the guitarists. With three tunes at each eatery, lasting for about 10 minutes, Danny and Roger had only worked for one hour in all - although discussing what and where to play, as we wandered round, had taken all evening. However, the financial outcome suffered a serious setback when over half the collected money was spent on three celebratory beers.

With Eva gone, it made a change to sleep alone. The beach also seemed much quieter. At the end of the next day, I was left by myself, with just my parasol and icebox, as everybody decamped to their tents, caravans and villas in the early evening sunshine. It was the best part of the day, but then Eva appeared.

"Hello, that was a quick trip," I said.

"You bastard, you just left me alone on that platform and came straight back to your beloved beach, didn't you?" raged Eva.

"I thought that's what you wanted," I said, astonished by the anger in Eva's voice.

"You do not love me. You were going to let me go half way across Europe and you do not care," continued Eva.

"If you love something, then let it go. If it returns then....," I started to quote before a handful of sand was thrown in my face.

"That is bullshit, you selfish bastard, you just do what you want to do, every time." Said Eva, in her ever-improving English, as another load of sand flew into my beard.

"Cut it out or someone will get blinded," I demanded., as I deliberately flicked sand at Eva, who was kneeling in front of me.

Handful after handful of sand flew between us with increasing force. By shutting my eyes just before impact, I was able to save my sight, but it was clear that I had upset Eva in some unknown way. She was definitely intent on hurting me. The only escape route open to me was to go into the sea; Eva was fully clothed, while I wore just my shorts. I made a dash for the water and dived in, relieved to wash the sand out of my hair. But as I surfaced and turned back to the beach, I was hit on the cheek by a clod of wet sand, thrown by Eva as she waded out towards me. Splashing as hard and as fast as I could, I sent a wall of spray towards my attacker, who continued her pursuit, undeterred. As she closed in, I turned tail and waded into deeper water as fast as I could, but Eva was in her element, even in jeans and a tee-shirt, the big German girl still had a huge capability in the water. Within a few powerful strokes her hands had grabbed the waist band of my shorts. My feet were then pulled from under me and as I submerged, I felt Eva's hands pushing down on my back. Quickly, I folded my legs underneath me and was able to push up from the seabed so that I could surface for air in the chest-deep water. I then jumped on Eva's back, taking her under as I grabbed a lung full of air. We both surfaced, gasping, but as Eva moved her hands up to hold me by the throat, we both submerged again. When we came up for air, I had reciprocated Eva's attempts at strangulation. As we tried to regain our footing, I attempted a head butt in the hope that some pain might bring my attacker to her senses, but I only succeeded in taking both of us back under the water.   Inexplicably, on the fourth occasion that we came up to breathe, Eva and I found ourselves kissing passionately, still holding each other firmly by the neck.

As we embraced, I looked over to the shore to see if anyone had witnessed our bewildering encounter, but the beach was deserted, which was just as well, because when we waded out of the water I had a massive erection. It was not wasted, as we went straight  over to the van to dry off and then directly onto the bed.  The post-fight sex was the best ever between Eva and myself;  whether it was because of the tussle or our arousal was caused by the deprivation of oxygen, I do not know.  We were like a couple of wild animals who did more damage to each other with our teeth and nails than we had done during all the sand blasting.

## Chapter Twenty-one

After the fight, Eva still had a fortnight of her holiday left, but it passed peacefully, as she concentrated on getting the darkest all-over tan possible.  Pat, Maggie and the kids started back for England after another week, which coincided with my brother, Paul, coming down to the Riviera for the first time.  He had only ever been on package holidays to Spain before;  but I had sent him a map and a letter giving instructions on where to find us.  Paul arrived during the early hours of the morning, but was gracious enough not to wake Eva or myself;  we found him, sound asleep, in his car when we got up.  Paul spoke no French, so was pleased when he found everyone spoke to him in English.  He fitted in quite well and slept in his car, parked amongst the camper-vans.

Eva finally went back to Karlsruhe on the train with the darkest tan in Germany and a promise from me to keep in touch.  Danny and Roger, the guitarists, concentrated their busking in Ramatuelle as there was too much competition in St Tropez.  R'dub and Karen had their dream come true when they were given the caretakers job at the Harvey villa. The season was coming to an end, with Richie Bishop and myself the only ones who had stayed for the whole summer.

Danny and Roger had the busking down to a fine art and played nightly at the four most popular restaurants in Ramatuelle.   It was still the same three tunes at each place, but the speed of playing had increased so much that it now only took about eight minutes, instead of ten. Richie, Paul and myself had heard the music so many times that we waited for the musicians at the Bar Tabac in the Place de l'Ormeau. Here we had discovered that the best value drink was the Ramatuelle Rose, at 19 francs. The chilled bottle of wine, with three glasses, worked out at half of what you would pay in an English wine bar, while everything else was at extortionate Riviera prices.

One night, two German women sitting at the next table noticed what we were drinking and followed suit. When Danny and Roger came in, after their evening's work, they too ordered a bottle of Rose and two glasses. The waiter was a bit peeved to see so many people drinking so much, so cheaply, but he kept bringing over the bottles – although the chilled stock from his refrigerated cabinets was exhausted and we had to make do with slightly warmer bottles from the cellar. Barbara and Collette from Bonn proved to be good company. I was surprised at just how well my brother, Paul, got on with the Germans. Obviously his dealings with Eva had given him the confidence to carry on conversations with foreign females, although the wine must have helped. Paul even arranged to meet our fellow rose drinkers same time, same place, the following night.

All the next day, everyone teased Paul about how Barbara, the one with glasses, clearly fancied him.

"I think we should give Ramat a miss tonight and go busking in St Trop," said Danny Rudd.

"You know we're seeing them German girls, don't make me go on my own," protested Paul.

"They're a pair of lesbians, if you ask me, they're only after you spending money on them," suggested Roger.

"No they're not, that Barbara's divorced," countered Paul.

"It must be fate, you breaking up with your Barbara after ten years, and then another Barbara comes along, just like that," I said.

"Well, at least when you're giving her one, you won't go moaning the wrong name," remarked Danny Rudd.

We did go to Ramatuelle that night, where the evening went well-nigh perfectly for Paul. Barbara was certainly not playing hard to get, although Collette made it quite plain she was not looking for anything more than a quiet drink. Soon after the buskers joined us at our table, Collette left her friend and returned alone to her campsite, leaving Barbara and Paul talking head to head, oblivious to everything around them. My brother was plainly getting on well with the girl from Bonn, but it was a shock when they stood up and announced that they were going for a drive into St Tropez. This meant that the four of us had to walk the four kilometres back down to our vehicles, as Paul had kindly insisted that we all go up to Ramatuelle in his car. Luckily for Danny and Roger, they had left their amplifiers in one of the restaurants, so that the batteries could be re-charged. They only had their guitars with them, but it was still a long hike back to the beach in the moonlight.

Paul assured us that our walk was not in vain, as he struck it lucky with the eager Barbara; his only regret was that it had been her last night at Ramatuelle. They had exchanged telephone numbers and addresses. I could not remember ever seeing my brother so keen on a female. The piece of good fortune that had clinched it for Paul occurred when he and Barbara were in one of the posh bars overlooking the Place des Lices. Barbara had just gone to the loo and Paul was sitting there, worrying about the size of the bill, when he felt something down the back of his seat. When Paul pulled the thing out, he found it was a single red rose, all done up in cellophane. A rose that a young gypsy girl had sold earlier that evening, which had been left by the previous occupant of the chair. Paul held the bloom under the table until Barbara returned, whereupon he produced it with a flourish. This was the first time my elder brother had ever given flowers to a woman; from the emotional and passionate response it had, he said it would not be the last.

The guitarists were relying on people to give them lifts at this time, because the automatic gearbox of their Cortina was leaking oil as fast as you could pour it in. In order to have a look at it, we built some ramps from pieces of concrete and old scaffold boards, onto which we towed the car. Richie Bishop, the bus mechanic from

Gloucester, then dropped the gearbox down from the engine, using the tools from my van. Richie's diagnosis of the oil problem was that the leak was caused by the worn seal on main shaft. A small part only costing a couple of quid, but due to the rarity of the old automatic Cortina, it was not a spare that was stocked by St Tropez's Ford agent. However, my brother Paul said he would buy on e in England when he returned and post it to Ramatuelle, as it was only the size of a jam jar lid, it would not be a problem.

The Cortina stood up on its ramps for over a fortnight before the part arrived from England, in a jiffy bag. Many people had said that it would never run again, but they were proved wrong when Richie had it back together inside an hour. We then all went into St Tropez to buy the correct amount of transmission fluid for the gearbox. The cost of the special oil was so high that it left Danny and Roger so broke, they could not afford to put any petrol in the car. But after a couple of nights busking, they did not need ferrying around any more, which was a good thing because Olivia was back on the beach.

It was mid-September which, by most people's reckoning was late to be starting a summer holiday. Olivia had been working at a bank in Paris as a holiday relief and now had a three week break before going back to college. My student lover was studying finance, with a guarantee of a job at the establishment where she had worked, if she passed her exams. Her timing fitted in well with the apartment in St Tropez which had been occupied in previous weeks by the owner and his family. The owner of the property was a distant relative of Olivia's and her sister, Sabine, who was also waiting to start at university in October. The apartment belonged to the father-in-law of Olivia's auntie, whose son (I later found out) was Olivia's lover. The uncle turned out to be a bit of a sugar daddy. Most of the high class underwear in Olivia's knicker drawer were gifts from him. I could hardly wait to see what new additions he had showered on his niece during the past year.

Olivia and I soon fell into the same routine as the previous autumn: afternoons on the beach, nights in the van. Once again, the parents were on the scene in the late afternoons, but looked upon me as their daughter's private windsurf tutor and knew nothing of our evening rendezvouses. Olivia had an intriguing lifestyle; I had never encountered a mistress before.

"Why do you go with an older married man when you could have anyone you want?" I asked.

"I have been with boys and they are terrible lovers. I prefer old men like you," replied Olivia.

"Hey, less of the old. I'm not as old as your lover, am I?" I retorted.

"No, you are at the age Sebastian was when we first became lovers," said Olivia, reflectively.
"How old were you then?" I pried.

"Oh, sixteen, but he was not my first," answered Olivia calmly.

"Does your family know about this Sebastian and you?" I enquired, thoroughly intrigued by the revelations.

"My aunt knows that my uncle has a lover because she discusses it with my mother, but nobody knows that it is me, not even my sister. My aunt tolerates it because Sebastian treats her very well. It is not unusual for a successful businessman to take a lover, especially in Paris," said Olivia, as if it was a natural, everyday relationship.

"And what does this Sebastian do, that allows him to buy you all these sexy undies?"

"He is a director at the bank where I have been working this summer. What are undies?"

The nights in the van seemed even better than I remembered; whatever sort of banker Sebastian was, it was not a merchant banker, the sugar daddy had taught Olivia well in the art of love-making. Although it was not that Olivia was some sort of slave, who did everything while you just lay back. Our love-making had a lot of tenderness, without any declaration of undying love. The young Parisienne never did anything I had not done before, but all that she did had never been bettered by any of my previous lovers. It was always smooth, with no awkward movement, as if our movements had been choreographed beforehand. Before Olivia, I thought I knew how good shagging could be, but she took it to a higher, dreamlike level.

It was the time of year when the grape harvest was about to start, but nobody seemed interested in finding any work. Richie Bishop set off back to England, reckoning he could easily find a job as a mechanic for the winter months. Danny and Roger, the guitarists, preferred to pick strings, rather than grapes. I thought about going up to see Francis Boi at Vidauban, for I knew he would need a tractor driver, but the nights with Olivia were just too good to miss. Each day saw fewer people on the beach, with only R'dub, his family, the musicians and a Dutch girl called Erin, coming for afternoon tea. Danny and Roger had met up with Erin at the top car park in Ramatuelle; she, too, had a Ford Cortina and had tagged along to the beach. Erin also went along in the evenings, at first to hear the music, but then as an integral part of the group, when she proved to be very good at going round with the hat. The takings went up by over 50% after the petit Dutch girl started going round the tables in her mini skirt, skimpy top and bare feet.

I found Erin very attractive, with her sparkling eyes and crew-cut. If it had not been for Olivia, I would have made a play for her. Both Danny and Roger were not the least bit interested in bedding their fellow Cortina owner. But it was a surprise when the sexy little Dutch girl started seeing R'dub behind Karen's back. There seemed to be a dark secret lurking somewhere in Erin's past, with questions as to why a 20 year old should be alone with just her car and virtually no other possessions, remaining unanswered. However, R'dub could not keep his secret from Karen; we figured that she found out about the affair just before R'dub came down to the beach with scratches all over his face.

Tarzan was about the only other person on the beach with whom I had regular contact. We had not spoken much since our evening with Eva and her mother, but he always said hello with a bone crushing handshake and passed comment on the physical appearance of whoever he had seen me with. It turned out that Tarzan detested Eva, even more than she disliked him.

"You should have drowned that German girl when you had the chance. It would have been self-defence. She attacked you. I saw it all. I could have been a witness for the defence," said Tarzan, without a trace of humour in his voice.

"I didn't think anyone saw what happened that day," I replied.

"There is not much that happens on this beach that Tarzan does not see or hear about," said the plagiste.

"And how have things been for you, romantically speaking?" I asked, having seen the well-built, fitness fanatic with several bathing beauties during the season.

"Well, there is one thing you could help me with. I have lost my English rose. She came onto L'Esquinade to use the toilet, which I told her was only for customers. So she hired a mattress for the day and then stayed with me for four days and three nights. Never once leaving L'Esquinade. She had no car and was alone, here in the south of France. Then my English rose disappeared with no "thank you" or "goodbye". I am thinking that maybe something happened to her. Will you keep a lookout for a beautiful English girl who is all alone?" asked Tarzan.

"I'm always on the lookout for just that sort of person, but now I know there's one out there, on the loose, I'll be extra vigilant," I answered as sincerely as I could.

During my last few days on the beach, Tarzan's English rose was never found and her disappearance remained a mystery. When Olivia and her family vacated their St Tropez apartment, I was not far behind them in heading north. I did offer to take Olivia back to Paris in the van, as I knew there was not enough room in the family Peugeot for four people and a months worth of luggage. But the mother and daughters already had return train tickets, while the father was driving back alone.

## Chapter Twenty-two

Back in the UK earlier than in previous years, I wasted no time in getting over to the Ipswich premises of Archie Fredericks.  My funds were low, so I needed a job urgently, but I did not let Archie know that as I nonchalantly walked into his porta-cabin office one mid-week morning in October.  Archie was on the 'phone, so I sat and waited while a conversation about the late delivery of a load to Rumania took place.  After every excuse you could imagine and a few highly improbable scenarios had been given to the irate customer, Archie put the telephone down and turned to me.

"That fucking Roland's screwing some Rumo bird; he's been gone nearly a month and still hasn't got to Bucharest.  When you go through Rumania keep an eye out for him and if you see him, tell him to stop pissing about and get his arse into gear 'cos the customers not very happy" said Archie, before I could even say hello.

"Does this mean that I've got my old job back then?" I queried.

"Yeah, take that X reg Merc that's standing in the yard.  Go up to London and load for Istanbul and Ankara. The old left-hooker will be back tonight and you can take that," replied Archie, who liked to keep his planning fluid and open to improvement.

Once again, I was working within minutes of looking for a job. The prospect of going to Ankara was a bonus for I had never been that far before. That afternoon, I loaded the trailer at the groupage warehouse in east London's old docklands, making sure the Istanbul was on the back and the Ankara goods at the front. When I returned to Ipswich, the left-hand drive Mercedes six wheel unit that I had driven during the previous winter was waiting to hitch up to the loaded trailer. The paperwork, carnets, permits and running money was ready in the office. After a quick trip up to Sainsburys in the van to get supplies, I left to catch the midnight ferry to Zeebrugge with some choice words of advice from Archie ringing in my ears.

"And I don't want to find out you've got some commie block flousie tucked away somewhere!" shouted the haulier as I pulled out onto the road.

"Me? And a commie block flousie, never," I replied as I wound up the window, "she's from Karlsruhe," I continued after it was closed.

Sometimes I wondered why Archie bothered with all the hassle of international transport operations. Sure, he had made good money in the early days of the Middle-East overland route, but by now the rates had been cut right back and there was little chance of money up front; also there was a good chance that your customer would go bankrupt before you were paid. Even with a good driver, who knew what he was doing, there were occasions when he would take a few days off, en route,

298

in order to visit girlfriends, or simply just sit on the beach at Kavala. With a bad driver, or one who was unlucky, it was a good result if the trip did not show a loss. All too often, breakdowns, accidents, drivers getting robbed or drivers robbing the company made the whole enterprise financially pointless.

Archie Fredericks had been in business for about 15 years, so had a lot of contacts; there was a never-ending stream of loads to and from eastern Europe coming through on the telex machine. Easily enough work for 16 trucks, if suitable drivers could be found. On average, Archie had a turnover of about 80 drivers per year. Some men came just to do one Middle East trip, before leaving after they had seen what it was like. A few drivers stayed while a few, like myself, came, went and then came back again. Most discontentment was about the money – the pay was poor; almost any reputable company was paying its drivers more for doing UK work than Fredericks paid for international trips. Archie had also found out early in his management days that whatever running money he gave a driver, it would always be spent. Therefore, the cash to buy diesel, pay tolls, buy visas and anything else was cut to a minimum. The amount was based on what Archie spent when he did the job as a driver many years before. You had to feel sorry for the boss - most of the drivers were fiddling their expenses, also there had been incidences of drivers abandoning their trucks when the going got tough. One of the worst occasions, when Archie got ripped off, was when a new driver, with plenty of Middle-East experience, was all set to leave the yard on his first trip for the firm. The ferry was booked, the truck was fuelled up and ready to go. The driver told Archie that he was just going to pop down to the supermarket to get some food, but was never seen again. Neither was the 1500 Deutschmarks running money that the driver had signed for, five minutes earlier.

There were two reasons why I could justify calling in to see Eva on my way through Germany. The weekend curfew on trucks was one excuse; while the other explanation was that I could go through Luxembourg and fill the trailer's belly tank with cheap diesel. Importing a load of fuel into Germany was strictly against the law – the authorities at the border town of Remich were very alert to the advantages that this route gave to drivers. In an effort to fool the Customs, I had left the tanks on the unit half full; on the trailer tank, I had forced a wine bottle cork up the outlet pipe so that when the tap was turned on, nothing came out. If I got caught, I would have to pay the duty on the diesel plus a fine for trying it on. Luckily, it was raining hard when I reached the border. The normally efficient and conscientious officials did not even come out to check the tanks. I kept my cool and showing I had nothing to hide, I casually telephoned Eva from the Customs office pay phone. My German girlfriend was pleased to hear form me. We arranged to meet at the fairground parking area – the same place I had stayed when I came to see Petra, two years earlier.

Late on the Friday afternoon, when I reached Karlsruhe, I found I was not the only one staying at Eva's house for the first time. Eva and her mother picked me up on the way over to the local dogs' home, where they had arranged to take on a rescued pet. At the kennels, Anna asked me to stay in the car while the mother and daughter went in to collect the animal. I soon found out why. The dog that Eva's family were giving a home to was the biggest St Bernard I had ever seen. A fully-grown, two year old, without an ounce of fat, but with severe behavioural problems. His name was Titan and he would attack any other dog he came across, also the dog would go for any man who was not sitting down. Titan did not attack women or children, but did not take a blind bit of notice of anybody's commands. Due to his strength and size, the St Bernard did exactly what he wanted.

All this became apparent during the car journey to Eva's home, as she struggled to keep the dog from invading the front seats as her mother drove. At the house, I briefly met Erland, Eva's younger brother, before he disappeared into his bedroom, never to be seen again. The lad was dead scared of the massive brute and I could not blame him. But I had been brought up with dogs, which made me think that I had the ability to get on with them. Titan just needed to be shown who was the master, then given affection – thereby earning his trust, while making him obedient. It was easier said than done.

I told Eva and Anna that I could not stay glued to my chair all weekend. I thought that if I confronted the dog, then we might become friends. The mother and daughter were not in favour of my idea, as they did not want blood on the carpet, but they did not have a chance to stop the fight because when I stood up the dog just came for me. Titan missed my forearm with his mouth, which enabled me to catch the dog in a headlock as he leapt passed me. I wrestled the mountain of dog flesh down onto the hearthrug, while aiming same well aimed punches to his muzzle - blows that I hoped went unseen by Eva and Anna. During the fight, I uttered such phrases as "Ah, he's only playing" and "I think he likes a bit of rough and tumble" but in truth, I was fighting for my life as the brute thudded his huge feet with their sharp claws into my body and attempted to get his jaws around any part of me that he could. The dog was only subdued when I lay across his legs with the headlock still in place. Slowly, I began to tickle Titan behind the ears and on the chest, while speaking to him softly, but when I released my hold and stood up, the dog came for me again. It took three more pinfalls, before my supremacy was acknowledged, after which, the dog never gave me any more trouble.

Eva's mother was so full of admiration for what I had done that she encouraged her son to make friends with the dog, but Erland was not willing to chance it. Eva thought that I had just been showing off, which led me to believe that her mother had not told her just what a problem they had on their hands. Whether it was a token of her appreciation for what I had done with the dog, or just modern German hospitality, Anna insisted that Eva and I have the double bed in her room, while

302

she slept in Eva's single. As a bit of fun, Eva pretended to be Titan, as we re-enacted the earlier dogfight between the sheets. It ended up with Eva on her knees, as I took her from behind; once again, the best sex between us had been preceded by violence.

Prior to meeting Titan, I thought all St Bernards were mild-mannered giants, typified by HG, the dog in the sit-com with the old man and his two good-looking daughters. Like everyone else, I knew the stories of barrels of brandy and heroic rescues on blizzard torn mountains. Bernadinas, as they were known in German, had a good reputation, but when you did come across a rogue dog, it was more dangerous than any Rottweiler. Anna, Eva and I took Titan out in the car on Saturday afternoon, so that Erland could come out of his bedroom for a couple of hours. The three of us drove to some woods where we walked the dog with no problem at all, mainly because we did not meet anyone. On Sunday, Anna had arranged for a tutor to visit the house in order to give her daughter a private maths lesson; Eva had missed a lot of schooling when her parents split up and was well behind in her studies. To stop the dog mauling the teacher, I offered to take Titan out for a walk by myself.

A super-model in a miniskirt would not have turned more heads than the St Bernard did when I walked him through the town. Luckily for the local population, everybody was travelling in their motorcars. When I glimpsed our reflection in a shop window, I thought how

Titan made me look small, he was the only dog I ever walked where the leash went upwards from my hands to his head, it was more like leading a pony. Understanding German was not one of my strong points, but on that afternoon I learned to lip read the German for "Gosh, look at the size of that dog."

Everything went well until we reached the woods, where Titan took off in pursuit of a squirrel. His charge caught me by surprise and nearly dislocated my shoulder, but I just managed to stay on my feet until we reached the tree that was giving refuge to the small furry mammal. After that, I made sure that I was the first to see any living creature that we came upon. This enabled me to either prepare myself for the tug of war, or in the case of somebody with another dog, drag Titan off the pathway and into the trees. Since our Friday night battle, Titan had not made one attempt to harm me, but nothing I tried would stop the beast from attacking anything that was not a female human being. As I sat on a park bench in the woods, Titan put his massive head on my lap, while I tickled him behind the ears. It pained me to think of what might happen to the magnificent animal and how sooner or later his spirit would be broken by a boot or a stick.

Back at the house, as darkness fell, everybody was looking at skiing brochures when I returned, exhausted, with a fit and lively Titan.

"Chris, would you like to join us on a skiing holiday at Christmas and the New Year?" asked Anna

"Yes, but I've never skied before," I replied.

"That is not a problem Eva and Erland are experts, they have been on skis since they were babies, they will teach you," said Anna proudly.

"Great, where are you thinking of going?" I asked.

"Switzerland, near the town of Brig. There is a chalet. I will telephone directly and see if it is available for two weeks," said Anna in her typical forthright way.

Eva's mother then telephoned Switzerland and made the reservation. Once more, I would be away from home at Christmas, but his time in better conditions than Rumania.

"It is good you are coming with us. You are very good with Titan and it will help us if you are there also," continued Anna, after the phone call.

"And it's good Titan is coming too. I might get lost or buried by an avalanche, then he can rescue me," I added.

"There will not be avalanches at Christmas. We will be fortunate if there is enough snow for skiing," said Eva, sternly.

"Well, it will be handy to have the dog there, with his little brandy barrel, just in case I get thirsty," I said, getting sillier in the hope Eva might join in the light-hearted banter.

"You cannot ski when you are drunk," retorted Eva.

"Oh, you've tried it then, have you?" I quipped, before Eva turned away to ignore me and rattle on in German with her mother.

At my request, Anna gave me a lift back to the truck that evening. I wanted to get going at 5.00 o'clock on the Monday morning, so I thought it would be easier for the family if I slept in my cab. Eva came along to say goodbye, having forgotten our little argument.

"Will you come and see us on your way home?" asked Eva, as we kissed beside the truck.

"It depends on what time I have," I replied, "but I will phone you when I get back to Germany, one way or the other."

"OK. Titan and I will miss you, auf wiedersehen," said Eva tenderly.

"I'll miss you two, auf wiedersehen pets," I said with a smile.

As the mother and daughter drove away, I wondered what Anna had done to deserve such a daughter as Eva, who made her life so difficult and then voluntarily take on a dog like Titan who was even more of a problem.

When I left Karlsruhe in the morning, I had two options open to me: one was to go flat out and try to tip in Istanbul on the Friday; the other was to take it easy, arriving at the Londra Camp during the weekend. I chose the second alternative and, typically, when you are not in a hurry, things went well, with no serious delays. With only ten tonnes in the trailer, the Mercedes trundled into Istanbul on the Friday afternoon, which gave me my second consecutive work-free weekend. However, I had forgotten that it would take all of the Monday for my agent to process the Customs' paperwork, so I was not unloaded until Tuesday afternoon. The goods were taken off at a warehouse, down by the waterside. For the first time ever, it had not been necessary to go across to eastern Istanbul for unloading, but it saved me nothing, as I still had to pay the £90 toll for the Bosporus bridge in order to get to Ankara

East of Izmit was all new territory for me. The main part of Turkey was not even on any of my maps as they all finished at Istanbul. To help myself, I had spent a lot of the weekend, casually picking the brains of other British drivers at the Londra Camp. They reckoned that I did not need a map as Ankara was on all the signposts; I was told of the whereabouts of all the police checkpoints; where I would have to stop, in order to have my TIR transit card stamped. Most of my helpful colleagues' advice also came with cautionary tales of a hill they called "Bolu" which proceeded the ominously sounding descent named "Death Valley". I was encouraged to learn that with only a part-load left on the trailer, weighing four tonnes, I should not have any problems going up or coming down.

It was a full day's drive across to Ankara, after I left Istanbul. The speed limit was 70 kilometres per hour, with plenty of slow and over-loaded local trucks to pass. These Turkish made six wheel rigids were nicknamed "Tonkas" by the Brits; they were built to carry 15 tonnes, but frequently carried more than 20, with their eight metre long loads piled as high as possible, with every cargo imaginable. The brightly painted cabs were decorated with an abundance of second-rate sign writing which contrasted greatly with the plumes of black smoke coming from the unsilenced exhausts. The Tonkas' incessant droning was only interrupted when an over-loaded tyre would explode with an almighty bang.

Just after the police checkpoint at the truck park, owned by SOMAT, the Bulgarian state transport company, I came to the hill they called "Bolu". The road snaked back and forth across the rising ground with a succession of blind summits that made me think I would never reach the top. Several Tonkas expired in their attempt at the long climb; some had overheated, while two others seems to have broken the half-shafts in their back axles as weight and gravity won the battle against the internal combustion engine. Not that coming down was any easier. A runaway Tonka had flipped over on the last bend of its descent, broadcasting sacks of corn into an adjacent field; while two others that I passed when I was close to the top seemed to be going downhill much too fast for the conditions. The worried look on the drivers' faces appeared to confirm it.

On the brief flat area at the summit, most of the Tonkas pulled over to let their engines idle, so that some of the excess heat could be dissipated, before they dropped down into "Death Valley". The road that descended into the valley was totally different from that of the climb as it was cut into the side of a steep gorge, with a rock face on one side and the drop into a dried up riverbed on the other. The hill they called "Bolu" was on relatively smooth terrain, with spectacular views across open countryside. The gorge road never let you see more than 200 metres ahead before it disappeared around another blind bend. Also, it was difficult to concentrate on the driving when your eyes were continually drawn to the shattered wrecks of cars and trucks that littered the arid canyon floor, in various stages of rusted deterioration. "Whatever gear you go up a hill, is the gear to come down that hill" is an old transport industry saying that certainly rang true concerning the descent of "Death Valley". The vee-eight Mercedes hardly needed more than a dab on the foot brake to slow it into the bends. The braking effect of the 15 litre engine, plus the closed exhaust manifold valve, held the rig adequately in check as I anticipated the gradient to flatten out long before it did.

It was nearly dawn when I arrived at the Teleks Motel on the outskirts of Ankara. After a few hours' sleep, I was awoken by the Customs clearing agent banging on the side of the cab. The shipping agency man in Istanbul had said he would telephone the Ankara office - true to his word, he had advised his colleagues of my arrival and saved me the cost of a taxi. This also meant that I did not get the chance to see the sites of Turkey's capital city as my delivery address was sited just next door to the motel parking area. By midday, I was empty and back on the road to Istanbul. The sun was coming up behind me, as I turned into Londra camp, 18 hours later.

A telex was waiting for me in Reception, but I did not bother to go and get it until late afternoon when I surfaced from a well-earned rest. Anyway, I knew that it was going to say: "To Chris Arbon. Load barbecues on account of House of Holland, London, from Roman Metal Export, Radauti, Rumania. Regards Archie Fredericks." It if was not a surprise that I was going to visit Marina and her tin bending friends again; I was surprised to find that my load was ready. After arriving in the middle of the night, I was looking forward to lazing around for a couple of days, but by midday the trailer was well on the way to being full. Marina was nowhere to be seen, but the security guard recognised me and sent over another factory girl to run my errands. All the barbecues were loaded and the paperwork was completed before it got dark.

With dry roads and an hour of daylight left, I set off across the mountain road, heading west towards the Hungarian border. My progress was good in the deserted countryside, but I knew that sooner or later I would have to stop for the night. Once again, I had to decide where I could safely park. The mountain road had many parking areas, set back in the surrounding forests, so I thought I would chance my luck and park up in the middle of nowhere.

At about half past four in the morning, I awoke with a jump and lay rigidly still as I waited for the noise that had roused me to occur again. Then it happened, two thumps and a scratching sound. Somebody was at the back of the trailer, either rifling through my storage boxes, or taking one of the spare wheels. Normal procedure in these situations was to start the engine while drawing the curtains, slam the gear stick into reverse and back over the villain before disappearing up the road a safe distance so that you could inspect any damage or loss. Why I did not do this, I do not know.

It was the first time in all my years of driving that anything like this had happened to me, but that was no excuse for ridiculous thing that I did. As the noises continued, I quietly dressed, grabbed the cigarette lighter that I used to light my stove, and pulled a can of WD40 from the toolbox.

Carefully unlocking the passenger door, I silently crept round the front of the cab with my lighter in one hand and the aerosol in the other. It was pitch black, but I could just make out the crouching shape of a body trying to break into the trailer boxes. As my finger pressed down on the button of the spray can, I flicked on the lighter to ignite the petroleum-based jet into a sheet of flames. The figure at the other end of the trailer rose up, turned towards me and roared.

"Oh, shit, it's a bear," I exclaimed, as I ran back round and jumped in the cab.

"Oh shit, it's a human being with a bloody flame thrower," probably thought the bear, as it scampered off into the darkness.

In the light of day, I inspected the damage, which turned out to be just a few souvenir claw marks on the trailer's paintwork. The bear seemed to have been attracted by the smell of some old empty food tins that had been left in the box, after a camion stew at the Londra Camp. To this day, I am always wary about getting out of the cab when I am parked overnight in lonely places. But if anything like that happens again, I am going to put plan A into action and drive away – I am definitely not going to use plan WD40 again.

The brown bear incident was the only hiccup of a trouble-free run back to the UK, but with having had two weekends off, I was running late, which meant I could not return to Karlsruhe. When I telephoned, Anna pleaded with me to take the St Bernard off her hands. The family was still struggling to control the animal. As I had bonded really well with Titan, I considered it for a moment. I thought of how handy a fierce dog would have been in a situation like I experienced with the bear.

But with the strict British rabies laws, it was out of the question – even though I would have had the biggest cab mut in history.

A few days later, I telephoned Germany and Eva told me that Titan had gone back to the dogs' home as he was too much of a handful.  I was at my brother's house when I rang, because I had called, primarily to ask Anna if Paul could join us in Switzerland for the Christmas skiing. Eva rang back later that evening to say it was not a problem. As Paul and Eva knew each other from the summer, I thought it was a good idea to make the party up to six. Also Paul could chip in for petrol and the cost of the ferry. Eva also asked when I would be going through Karlsruhe again, but I did not know.  It turned out that after the one trip to Turkey, I did the Italian run for the rest of the year, so my next visit was at Christmas.

## Chapter Twenty-three

Paul was more excited about the Swiss trip than almost anything else I could remember him doing. It seemed that the summer weeks on the beach had lit the flame of adventure in his life. My brother was also still in regular contact with Barbara from Bonn, who worked in the national headquarters of the German telecommunications company. Paul's love interest from the summer had easy access to free telephone calls as she worked in the international enquiries department. Every Saturday morning would see the pair having hour long telephone conversations at neither one's expense.

When it became evident that Paul and I could fit in a visit to Bonn on the way down to Karlsruhe, my brother insisted we should take the night boat from Felixstowe to Zeebrugge. This gave us an early morning dash across Belgium, a short stretch of autobahn to Cologne, then we followed the river Rhine south to Bonn. By lunchtime we had found Barbara's home, just a few hundred metres from the river and within earshot of the constant droning made by the heavily laden barges struggling up-stream towards Switzerland.

Barbara was pleased to see us. She had gone to a lot of trouble in preparing a three course meal, based on the traditional English roast beef Sunday lunch. It was an amazing little home; about ten years old, at the centre of a five house terrace that was one of many on an edge of town estate. Nothing too remarkable from the outside, but the interior was packed with high quality furniture, sculptures, pictures and object d'art, all mixed in with every possible piece of modern electrical equipment imaginable. It was as if Barbara had recently moved from a mansion to a cottage, but had kept everything that filled the larger property. Every room was on the topside of cluttered; it was impossible to walk anywhere without having to turn sideways and edge your way through. I knew Barbara had not long split up from her husband, so I wondered if she had moved in since the break-up, but it turned out that he had left her, taking all his things with him.

The excellent meal was followed by a tour of Bonn in Barbara's Fiat Panda. Paul and I thought Barbara was in a bad mood when we drove off in the car, because she roared away, went flat out before braking late at every junction and seemed to be wearing blinkers as she only ever looked straight ahead. After running at least half the red lights on the way into the town centre, we visited Beethoven's old house, which was now a bar. Over a beer, Paul and I found out that Barbara always drove like it was the wrong time of the month, without ever having an accident. Thankfully, the white knuckle ride back to the house maintained her record. It was a lot later than we had planned when we left Bonn for the thrash down the autobahn to Karlsruhe.

"Talk about bring on the scary driving" I said, as we turned onto the south-bound slip road.

"Yeah, not half, and what about all the stuff in the house?" replied Paul, who had been quietly reflecting.

"I couldn't live like that, I'd be scared I'd knock something over."

"Oh, I could, all that gear was first rate, top of the range, no expense spared."

"So when are you moving in then?"

"Huh, I don't know about that."

"But you would do, wouldn't you?  There's plenty of work for carpenters over here and you'd be well looked after.  Barbara thinks the world of you," I said, forcing the pace a bit too quickly.

"That'll take a lot of thinking about," said Paul, as he began his contemplation and did not say another word until we reached Karlsruhe.

Eva was out when Paul and I arrived, just before midnight.  Since my last visit, the young German girl had passed her driving test.  She had gone out in the car to collect the sixth member of our skiing party from the station.  Sylvie was Eva's long time French pen-friend, who lived in Paris.  For her too, it was going to be the first time on skis.  Paul volunteered to sleep in the van, but Anna had made up a camp bed for him in Erland's room;  while Eva and I, once again, had the double bed in the master bedroom, as the generous mother slept in Eva's room with Sylvie.

Bright and early, after a cereal breakfast, we loaded the German family's skis into the van, before racing down to the Swiss border at Basle; Eva driving her mum's Opel, while I tried to keep up in the graffiti ridden Volkswagen. A quick count up of the Swiss police and Customs officials came out in favour of the Zap-Pow mural as we chatted while purchasing our road tax stickers. The light hearted banter might have been because it was Christmas Eve, but it was a stark contrast to the over officious reception I always got when I came through the same border with a truck load of imports. The race continued across Switzerland, down to the village of Klandersteg with the VW coming in just ahead of the Opel. The village was at the northern end of a tunnel, that provided a rail link to Gloppenstein in a southern Swiss valley - here the vehicles were driven onto the train. Once on the train, the occupants remained in their vehicles for the journey. Eva came to sit in the van, nothing had been pre-arranged, but she had plans for the break between our driving.

"Paul, you can go and sit with my mother and brother, while we are on the train," suggested Eva, in a tone that was stating it as an order, rather than an option.

"But I hardly know them, I'd rather stay here," protested Paul, not recognising the reason for the request.

"Well this will be a good time to get to know them. Chris and I want to be alone," said Eva, bluntly.

Paul glanced across to me, as I nodded my head sideways in the direction of the Opel parked behind us. Without any more protest, my brother reluctantly got out and went to the car, just before the train pulled out of the station. Paul always had difficulty in thinking of things to say to strangers; sitting with newly acquainted foreigners in such bizarre circumstances could not have been easy. I am sure he only did it because Paul thought he owed it to me, as I had been able to arrange for him to come on the holiday.

The sex was bad, but I never told Paul, as I preferred my brother to think that the effort he made in over coming his shyness was worthwhile. The van was so full of skis, suitcases, sports bags and boxes of food that there was not enough space to recline the rear seat so that we could lay on the bed. Coupled with the fact that neither of us knew how long the rail journey would take; everything was rushed and cramped. We both just took off our jeans and tried a variety of positions that suited one of us but not the other. The one with Eva kneeling on the rear seat with her head amongst the suitcases seemed the most sensible way of solving the problem; but Eva complained of it being unloving. Although a few months earlier, after my fight with Titan, doggie-doggie had been excellent for both of us. We tried it with me sitting on the bench seat and Eva facing me with her knees spread. That did not work, although we had successfully done something similar on a kitchen chair. Finally, Eva sat on the seat with her bum edged to the front of the cushion, her right leg was on the sink unit and her left foot wedged against the door handle. I knelt in front of her, but was just too low, so I had to raise myself up by locking my arms straight while taking all of my weight on my wrists. Having done it the night before, it seemed to take forever. Eva and I then pulled on our jeans at the same time the train came out of the southern end of the tunnel. My partner never said if it was good for her or not, but the only thing I can say is that now I have done it on a train.

The chalet was set on the lower slopes of a south-facing valley, which looked as if it had come from the front of a chocolate box. The ground floor was the home of the owner, while the first floor was reached by a wooden staircase on the side of the building. Upstairs were three good-sized bedrooms, a bathroom and a living area, which combined the kitchen with a dining room. All the walls were wood panelled and all the windows were triple glazed. As darkness fell, a light snow shower started, adding to the Christmas atmosphere, as we all carried the gear up into the chalet. Anna then took Sylvia, Paul and me over to a nearby shop where the owner rented out to us the necessary skis, boots and poles. Everything was now all set for skiing on Christmas day.

The evening was spent dining on the Raclet cheese dip that Anna had brought specially. At midnight we exchanged presents. I felt bad that I had not brought anything for Sylvie, but Eva really liked the leather jacket that I had acquired when I was in Istanbul. The night had a true Christmas feeling to it, with everyone happy and smiling in the warm chalet, while the odd snow flake still fluttered down outside.

It must have been the cold air on my face that woke me up in the middle of the night. As I reached over to find an empty space where Eva should have been sleeping, I wondered what was going on. The French doors that led onto the small balcony were wide open. I could see the naked body of Eva silhouetted in the moonlight.

"What on earth are you doing out there at this time of night, with nothing on?" I whispered.

"I am changing the air in the room," replied Eva, "why don't you come out here and make love to me? It is such a beautiful night."

The invitation was just as big a shock to my system as the cold air, but there was a huge positive reaction from below my waistline. I gingerly slid out from under the duvet and went outside, under the stars. The whole valley was asleep, as I embraced Eva in the still night air. We kissed passionately, as our hands moved firmly across each other's body in an attempt to create heat by friction. Our mouths moved from mouth to neck to chest and back to mouth with unprecedented speed, as a frenzy of movement combated the cold. Eva then brushed the snow from the top of the wooden rail at the corner of the balcony and pulled me towards her as she edged up to sit on the cold timber. With blind faith in the workmanship of an unknown Swiss carpenter, we made love. Eva put her life in my hands as only my knees, jammed between the balustrades, stopped us from tumbling over the ten-foot drop into the garden. A romantically positioned snowdrift might have saved us later in the season, but with just a couple of inches of the white stuff on the frozen earth, we would have suffered severe injuries and acute embarrassment had we have fallen.

As we writhed together, the heat generated by our hands subsided, as the priority for keeping a firm grip made our movements less effective. WE both began to shudder, for Eva, it may have been an orgasm, but for me, it was because my bare feet were turning blue. It took all my strength to carry Eva back, through the French doors, as she crossed her legs behind my back and hung on round my neck. Eva was disappointed that we did not accomplish the journey without a withdrawal, but I was more interested in getting back in the warm. Rubbing two bodies together under a duvet has got to be the most pleasurable way of restoring body temperature to normal; with Eva laying on top of me, while I firmly caressed all of her body that I could reach, we soon climaxed.

We stayed huddled together and sleep came quickly to us both. But before dawn, I was awake yet again, once more because of the cold. This time Eva had rolled away from me during the night, taking all the covers with her and behind me were the French doors that had remained open all night.

First thing after breakfast, we were all on the nearby nursery slopes; while Anna and Erland took the cable car to higher ground, Eva gave Sylvia, Paul and me our first lesson. Eva demonstrated the same prodigious talent for travelling on snow as she did for moving in water, but her patience was non-existent. The morning turned into one long moaning session, as the three novices failed to get everything right first time. However, in the afternoon, things were much more enjoyable as Erland took over the teaching and Eva took his non-transferable ski pass up the mountain. At dusk, all of us were getting the hang of skiing with "benz zee knees" being the catch-phrase of the day.

That night, Anna brought out the Raclet kit again, while I brought out the Blue Label Smirnoff duty free. There was a 24 can carton of Coca-Cola, plus some 7Up, so soon after dinner everyone was relaxed, as the easily drinkable, long vodka and whatever took effect. I know I had too much to drink, which made me say things I would later regret. I was only joking when I made a remark about Eva's new habit of cigarette smoking; but the phrase "like kissing an old ashtray" seemed to trigger a very bad reaction. Eva retired to our bedroom in a huff. When after a while Eva did not re-appear, her mother went to check on her. I thought I had better show some concern, so I went too. Eva was changing the air again. She was standing out on the well constructed balcony, in the light of the full moon. Soon all six of us were standing outside, admiring the amazing visibility caused by the fallen snow reflecting the moonlight across the valley.

"It is nearly bright enough to ski," commented Erland.

"Do not be crazy, you could fall and hurt yourself; no one would find you until morning, " said Eva bleakly.

"Tobogganing would be more fun," I suggested, in an attempt to side with my girlfriend.

"Yes, let's go to the place where we skiied this afternoon," enthused Erland.

"You have had too much to drink," warned Eva.

"Yes. You will have to walk. Leave the car here," chipped in Anna.

The conversation continued for a while, but everyone declined Erland's invitation for some midnight fun, except me. Just the two of us set off down the lane, towing Erland's yellow, plastic sledge behind us. The deserted nursery slopes were ideal for sledging. We had the ideal tool in the purpose built toboggan with its two levers that could be used either as a method of steering or as brakes. Erland and I took it in turns to hurtle the 300 metres or so, downhill across the snow, while the non-sledger rested, after his strenuous climb back up to the top.

Not long after we started, Erland noticed a figure coming toward us. We thought it would be Eva, wanting to join in the fun, but it turned out to be Sylvie.

With her small stature, the French girl was able to fit on the enlarged plastic tea tray with either Erland or myself; Sylvie quite happily made every descent. The extra weight gave extra speed, but control was well nigh impossible. Every run with two people aboard ended in a crash before the bottom. After one such mishap, I ended up with Sylvia lying on top of me, as we came to a halt in the snow. Quite unexpectedly, Eva's pen friend gave me a big wet kiss on the lips, before running off up the hill, giggling. On our next run, I felt that the French girl's weight distribution was deliberately designed to make the sledge uncontrollable. Sure enough, just after half way, I was on my back, sliding headfirst downhill with Sylvie laying on top of me. She even planted her big sloppy kiss before we came to a halt. I do not know if Erland was getting the same treatment, but the little Parisienne certainly liked her cuddles. Sylvie always sat at the front, between my legs, with her knees tucked under her chin. I could just about cross my feet in front of her. After a few runs downhill, I abandoned the steering handles in favour of holding on to her shins. There was a kiss at the end of every run; a couple of times, to add variety, I contrived to finish up laying on top of Sylvie. Then it was my turn to kiss her, before running off up the hill, leaving Sylvie to pull the sledge back to the top.

Eventually, the uphill climbing became too much for us and we decided to call it a day. On the last run down, the three of us all squeezed onto the metre long plastic projectile for the fastest decent of the night. As we set off, I suddenly thought about the prospect of Sylvia giving me a smacker, right in front of my girlfriend's brother. But I need not have worried because, at the first major bump, I came off the back, while the other two continued without me all the way to the bottom. During the trek back to the chalet, Erland reckoned it was the best fun he had ever had in his life, Sylvie said nothing, but then I realised she had not said anything all night, just kissed and giggled.

Trying to be as quiet as I could, I crept into bed, hoping I would not wake Eva, but as I cuddled up behind her, I got an elbow in the ribs.

"Get off, you are cold," said an unwelcoming sleepy voice.

At midday, I awoke to find myself alone in the chalet, with the other five having gone cross-country skiing. When they all came back, Paul had enjoyed himself following the trails through the trees a lot more than he did on the nursery slope, but he thought that something was seriously wrong because Eva and her mother had been jabbering away in German all day. Then, right on cue, Eva came into the room.

"Chris, my mother and I want you and your brother to leave our chalet immediately," announced Eva, "you can rent another chalet and stay in the area so that you can continue skiing, but you must move out before tonight."

"What's brought all this on then?" I asked in a state of shock.

"You do not love me any more. You say I am an ashtray. You prefer to be with my brother and my pen friend. You drink too much. My mother says you are a bad influence on her, as every time she meets you, you get her drunk," revealed Eva.

"Oh, is that all?" I said jokingly.

"It is enough. My mother and I have agreed that if you do not leave tonight we will call the police. I will go and pack your food, while you pack your clothes," ordered Eva, before marching out of the room.

"I thought something like this was on the cards," said Paul.

"What do you reckon we should do about it?" I asked.

"Oh, let's just get the hell out of here. We can't stay now you've upset them two so bad," replied Paul.

"Where to? We can't go back to the UK with the ferries now on strike," I inquired.

"Anywhere away from here. I don't care," said Paul, not even wanting me to try for a reconciliation.

"What about Ramatuelle? We could go down and see R'dub and Karen at the villa," I suggested.

"Yeah, sounds fine to me, let's get going straight away," said Paul.

Anna went with Paul to take the ski equipment back to the rental man. There was a stingy rebate, but I was past caring. I loaded the van whilst they were gone, passing Sylvie in the hallway on my last journey.

"Where are you going?" Sylvie asked innocently.

"St Tropez. Do you want to come?" I replied.

But before Sylvie could answer, Eva, who had heard my invitation, came out of the kitchen to put her arm round her pen friend and give me a steely glare.

"Titan was a good dog. It's the family that's the problem," I commented, as a parting shot.

"That is unfair," replied Anna, as calmly as she could.

It was unfair too. The mother had an unenviable job bringing up Eva and Erland on her own. Anna was close to tears when she closed the door behind us. Snow fell on the higher ground that night, but it rained steadily on the van roof as Paul and I parked on a Swiss motorway service area to sleep.

After crossing into France near Chamonix, I was driving on familiar roads, as we followed the route down

Mont Blanc, towards Bourg-en-Bresse and then the autoroute to the south. R'dub, Karen and the boys were pleased to see us, if a bit surprised. Paul and I were surprised to see a lime green sledge identical to Erland's yellow one, leaning against the side of the cottage. Coincidentally, R'dub had driven the family up into the mountains behind the Riviera to do some tobogganing that very day.

Not much happens in St Tropez over the Christmas to New Year period, although the local chamber of commerce had put up a few festive lights and relaxed the car park charges. The only tourists, besides Paul and myself, seemed to be Italian families in their weird looking coach built camper vans who congregated in the main car park by the port. All the big yachts that always took pride of place in the harbour had gone to cheaper moorings in Turkey for the winter. The beach looked a mess. The winter storms had washed the sand into unfamiliar positions, while driftwood, seaweed and empty plastic bottles littered the scene. Like every stretch of sand, on every day of the year, there were people out walking with their dogs, but not a single boat or windsurfer could be seen out in the choppy bay.

The hamper of food that Paul had been given by his company as a Christmas bonus had hardly been touched at the Swiss Chalet, but now at the Lewis family home, R'dub delighted in delving into the box and bringing out traditional British goodies to eat. In the two days that Paul and I stayed, the supply of food worked out even so our visit was not a drain on R'dub's limited resources. The boys were now attending the local Ramatuelle school, spoke fluent French and played for the village youth soccer team. Overall, they seemed happy, but R'dub in particular, was looking forward to the start of the summer season when he could have the company of a few more English speaking people.

We could have stayed longer, as the hamper was not completely empty, but during a conversation with my brother, I mentioned that we could go back to England via the farm in the Dordogne. Paul was keen to see for himself a place he had heard so much about, while I think he also wanted to inspect my attempts at house renovation. Leaving behind the unfinished jars of marmalade and jam, along with some shortbread and assorted savoury sauces, we said farewell to the Lewis family until the summer.

The cross-country trip to the Dorgogne was made during the coldest weather that central France had experienced for several decades. But Paul and I thought nothing of it at the time, as we visited the Pont du Gard, traversed the corniche of the Cevennes and ran down the spectacular Gorge Du Tarn. A bit belatedly, I telephoned Rupelon to check if there was anybody in residence. Marianne answered and told us to get there as soon as possible. It did not take long to figure out why we were so welcome – the whole water system of the long house was frozen solid. The blame for the catastrophe lay at the feet of Rupert and myself, as we had naively installed the pipe-work without lagging. In remedying the situation, there were, however, a couple of things in our favour. One was the fact that the black plastic pipes had only ever been draped loosely across the rafters of the barn and through the unused loft space, en route to the kitchen. The other fortunate point was that my brother had worked in the building trade all his life and dealing with a problem like this was child's play to him; even if he did not hold back in letting the culprits know what idiots they were.

Paul's solution to the predicament was typically forthright, with no half measures. He just completely dismantled the whole network of pipes that ran to the kitchen and bathroom. Rupert and I were ordered to light a bonfire in the yard, then, when all the frozen pipes were coiled up and secured with bale string, they were hung from the washing line, above the flames. Working on the principle that heat rises, it was a tricky job, suspending the pipes at just the right height so that the ice melted, but the black plastic did not. With constant attention, the task was safely accomplished. Meanwhile, Paul had taken the loft insulation from above the living area, in order to cut it into foot wide strips, with the help of long lengths of bale string, the pipes were then wrapped and bound in glass fibre before re-installation. The long house was re-plumbed and lagged in less than a morning, much to Marianne's delight. The lady of the house was now six months pregnant and grateful that the loss of running water would not occur again, before or after the baby was born. Sadly, nobody got to take a shower as the gas bottle that fuelled the instant hot water heater in the bathroom was also frozen solid;  even Paul did not fancy thawing it out over a bonfire.

New Year's Eve was spent at the house of Marianne's old school friend, Francine, who lived in the neighbouring village of Champ des Galles.  Francine's family actually owned the whole village and had done so for nearly a thousand years, so it was to be expected that we saw in the New Year at a manor house still languishing in the last century.  Even Rupert contributed to the time warp theme by driving the four of us over to the manor in his newly acquired Vauxhall Velox.  The car was well over 20 years old, but was in as-new condition due to its previous sheltered life on the island of Malta.

The strange night even rivalled the New Year I spent in the cabin by the lake with Regine and friends.  There was no television and the radio that gave the time at midnight was probably the newest thing in the house. There were electric lights, but Francine preferred candles, to maintain the atmosphere as a dozen of us sat and played gin runny around two antique tables.

I thought Paul would have hated the bizarre circumstances of the New Year, partly because it was not his scene at all, but he enjoyed himself, finding everybody kind and friendly, considering he had never met any of them before.  I told him it was because Marianne had told the story of how he had re-piped the long house in a morning and even in rural France, people knew the value of a good plumber.

Paul and I came back to England at the same time as we would have done if we had continued our skiing holiday. It had all turned out very differently from what we had planned; but Paul reckoned it was better than sitting about watching Christmas television on his own. As soon as Paul got back to his house, he telephoned Barbara, who asked why we did not think of going back to Bonn? I told Paul that if he had mentioned it, then we could have done it. As for Eva, I never heard from her again and I have not been skiing since.

## Chapter Twenty-four

The first full week of January saw everybody back at work and as I started another trip to Istanbul, it seemed that every other Middle East haulier had also waited to get the Christmas break over and done with, before heading into the inhospitable east European winter. There were already seven British trucks parked at the Pilsen Motorest when I pulled in, just after dark. To stop the fuel lines freezing, all the trucks had their engines running at fast idle. If you had switched them off, it would not have been long before the antifreeze would have started to gel, such was the severity of the bleak Czechoslovakian weather. The British drivers had retired to the restaurant, leaving the ignition key in, but making sure they locked the cab doors.

I knew all the faces and most of the names, Ricky Port seemed to be in charge and had with him a huge wad of Czech krona. Apparently, he had changed up a very poor quality forged £50 note at an hotel in Prague on his last trip. Now he was trying to dispose of the proceeds from his black market dealing. To do this, Ricky bought all the beer, all the food and even a girl for his mate from Wales. At the Londra Camp, I had drunk with Ricky several times before; he was always generous when it came to getting the beers in. Some people found the impressively built Welshman to be threatening and gave him a wide birth, but Ricky had always been friendly towards me, with helpful advice emanating from his well told stories of disaster, confrontation and the inevitable violent results. Ricky Port went to the original school of hard knocks and followed that by attending the university of life. On nights like this, he was in his element, with his mates, his stories and his Kenny Rogers tapes playing on the restaurant's stereo. The night only ended when we had drunk every bottle of beer in the place and the wine was found to be totally unpalatable.

All the engines of the trucks were still running in the morning. Sleeping in the Mercedes with its vee-eight motor rumbling was not my first choice for a peaceful night, but if my right Timberland was laid on the accelerator pedal in a certain way, the engine speed rose to a steady purr which freed me from the irritating vibration of normal tick over. There was the added advantage of waking up to a warm cab, even though most modern vehicles had independent warm-air heaters, these were always the first things to pack up at the first sign of a severe frost. The curtains of the other Brits were still firmly closed when I pulled on to the snow covered road in the direction of Prague. From the previous evening's conversation, I had concluded that the others were going to run together in pairs, but I was not too concerned about being on my own, if I was in front. Sooner or later, somebody would come to my assistance, if I had any difficulty.

Trouble was not long in tracking me down as the mercury stayed firmly at the bottom of the thermometer. Slowly, but surely, I felt the drag of the trailer brakes coming on, when my foot was nowhere near the centre

334

pedal. On investigation, I found nothing obviously wrong, but presumed it was due to the air valves on the trailer freezing shut. An easy cure to this problem was to disconnect the air lines between the truck and trailer in order to pour some methanol down the pipes, hoping the inflammable fluid would mix with any ice in the frozen valves, thus lowering the freezing point temperature of any liquid. I used all my spare methanol on the remedy and got back behind the wheel to find the brakes working perfectly.

However, about 20 minutes up the road, the same thing happened again. I spent half an hour poking about and standing around, looking baffled, but then found that the problem had gone away all by itself. Annoyingly, this turned out to be the start of a sequence of stops, which allowed for 20 minutes driving, followed by 20 minutes of waiting while the brakes thawed themselves out. The logical source for all this trouble was the container that gave a constant methanol supply to the whole pneumatic pipe system, but I had made a point of having the reservoir topped up before I left Ipswich. I had even watched the fitter do the job before asking him to let me take his half full methanol bottle with me.

I gave the whole situation some serious thought; finally working out that it was the heat from the engine thawing out the brakes, as the weather had not warmed up at all. This led me to believe that it was one of the air valves situated behind the engine, above the gearbox that was the culprit. Sure enough, when I poured half a cup of hot tea over the valves, the brakes released immediately. The valves were the cause of the problem but hot water was not a practical cure. I decided to check the methanol reservoir to see why it was not doing its job. On taking it apart, I found the area that should have contained methanol was one big block of ice. It was not the fitter's fault when he told me the container did not need much filling – how was he to know that it was already full of water. Pouring all my spare methanol into the trailer pipe work now showed itself to have been a bad move, but I was not going to be beaten. After hack sawing two foot off the end of the exhaust pipe. I laid under the truck in the snow and hammered the remaining pipe towards the misbehaving valves in a last ditch attempt to keep them warm.

The overall result of my pipe bending was that at speeds of over 30 miles per hour, the wind chill factor brought on the trailer brakes, so I resigned my self to slow, steady progress while thinking about where I could purchase some methanol.

The Brits behind me were favourite, but they still had not caught up, even with all my stopping. Help came from a Dutchman parked on the services at Brno, he had no spare methanol, but advised me that Scotch whisky worked just as well and added that my best chance of getting a cheap bottle was at the duty free shop at the border. For once, alcohol cured a problem rather than giving me one; I bought a litre of Metaxa, Greek brandy, which was on special offer.

The cold weather that had frozen pipes in France and trailer brakes in Czechoslovakia, seemed to be all across Europe. The temperature never rose above freezing point all the way to Turkey, but the brandy did its job as well as providing me with a body warming night cap before I went to sleep with the engine running.　My load of diesel engines had been delivered to Izmit before I saw Ricky Port and the rest of my Pilsen drinking partners again.　I was back at the Londra Camp, having a day off, before I tackled the arctic conditions in Rumania, when they rolled in.　All of them had enjoyed an incident free run – the only problem they had was in spending all of Ricky Port's krona, which had taken another two nights at the Motorest after I had left.

The weather in the Balkans was as grim as I had expected. The 4 x 4 tractor tow up Cobblestone mountain cost 40 Marlborough and I had perfected the art of snow chain fitting so well that putting a chain on each outside wheel of the drive axle took less than 10 minutes.　Snow chains gave excellent traction, but could only be used on snow or ice covered surfaces;　they also tended to break, throwing themselves off at speeds over 20 miles per hour. This fact I had found out to my cost.　The chains were only repaired with the help of my brand new padlocks from the trailer boxes.

Up at Radauti, the barbecue making workforce finally seemed to have got their act together.　This time, there was no waiting around for things to be manufactured. I wondered if this had anything to do with Marina not being there any more. The same little blonde who had gone to get my bread the last time, came out to see me again. With what seemed to be a corkscrew perm, Olga seemed quite attractive, even in her cheap, ill-fitting nylon tracksuit, but she had the disconcerting habit of holding her hand over her mouth when she talked. I did catch her name, but I did not understand anything else, so she might as well have kept her mouth shut. The kind-hearted part of me thought Olga was probably acutely embarrassed about her poor dental condition; while the cynical side figured the girl was definitely carrying a sexually transmitted disease. Due to an inexplicable loyalty to Marina, I did not invite Olga to share my evening meal, before heading back to the UK, after my fastest ever barbecue turn-around.

My newly found prowess in snow chain fitting was a big factor in my decision to take the Transylvanian mountain route across Rumania. By the end of the first day, I knew it was the bad option. Progress was slow, as darkness fell. I was stuck at the bottom of a particularly steep incline, with only the knowledge that all the brown bears were in hibernation to console me. At the crack of dawn, I was out with one of the world's most travelled shovels, trying to guess if the raised humps on the snow covered verge contained heaps of grit. Invariably they did not, so I had to make do with chunks of turf to provide my grip.

It took over two hours to give the 300 metres up to the brow of the hill a liberal sprinkling of dirt, stones and grass.  Once I began moving, I did not want to stop again, on this or any hill, so I brewed up a cup of tea and had something to eat before I started.  While I was drinking my well earned cuppa, a snow plough came over the top of the hill, pushed all my hard work into the side of the road, swerved round me and disappeared out of my rear view mirrors.  I was stunned, not only because I had wasted the whole morning, but I had never before seen a snowplough in Rumania.

In frustration, I attacked the hill as it was, gunning the Merc at full throttle in third gear.  All this did was to spin the wheels and the offside snow chain flew into a hundred pieces.  Fortunately the snow plough returned an hour later, when he put me on the end of his tow chain.  For the next 40 miles I was towed up hill and down dale until the driver came to his home town.  At times, I thought the snow plough driver had forgotten that I was still attached; but he was only trying to maximise his Kent cigarette income on a mileage basis.  The driver was well pleased with his 200 king sized.  I felt for a thousand, he would have pulled me all the way to the Hungarian border.

Out of Rumania, it was no warmer, but driving conditions improved as I got further west.  For the last leg of the journey, my sole surviving snow chain was able to stay hanging on, its hook at the back of the unit – shining brightly, like it was made of stainless steel, for a few days, before slowly returning to its usual rust.

I followed the Turkish trip with a month of Italian

runs, but even Mt Blanc could not give me the hassle of Transylvania.

After Christmas, Ron Carrick, the voyeur from the Pigale, had come to work for Archie Fredericks, but our paths had not crossed until one Saturday morning in the yard. Ron took great delight in telling Archie about our Istanbul adventure. Normally the boss took a great interest in his drivers' sexual exploits, but this time, he had other things on his mind. Archie had sub-contracted a trailer load of diesel engines to a small London-based haulage company. A month after crossing the North Sea to Belgium, the goods still had not arrived in Istanbul. News had just come through that the company had folded, with the trailer-load of diesel engines stranded on the Hungarian-Rumanian boarder. Archie had no option but to send someone down to Nadlac to finish the job. With only Ron Carrick and myself to choose from, Archie gave the job to me. To help cover the costs. Archie arranged to me to take an unaccompanied Bulgarian trailer as far as the Czechoslovakian border. I shipped out of Felixstowe bound for Europort on the Sunday evening.

The Bulgarian registered trailer was destined for Tehran and was loaded with bandages, a frequent export to war-torn Iran. Willi Betz BV organised the loads carried by the state owned Bulgarian trucks – it was one of the communist country's biggest hard currency earners. First thing Tuesday morning, I dropped the trailer off at Willi Betz's depot, just east of Amberg. From there, I set off across Czechoslovakia and Hungary with just the tractor unit. All the border officials took great delight in pointing out that I had lost my trailer en route, but the guys on duty at Nadlac, on the Rumanian border, knew just what I had come for.

The Fredericks' trailer stood over to one side, still within the frontier compound, so it had not suffered any pilfering and even the Customs' seal was in tact. At the front of the trailer was a ten year old Seddon Atkinson unit that had seen better days. Eight of the ten wheel studs on the offside drive axle hub were broken and the wheels had been pushed under the unit. The Rumanian guards referred to the Seddon driver as Dave; they spoke of him as a good friend. Dave had obviously got to know every one pretty well during the ten days that he sat with his crippled unit, before returning to the UK with a homeward bound British truck.

I put one wheel back on the Seddon Atkinson, but I could not get the engine to start, even with jump leads. In the end, I dragged the unit out from under the trailer with my Mercedes. The Rumanians were keen to know what I was going to do with the broken down Seddon, as it was obvious I could not take it with me. I told them to look after it for me and that I would return, once I had an empty trailer, in order to take it back to Britain. There was not much chance of that happening as the non-runner was not even Archie Fredericks' property, but my explanation kept the Customs officials happy. After getting the vehicle registration numbers changed on the paperwork for the load, I went round and doled out ten packets of Kent cigarettes to the border guards, in my gratitude for the way they had watched over the trailer. By midday on Wednesday, I was crossing Rumania.

The tension between the Bulgarians and the Turks had been steadily rising during the first months of 1986. Things had come to a head during the time of my passage through the two countries. The Bulgarians were trying to force the ethnic Turks in south-east Bulgaria to take on Cyrillic names and renounce their Turkish heritage. While Turkey had given citizenship to an Olympic standard Bulgarian weightlifter who had recently defected. To aggravate matters, the Turkish prime minister had adopted the teenage strongman as his son, which had brought the situation dangerously close to conflict.

There was a great deal of military presence at the border, but the circumstances worked in my favour, as no Bulgarians were crossing into Turkey and no Turks were coming the other way. Mine was the only truck at the tense, but normally busy, crossing point that had on one occasion taken me four days to negotiate. This time it took four hours. I was in Istanbul by midday Friday.

Just how desperate the truck factory was to receive their engines was shown when the shipping agent implored me to get over to Izmit that afternoon, for Customs' clearance. He was grateful that I knew where to go and what to do, but it took me some time before I made him understand that I had only left England on the

Sunday evening. When the agent realised I had come out to recover the trailer, only then did he stop blaming me personally for the late delivery. Three workers stayed on late at the truck plant and I was tipped on the Friday evening, which just goes to show how Turkish bureaucracy could be quickened up when it suited them. Even Archie was impressed with the speed in which I had done the job - it was the first time I had heard him say "thanks".

With all the cold weather in late December and January, I had expected it to have warmed up a bit in Rumania; but, if anything, it was colder still, as I made my way up the main road from Bucharest to the Soviet border. Just how cold it could get in the middle of February was shown to me one night when the Mercedes' engine died, just north of the town of Roman. The German made anti-freeze fuel additive called "Long Drive" said on the bottle that it was good for minus 24 degrees centigrade. I could only presume that it was minus 25 when the diesel in the fuel lines froze and I came to a halt in the snowy wastes of the windswept Rumanian plains. That night, I went to bed fully clothed, inside two sleeping bags, with my sheepskin coat over my head and I still shivered.

In the morning, I turned the engine over, but it would not fire. Careful not to run down the batteries, I left it and hoped the sun would warm things up. The sun never came through the clouds all day, so I had to resort to filling empty food tins with near solid diesel and lighting little fires under the truck. At the end of the day, the motor still would not start, plus my camping gas bottle in the cab would not light because it, too, was frozen. Back on the bottom bunk, I shivered through another night, after chewing on a couple of rock hard Mars bars.

Day two was much the same as day one, with only the arrival of a couple of Bulgarian trucks, on their way back to Sofia from Kiev, to relieve the monotony. The drivers obviously thought there might be some handy bits and pieces to be had from an abandoned British truck, but they left empty-handed after boiling me some water for a coffee. The Bulgarians also gave me a swig from a spirit bottle that reminded me of Camping Roma, as it burnt its way down my throat and into my stomach. My only other visitors were an old couple in a horse drawn sled. I swapped 20 cigarettes for a loaf of bread, but declined the offer to go back to their place. The little fires in the baked bean cans burnt for about three hours at a time, but had no noticeable effect on the frozen engine.

On the morning of the third day, I figured that the wind blowing underneath the truck was taking most of the heat away from where it was supposed to go. To stop this, I got out the world's most travelled shovel and built a wall of snow against the front and sides of the tractor unit. With the addition of a couple of extra cans, whose contents I had consumed cold, the little fires started to give off some perceptible warmth. When it was getting dark, the battery spun the starter for the umpteenth time, but with success, as the vee-eight came to life for the first time in 72 hours.

The fourth night was just as cold as the previous three, so I kept the engine running, the fires burning and the snow walls in place. From now on, I would only run in day light when temperatures were, hopefully, higher. It took over a week to go from Istanbul to Radauti. It was the best part of another week before the barbecues were ready to load. By the time I got back to the UK, I had been away for the best part of a month. What had started out with my quickest ever run down to Istanbul, finished up as my slowest ever round trip. As Archie Fredericks only paid you for the trip and not the time it took, I would have been better off staying at home.

But I plugged away with trips to Turkey, Italy and one to Spain as winter eventually turned into spring. I was down in Rumania when the nuclear reactor at Chernobyl blew up. Nobody knew what was going on. The Germans washed the truck and collected all the water when I came back to the west - what good it did and where the water went, I do not know.

On the way down to Barcelona, I picked up a couple of Australian hitchhikers who were doing their big European back pack tour. The boy and girl came with me to visit Rupert and Marianne at Rupelon, where my arrival coincided with the French weekend truck curfew. Baby Marie-Claire had arrived two weeks earlier. Rupert was already planning a big get together for the christening, during the first week in June. The Aussies welcomed the two-day stay on the farm which gave them an unexpected insight into French sheep farming which contrasted so greatly with the immense scale of things in Australia.

My passengers continued with me, all the way to Barcelona, on the Monday. The Spanish work seemed to be similar to the Italian runs, complicated Customs procedures which took an eternity, plus the need to be 100% vigilant. As a new partner in the European Union, things in Spain were simpler than they had been, but it also meant that every continental haulier was trying to get in on the action. Return loads were at a premium as the Spanish freight companies tried to keep all of the export work for themselves.

Mickey Salmon, another Archie Fredericks' driver, on his first trip to Spain, had the misfortune to come up against the nightmare of Spanish red tape. His load of sports goods was imported with the paperwork marked "Made in Britain" but on inspection, it turned out that most of the golf clubs were made in Taiwan. The load, the truck and the trailer were promptly impounded, with Mickey only escaping incarceration by the skin of his teeth. Archie's driver was spending his seventh day at the Zona Franca in Barcelona, waiting for the duty, taxes and fines to be paid, when I arrived. Mickey was flat broke, not due so much to his Customs delay, but mainly because he visited the Ramblas every night where he had something going on with an Argentinean bar girl. All the spare cash I had on me was in Italian lira, but Mickey had no hesitation in relieving me of 250,000 and ordering a taxi to take us downtown.

In the Ramblas bar, I had no trouble picking out Mickey's girl. As we came through the door, she turned towards us, as if holding an imaginary machine gun:

"Huh, huh, huh, huh, huh, huh!" went the Argentinean in a hoarse staccato laugh.

Mickey did the same, then they shouted out in turn,

"Malvinas""

"Falklands!"

"Malvinas!"

"Falklands!"

Slowly, they closed in on each other, still shouting, circling in the space in front of the bar, before embracing passionately - much to the amusement of all the other patrons.

Mickey introduced me to Suzannah, as a good friend who had just given him a quarter of a million lira. I do not know if the hostess made a mistake in her exchange rate calculations, but she got straight on the telephone to her sister and told her to come over for a drink. Suzannah was certainly the most stunning Argentinean girl I had ever set eyes on – even if she was the first Argentinean girl I had met. With her long black hair and long brown legs, if Mickey had told me she was a former Miss Beuno Aires, I would not have disputed it. Suzannah was about three inches taller than Mickey. When Maria, the sister, turned up, she was three inches shorter than Mickey. As I was three inches taller than Suzannah, I thought things should have been the other way around, but as the machine gunners got on so well, I did not mention it.

In fact, Mickey got on well with everybody, with his ready smile and cheery "hello", he soon made friends, even without the slightest command of any language except English. The stocky north Londoner, with his happy-go-lucky attitude seemed to handle himself well in all foreign situations, without having to think about it. A welcome change from many hard drinking Brit truck drivers who could be a real embarrassment when they had sunk a few beers.

Size did not matter when the four of us sat on our bar stools. While Mickey and I drank San Miguel, the girls were served with the Hostess Special, which was expensive, but probably not very potent. Maria sat close with her hand on my knee, as we talked about the price of land in various parts of Argentina. The younger sister wore a black mini skirt and pink lambswool vee-nick sweater with no blouse underneath. With a bit more meat on her than the pencil slim Suzannah, it was difficult not to keep looking down Maria's top and at the little crucifix that hung in her cleavage. I was just thinking what a sure thing I was onto and wondering how much it was going to cost, when this guy in a cream suit came in. He shook my hand before whispering something Spanish in Maria's ear. Then, with a quick squeeze of my leg and a kiss on the cheek, Maria left the bar with the cream suited guy. Mickey and Suzannah were so wrapped up in each other that they did not see Maria leave. Without interrupting them, I finished my beer and got a taxi back to the truck, leaving Mickey to pick up the tab. I had done from just south of Limoges to Barcelona in one day, so I was looking forward to my bed with or without a sexy little Argentinean for company.

Having spent a week hanging around the Zona Franca, Mickey was a great help the next morning when it came to getting my paperwork through Customs. Almost everyone called him by his first name as they shook hands, but they all shrugged their shoulders when Mickey asked how long it would be before he finally got going again. For a change of scene, the stranded driver came for the short ride across town so that he could help me tip my part load for Barcelona.

"Maria was a bit upset that you left before she got back last night," said Mickey, as we stripped out the side of the tilt.

"She didn't say she was coming back, how was I to know? Anyway, I'd had a long day, I was knackered," I replied.

"They'll both be down there again tonight. I told 'em we'd be back," continued Mickey.

"Yeah, but I'll be tipped here by 1.00 o'clock. I should be getting down to Valencia so I can get this other stuff off," I protested.

"Don't you fancy yours or summat?" queried Mickey.

"It's not that. I just can't afford it. How much did you spend last night?" I asked.

"Oh, about half of them lira. The way I see it, our boys went down the Falklands in '82 and fucked them Argies. Now we've got a chance to fuck two for ourselves. With that Suzannah, I give it to her as hard and as fast as I can. She loves it," bragged Mickey.

"What sort of war is that? When she loves it. Do you expect somebody to give you a medal when you get back to the UK? I'll tell you, when Archie finds out what you've been spending his running money on, you'll be facing a firing squad," I warned.

For the rest of the time we were unloading, Mickey carried on trying to persuade me to go down the Ramblas that night. I was tempted by the thought of seeing Maria's tight-fitting woolly top come off over her head, but in the end I drove Mickey back to his truck and went straight down to Valencia.

At the chemical plant, where I delivered the remaining oil drums, there was an export load waiting for shipment to England.    I left Valencia less than 24 hours after arriving.  Mickey Salmon was still stranded in Barcelona when I got back to England, and I had lost a day when the bearing in the universal joint at the front of the propshaft broke up, just south of Paris.  I wondered how much cash Mickey must have been getting through, as his trip entered its third week.  I never did find out, as I had left for the summer before I saw him again.

## Chapter Twenty-five

The Christening at Rupelon was less than a month away, so I planned my visit as part of the journey down to the beach. After an Italian trip, I handed in my notice, did another run to Milan and timed it just right so that I had a couple of days to get the van ready. Meanwhile, Keith Connery had got in touch, so we arranged to travel down together in the van, along with his French girlfriend, Katrina. The van was one of many British registered vehicles heading for the Dordogne that weekend. From midday, there was a steady stream of arrivals at Rupelon. Except for Rupert's family, all the British were known to me, from either the beach or the grape picking. On Marianne's side, I knew most of her family, but not many of her French friends.

The Christening was scheduled for the Sunday morning; Saturday was spent lazing around in the hot June sunshine, drinking and watching a whole pig spit roasting over a pit of burning logs. Some of the guests, I had not seen for several years, so it was interesting to see how attitudes and priorities had changed. Nobody but me seemed to view the beach as a permanent part of their lives anymore. For others it had been just a pleasurable episode, but now they had moved on.

Most ex-beach bums now lived in a world of mortgages, car loans and good career prospects. Only Danny, with his dedicated guitar playing, and Irish

Danny Oakes, with his wandering chef existence, were maintaining positions with me on the lower rungs of the social ladder.

As the bar owners of Vidauban would confirm, the British idea of a party differed greatly to the French concept in one major aspect:   alcohol consumption. Rupert's English speaking guests drank huge quantities of wine and beer, while the French speaking locals hardly touched a drop;  with the one exception of Marianne's brother, Pierre, who single handedly matched the hardest drinking Britons, drink for drink.  The Saturday night partying strayed into Sunday morning, which was unfortunate for Pierre as he was baby Marie Claire's uncle and was expected at the church service.  Paddy Botley was a godfather, he too, had an enormous hangover. The drinking partners only just made it to the church on time.   I was one of many who missed the baptism. Like most of the grape picking fraternity, I only surfaced when everyone had returned to the farm, at noon.   After a lunch of cold roast pork, the drinking started again. Once more, going on into the night.   I wondered how the sober members of Marianne's family viewed this traditional British and Irish behaviour, but never plucked up enough courage to ask.

On the Monday morning, everybody sleeping at the farm said their goodbyes and went their separate ways. Most of the English contingent headed for various ferry ports:  Keith and Katrina went down to Biarritz to visit her parents, so I was the only one going to Ramatuelle.

My route was the reverse of the one taken by my brother, Paul, and myself during the days between Christmas and New Year. It was now warmer, greener and busier through the Gorge du Tarn, as hordes of caravan towing Dutch cars made early season expeditions into central France.

Back on the beach there was no Tarzan, but R'dub, Karen and the boys were still at the villa. They introduced me to Diana, an English girl who was looking after her father's caravans on the Croix de Sud campsite. Diana's caravans were rented out to holiday makers, one of whom was introduced to me as Mary who, it turned out, was Tarzan's English rose from the previous summer.

"I hope you know that I've spent the last nine months looking for you, after you disappeared so suddenly," I said, laying it on a bit thick.

"Now you've found me, what are you going to do with me? Tarzan's not about this year, is he?" asked Mary, suggestively.

"Might as well keep you for myself, then," I flirted.

"If you're man enough," stated Mary, confidentially.

That night, I slept with Mary on a pair of sun-loungers, under the awning of one of Diana's caravans. After drinking and talking until way past midnight, it was just a case of laying back and closing our eyes. The only thing that happened was that Mary was savagely attacked by mosquitoes. I was untouched by the blood-sucking pests, so it must have been something about the taste of the English rose that made her so desirable. It was not the first time that Mary had suffered this way; her fear of a bad reaction was confirmed, when the bite marks reddened and swelled up alarmingly. All I could do to comfort Mary was to offer her a bed in my 100% mosquito-proof Volkswagen camper.

To my surprise, Mary took me up on my offer of a safe haven and for the remaining two weeks of her holiday, I managed to keep the insects away. My main defence was the nylon mesh sheeting that I pegged to the soft rubber sealing strip of the side door surround. It allowed for the door to be open in the evening, with good air circulation and maximum protection.

During the night, we relied on the roof vent, which was also netted. To give my guest total peace of mind, every night, before settling down to sleep, I made a thorough search of the van's interior, armed with my trusty fly swat, while listening for the telltale whine of the mosies in motion.

As grateful as she was, Mary never let me make love to her during her stay in the van. Once again, the question about contraception was asked, yet again I had forgotten to buy any. For the second year in a row, my first love affair of the season was all fingers and tongues. What we did do, gave both of us a lot of pleasure, so it did not matter that I never made a home run. R'dub would have given me a hard time if he had known, but he, like everyone else, thought that we were doing it.

Mary and I saw a lot of R'dub during our time together. Our visits to the cottage in the grounds of the villa usually included a dip in the pool. As there were no clients in residence during the first week, on a couple of occasions, we spent the whole day living the high life. The second week of Mary's holiday coincided with the renting of the villa by a rich Irish businessman, his wife and her friend. But R'dub could not resist inviting everyone round for a swim and a barbecue when he knew his clients were booked up to dine in St Tropez.

Irish Danny was back on the beach, after losing yet another cooking position. It was his first visit to the villa when R'dub challenged everyone to an under water swimming competition. One length of the fifteen metre pool was the best I could do, while both the Lewis boys beat my effort and the eldest did two lengths. R'dub did three lengths easily without surfacing, which left Irish Danny to go last. In an attempt to get more speed, Danny chose to swim naked, as he reckoned his cut off jeans restricted his progress. But just as he dived in, the headlights of a car appeared at the far end of the drive.

"Quick, quick," shouted R'dub, "it's the clients. Grab your stuff and let's get out of here."

"Everybody back to the cottage, before they see us,"

yelled Karen, as we all bundled up our clothes and ran barefoot down the garden.

"Where's Danny?" whispered R'dub, when we had assembled safely behind the fence, in front of the cottage.

"In the pool," replied Christopher.

We all peered round the fence, as the car lights came to a stop at the villa and were then switched off.

"Hey you, what do you think you're doing in my pool?" came an Irish voice from out of the night.

"About two lengths under water," came the equally Irish sounding reply from Danny, who, at the same time, came fleeing down the path and ducked behind the fence.

"Oh man, that was weird," panted Danny, "you lot disappearing like that and then some guy shouting at me."

"Yeah, but think how weird it must have been for him. He comes home to find a naked man in his pool. He shouts at him and then gets shouted back at, in the same accent," remarked R'dub as we all went into the cottage for a beer.

It was the last time I went to the villa with Mary. A

couple of days later, we went over to Frejus to see the Eurythmics in concert. We went there with no tickets, but need not have worried, as there were still plenty for sale. The venue was in the old Roman amphitheatre which had almost unlimited capacity out in the open air. Big Audio Dynamite played support. It was a great night with Annie Lennox on top form. To show how grateful she was for the mosquito free sleeping quarters, Mary bought the tickets and the pizzas afterwards.

From Frejus, we headed north to the Gorge du Verdun, to spend the last two full days of Mary's holiday away from the beach. It was all new to the English rose. She loved the splendid scenery, probably more than anyone that I had accompanied into the mountains. Mary certainly took more photographs than anybody else. As if to prove that I did not know it all, Mary led the way when we climbed up the path to the small church, built into the cliffs, high above Moustiers Ste Marie. The village was a few kilometres from the lake and the largest shopping centre in the area. Before, I had only used the place to replenish supplies, thinking it to be just a tourist trap with its endless racks of swivelling postcards outside every shop. On closer examination, most of the postcards showed the church on the hill, along with the star that hung from a chain, suspended between two cliffs.

It was a long walk up the steps' twisting path to the church, but the spectacular view from the top made it worthwhile. From looking directly down on top of the village roofs, you could raise your head and take in the whole Verdun valley, with the shimmering water of the lac de Ste Croix reflecting the steep cliffs on the far side. The air was still and hot, as Mary and I entered the empty church with its cool dark interior, lit only by a handful of candles, burning beside the alter. In silence, Mary explored, while I thumbed through the visitors' book, before adding my name and vehicle registration. Back outside, both of us looked up at the star on a chain, simultaneously, concluding that its size on the postcards was totally out of proportion to the real thing.

"I wonder if they do weddings up here? Its such a romantic place," Mary thought out aloud.

"We could ask and maybe book it for the same time next year, if you want?" I said with the intention to shock.

"Was that some sort of marriage proposal?" asked Mary, coolly.

"Yeah, why not? You and me. Its about time I settled down," I said, hardly believing what I was saying.

"I'll think about it," replied Mary, as she came towards me, kissing me on the lips, while tweaking my balls at the same time and then starting her descent back to the village.

I never brought up the subject again before Mary

left the next afternoon. After our church visit, my English rose became uncharacteristically quiet and withdrawn. Maybe she was thinking about my proposal, which is what she said she was going to do. It may have been a spur of the moment thing, but the more I thought about it, the more I found the idea appealing. Mary was definitely the sort of girl I could take home to meet my mother. Good looking, nice body, same middle-class background, a one year old car and a job as a freelance mobile hairdresser that brought in 400 quid a week. Not bad for a girl who would not be 20 until the first week in August. Mary flew back to London from Nice; I took her to the station at Les Arcs on my way back to the beach. Unlike the year before, with Eva, I stayed until the train departed. It was the classic railway farewell, with promises to write every week and meet up again in England at the end of the summer. One last lingering kiss, then a wave as the train pulled out, going the wrong way for Nice. It was a heart-stopping moment as visions of empty aircraft seats flashed through my mind. I pointed east as my English rose went west, but not knowing where exactly Les Arcs was, Mary could not see the problem and just continued waving. She was still waving, after the two car stop-at-all-stations train had crossed the points on to an outside track and came trundling back through the station, heading for Nice.

# Chapter Twenty-six

When compared to other years, my late arrival on the beach made the season go so much quicker. After just a few days with only Irish Danny for company, all the familiar faces started coming back. Regine and Pascaline, Eric and Ingo, Ingmar and Carsten, even Pat and Maggie seemed to be ahead of themselves. Danny found himself a nice girlfriend in Lynda, who came from Wales; while I was pleasantly surprised when Olivia turned up unexpectedly. She had just one week before starting her summer banking job, but said that she hoped to be back for the whole of September. Olivia had just taken the final examinations of her college course, but was not hopeful of passing. The student thought that if she was good, then maybe she would still be offered a permanent position, even if her results were poor. I did not ask if that meant being good at her summer job or being good in bed.

A couple of rainy days in Olivia's week stopped her from getting the expected tan, but gave me plenty of time to be with her in the St Tropez apartment. Olivia's younger sister was there, but we saw little of her as she mixed with a rich partying crowd that never left the Byblos discotheque before dawn. The apartment was on the second and third floors of an old terraced building in the traffic-free maze of streets behind the port. The second floor had two bedrooms and a bathroom, while on the third floor was another bathroom, a kitchen in the corner of the big living area and one more bedroom. The unusual layout explained how Olivia was easily able to avoid the attention of her parents when she came in at dawn. It also let her sister sleep all day, while we had the run of the third floor. I welcomed the chance to sleep in a proper bed for a change, while Olivia liked having me around as she had come down from Paris by train and needed the van for transport to the beach. The only disappointment was that the apartment did not have a washing machine. The week went far too quickly for my liking; the highlight was the first afternoon that it rained. Olivia and I made love for hours as the water from an overflowing gutter cascaded passed our open bedroom window. Later, we dodged from doorway to doorway as we shopped for dinner. Olivia cooked an excellent stir-fry with rice, which was washed down with a fine bottle of wine. Then we went straight back to bed, after soaking in a hot bath with a mountain of bubbles.

My staying at the St Tropez apartment during the inclement weather did not go down too well with Irish Danny who, with Lynda, had to trek up to the old abandoned villa to take shelter. But things soon dried out and as Olivia made her way back to Paris, so Danny telephoned the hotel in the Dordogne in order to get his old job back. Irish Danny set off hitch-hiking early the next morning, leaving Lynda to continue her holiday on the beach. Lynda had started her summer in the company of Sarah, a friend who worked with her as a chambermaid at a Chepstow hotel. The pair had hitched together to the south of France, but split up when Lynda went with Danny and Sarah met a guy from Stuttgart. When the German went back home, Sarah went with him, which left Lynda with Danny. Now Danny had gone, leaving Lynda with me. We sat together all day under the parasol; as evening came, I gave Lynda a windsurfing lesson on the calm, shallow water, just off the now deserted beach. Lynda did well, sailing for over 200 metres in perfect beginners' conditions.

"You done really good for the first time," I said, "are you hungry after all that exercise? Would you like to eat at the van tonight?"

"I'd love to," replied Lynda, as she helped me carry the board and rig into the car park.

Lynda had eaten at the van before, but only when Danny had been in charge of the cooking. It was going to be difficult to impress her with my limited culinary skills, but Lynda was easy to please and was more interested in going through my music cassette collection than the quality of the food. After, Lynda insisted on doing the washing up, we finished the wine, while listening to John Martyn.

"I suppose I'd better go find myself a nice piece of sand to sleep on," said Lynda finally.

"You can kip in here, if you want. It's far more comfortable," I offered.
"Oh, thanks. I'd like that," answered Lynda.

We made up the bed and locked the doors. Lynda seemed to have no qualms about laying naked next to a man she had never even kissed. We lay on our backs in silence, with a six inch gap between us.

"Tell me a story," said Lynda.

"Once upon a time, when I was on my first trip to Rumania, I had gone to a town called Piatra Nearnt, up in the Transylvanian mountains, to load knitwear for London. The stuff wasn't ready, so I drove to this lake outside of town, where I parked the truck beside the water. When I woke up in the morning, this old Volkswagen camper was parked beside me. It had German registration plates that began with the letter 'B' so I knew it came from Berlin. During the morning, I got talking with the owner, who said his name was Ziggy. The guy was in his fifties and a real old hippie: long hair, goatee beard, the lot. We drank coffee and talked all day. He had excellent English and told stories of his travels. In the evening, Ziggy said he would let me in on a secret, because he thought he could trust me. He told me a story about his parents. He said his father had been an officer in the German army during the second world war. Ziggy's old man had died some years ago, but his mother had only recently passed away. Before she died, she gave her son a map that her husband had given to her, years before. It was a treasure map. It contained details of treasure looted by the German army during their occupation of Rumania in the war. The map showed part of the Transylvanian Alps and Ziggy pointed out the lake where we were parked.  He said that if I helped him find the treasure and get it out of the country in the truck, he would go halves.  We shook hands on it.  In the morning, we went off in his VW to find the spot marked with an 'X'.  The map showed four churches and when a line was drawn to the opposite church, the crossing point was the site we were looking for.  It was rugged terrain which was impassable to vehicles, so we had to explore on foot.  But on the second day of our search, we found a cave, close to the summit of a mountain, from which we could see all four church towers.   The cave was not particularly well hidden and showed signs of recent occupation, probably by local children, out camping. With our torches, Ziggy and I explored every inch, but found nothing, in a place that would have been visited many times in the last 40 odd years.  Ziggy was sure his father would not have chosen such an obvious hiding place, so we combed the surrounding area for more clues.  But we had to return to the cave when a thunder storm caught us in the open.   While we sat on the dusty floor, waiting for the rain to stop, Ziggy kicked at the ground with his heel and unearthed a large metal ring, the size of a dinner plate.  The ring was linked to another, which was set in the rock floor.  As we scraped away at the loose dust, it became apparent that a block was set into the cave floor and it could be pulled out, using the ring. The combined strength of Ziggy and me could not budge the block, so we went back to the nearest village to borrow a six foot long scaffold pole from a building site.  Using a convenient rock as a fulcrum and the pole as a lever, Ziggy and I then managed to lift out the block.

It revealed the entrance to an underground chamber, ten foot square and ten foot high. Leading down to the bottom, through the two foot square hole, was a wooden ladder. From the top, we shone in our torches and could see stacks of old ammunition boxes, overflowing with jewel encrusted alter plates and gold chalices. We both climbed down the rickety ladder to inspect our new found wealth. It was beyond our wildest dreams, with jewels, gold and silver, plus a huge pile of old rolled-up paintings laying in one corner. Ziggy went back up the ladder and I built up a pile of boxes so that I could have something to stand on, as I passed up the treasure. It was heavy work, but I didn't mind sweating when the rewards were so great. Soon, all that was left was the pile of stuff that I was standing on and the paintings, which we decided to leave. By balancing each box on my head and climbing the decaying ladder, I managed to get all the boxes up to Ziggy. I had just gone back down to pick up my torch and was climbing the ladder for the last time, when Ziggy somehow managed to drop the block back into its tight fitting hole. It missed my head by less than an inch, but it made me drop my torch and my right foot broke the step that it was on. The torch bulb broke as it hit the stone floor. In the pitch darkness, I tried to regain my footing, only to find that one side of the bottom half of the ladder had fallen away. All my weight was on my left foot, I clung on desperately, while I waited for my eyes to adjust to the darkness. They never did, as there was no light source to help them. Shouting for help didn't help either, as the only person who might have heard was Ziggy and he knew of my predicament anyway. I tried thought transfer, by thinking things such as "Come on Ziggy, there's enough here for both of us" and "OK, but let me out of here and you can have it all." It seemed like hours, as I clung on, anxious not to fall down, in case the hole opened up again so that I could climb to freedom. I said nothing in the darkness, as my thoughts ricocheted from past, to present, to future. It was then I noticed that the trouser of my hanging right limb had gone taut. In the inky blackness, something had attached itself to the material and there was definitely a weight of some sort clinging to me. When I had my torch, and now in the darkness, I had not seen nor heard anything, but I was in no doubt that there was something pulling my leg like I'm pulling yours."

Seconds after delivering the punch line, I found out why it was so called; as a torrent of blows rained down on my body.

"You asked for a story and you got a story. Why are you hitting me?" I asked, as I covered my face with my forearms.

"You really had me going," said Lynda, still thumping my chest, "there must be a better ending than that."

"No, that's all there is," I replied.

To stop the onslaught, I grabbed Lynda, first by one wrist and then the other. Undeterred, my irate listener pulled herself onto her knees while pushing my arms down beside my head, into the pinfall position, as I lay on my back.

"Kiss me," I murmured, as Lynda leaned over me.

Slowly, she lowered her lips onto mine; within a few seconds, our tongues were battling their way down each others throats, while Lynda moved one leg across my body and lay down on top of me. Without relaxing my grip on her wrists and without our lips parting, Lynda positioned herself perfectly as my gentle upward probing found a warm, moist welcome. But it was all too much for me, to be underneath, all at once, I pushed Lynda's legs out straight, tipped her off and rolled over on top of her. Little yelps came each time I thudded into her and while I shuddered to a climax, it felt as if the suntan on my shoulders was being torn away by her fingernails, as Lynda came too.

There was no six inch gap between us when we lay down together again. It was not long before we made love once more, before finally falling asleep. Physically, Lynda was remarkably similar to Eva, even down to the same short hair. So much so, that R'dub started to call Lynda "Eva" by mistake, although he could have been trying to wind me up. However, their personalities could not have been more different: with Lynda being probably the most easy-going British girl I had ever met. She did not wear my clothes, as Eva did. In fact, Lynda seldom wore anything. The impressively built teenager liked to go naked, even in the van; she would sit in the back, with the side door open and not give a damn who saw her. On one occasion, when going up to Ramatuelle, I noticed car drivers looking in, as we waited at a junction.

"Don't you think you should put something on?" I enquired.

"Oh, OK, if you say so," Lynda replied lazily, as she reached over for her hat.

Lynda was not an exhibitionist, it was more that she just could not be bothered to dress. Away from home for the first time, she did not have a care in the world. One evening we parked at the Moulins des Pallais, to watch the sunset and have our evening meal. As usual, Lynda had nothing on; when we had finished the washing up, we kissed and cuddled against the side of the van. Except for us, the hilltop was deserted until a BMW pulled across the back of the van.

Lynda did not appear to notice it, as the driver switched off his lights and engine. I figured it was probably only a courting couple, out for a drive, but I was not expecting Lynda to go down on her knees and give me head, right beside their car, even if it was almost dark.

I do not know how much our neighbours saw of our silhouetted shapes. They must have either been disgusted or embarrassed because they backed out of the car park soon after we started. Not wishing to invade our privacy any more than possible, the BMW kindly kept their headlights off until well down the hill. Later, we drove back down to the beach, giggling.

"What if they'd turned their lights on?" I asked.

"What if they'd had a camera?" Lynda asked.

"What if they had got out and asked us to stop?" I asked.

"What if they had come and asked to join in?" Lynda asked.

"Betcha they've gone off somewhere and are doing it right now," I suggested.

"Yeah, same position, same everything," added Lynda.

"You just didn't want to stop, did you?" I remarked.

"You couldn't stop me if you wanted to," stated Lynda with a laugh.

Back at the beach, we joined Pat, Maggie and the kids for our regular game of cards. Pat was teaching Sean and Alice the game of poker; each night saw us playing for a huge quantity of matchsticks that the family had brought with them. Lynda was getting tuition from me, as well as any cards from my hand that would give her two pair or better.  Invariably, the matches all ended up in front of Lynda – much to the disgust of the children and to the amazement of Pat, who had never played with anyone so lucky.

One night, Sean and Alice asked about a trip up to the Gorge du Verdun, like the one they had enjoyed the year before.  Pat was reluctant to drive for any amount of time, as it interfered with his drinking, but after Maggie insisted that a change of scene for a couple of days would be a good idea, the man of the house decided to give it a go.

The next morning, everything was all set in the VW but the old ambulance showed little sign of readiness.

"You go on ahead," said Pat, "we'll rendezvous at the bridge sometime this afternoon."

"Are you sure you don't want us to stay together, in case there's any problems?" I asked.

"No, I'm going to take it slow.  I'll only hold you up. See you up there," replied Pat, as he took the cap off his breakfast bottle of Kronenbourg.

Lynda and I left the beach car park to drive up to Ramatuelle in order to do some shopping.  I also checked the Poste Restante, while Lynda telephoned home to Wales from one of the metered 'phone booths.  Mary had sent me a long letter, thanking me for a wonderful holiday;

she showed her appreciation by enclosing two self-taped Chris Rea cassettes, along with some photographs of our time together. At the Lac de Ste Croix, it was a scorching hot, windless day when we arrived. The only place to be was in the lake, where the top two feet was luke warm, but the deeper water was refreshingly colder. There was little chance of windsurfing in the still air, but the board saved us the cost of hiring a canoe. I dug out an old paddle from the depths of the van and went up the gorge sitting on the windsurfer. Lynda swam alongside for a long way then, when she tired, she held on to the back for a tow. It was only when she clambered aboard, to sit behind me, that I noticed she was not wearing a swimsuit. Practically all the occupants of every canoe and pedalo stared at Lynda, but no one said anything more than "bon jour". The river traffic thinned out when we were further upstream. It was good to see that some women were going topless, but I do not think Lynda gave a second thought about being naked.

Very few of the rented canoes made it to the end of the navigation as the hour time limit required them to turn back earlier. It was here at the first shallow stretch that Lynda and I found a large area of thick squelchy mud. Several families, with two hour canoe charters, were embarking on an hilarious mud slinging fight with everybody getting well and truly plastered. Some people were so totally covered in mud that they booked like statues. It all came off when they dived in the river, although the water was half the temperature of the lake. After the mud splattered canoes returned downstream,

Lynda and I ventured onto the mud flat, having previously kept our distance, in fear of being pelted. The mud was the smoothest, creamiest and most sticky I had ever encountered. Lynda and I stepped off the windsurf board and sunk up to our shins, with an amazing feeling as it went between our toes.

"Will you make me into a statue?" asked Lynda, as she suddenly laid down in the fudge and rolled her naked body around.

"Yeah, why not. You've not got anything else on, why not wear a coat of mud?" I replied, adding, "if I pull the board out, you can stand on it for a base."

Lynda tried a few poses, such as standing to attention, standing at ease and one with her legs open and her arms outstretched. I suggested "throwing the discuss" but it was difficult to stay still; in the end, my model settled on the 'starting to run' pose. Not the hundred metres sprint crouch, but the 1500 metres lean forward start, which was more comfortable to hold  Lynda already had a lot of mud on her body, but as I took handfuls of the goo and spread them all over her, I found it to be one of the most sensual things I had ever done with a woman. I lingered over giving her breasts a smooth, even coating and as I slid my hands between the cheeks of Lynda's bum, I had a tremendous hard on.  The layer of mud was about a quarter of an inch thick;  it had begun to dry rock hard by the time I got round to the statue's face.  Her eyes, ears, lips and hair were left clear, as I dabbed the mud on with my fingertips, in a texture that artexers call 'rough cast'. When I had finished, I stood back to admire my handiwork.

"Are you feeling horny or what?" said Lynda without moving her lips.

"Yeah, not half. Its all that touching. I could do it right hear and now," I whispered.

"No way. I don't want this stuff inside of me," protested the ventriloquist.

"Why not? You've got it every where else," I teased.

"Don't you dare! Anyway, you can't, here come some boats," said a relieved Lynda.

I turned round to see two canoes coming up-steam, carrying a family of four between them.

"She is very good," said the father in English, as the canoes ran aground on our mud flat.

"Yes," I replied, puzzled as to how they knew we were English.

"May I take a photograph?" asked the well mannered mother.

"Sure," I answered quickly, without consulting

Lynda, who had suddenly become an object rather than a human being.

After a couple of pictures , the teenage daughter leapt out of her father's craft, peeled off her tee-shirt, threw it in the canoe and struck a topless pose on the mud. The girl said something in Dutch which I took to mean: "Can I be a statue too please daddy?"   As she stood there in just her bikini bottoms, her father made a short speech.

"No, it's just a boy friend, girlfriend thing.  Gosh, is that the time, we had better get these canoes back to the lake."

Lynda was drying out fast, as the family said goodbye and paddled away.

"I wish we had a camera, I'd love to see what I looked like," muttered Lynda.

"If you can stand still for a bit longer, I can float you down to the bridge, if you like.  Pat and Maggie will be there by now. They've got a camera," I put forward.

"OK that'll be great," said Lynda.

We did not realise it would take nearly an hour to do the journey with me pushing the board.  The water was very cold;  it started off OK when I was wading in the shallows, but as it got deeper, it got colder, by the time I had to start swimming, I began to wish I had never thought of the idea. Every camera on every canoe and pedalo was aimed at Lynda, as we encountered more and more river craft. Nobody commented directly on the strange site of a naked mud-covered woman floating by, but it must have seemed very bizarre. The mud had now completely dried to a light biscuit colour, no darker than Lynda's tan; it had cracked all over, resembling a hard boiled egg ready to be shelled. Lynda had stayed still for well over an hour. I was wondering just how long I could keep on pushing the board before I got cramp, when Lynda fell off. The water clouded to brown as the mud came off of the statue; she then surfaced and clung onto the windsurfer.

"What happened?" I asked.

"I don't know. I must have fallen asleep. I woke up when I hit the water," said a disappointed Lynda.

"You must have fainted in the heat. Let's go under the waterfall. You can have a shower to get clean," I suggested.

We clambered aboard the windsurfer and I paddled over to where the water came racing off the mountain. It was colder than the river, but was just what Lynda needed, as she was rinsed and refreshed, all at once. It was mid-afternoon by the time we returned to the car park. Pat and Maggie still had not turned up, so we would never have got a photograph of the statue anyway. After a late lunch, Lynda seemed to be troubled by something which was most unlike her.

"What's the matter? Are you fed up because you fell in?" I asked.

"No, it's not that. I've decided to go home. I'm going to hitch back, starting today," said Lynda.

"What's brought this on? I thought you liked the beach life," I said, totally surprised by Lynda's decision.

"R'dub said that no girl that's come to the gorge with you has ever been seen again," continued Lynda, hesitantly.

"He's winding you up. There was only Mary and I took her to Nice airport to fly back to England," I protested.

"How do I know that? It's only your word against his," said a worried looking Lynda.

"Well, while you were on the 'phone this morning, I checked the post and there was a letter from Mary, you can read it if you want. Also the tape playing right now, was with the letter," I replied, as I handed the envelope to Lynda.

"I wondered where Chris Rea came from. No, I don't want to read it, it's to you. But I'm still leaving," said Lynda.

"Why do you have to go? We get on so well and we're having a good time, aren't we?" I pleaded.

"That's just it. I'm having a great time, but Mary writes and sends tapes. Olivia will be back in a couple of weeks. There's no future for me in your life. I might as well go now. You're just using me to fill in the gaps," blurted Lynda.

"Me, using you? Hang on a minute. You get a comfy bed, a roof over your head, a place to stash your gear, get driven around, cooked for, pay no rent, I even scrub your back in the shower," I gushed.

"Yeah, OK, but you get sex and I scrub your back as well," complained Lynda.

"I seem to remember you were the one who first got physical. It's not as if you're continually fighting me off," I moaned.

"I know, we've had a good time and get on well, but you forget, I've met Olivia. I've seen how you get on with her. What's going to happen if I'm still around when she comes back?"

"We'll just have to cross that bridge when we come to it, I don't know."

"Yeah, I know what you want, three in a bed and I know what these French girls are like."

"Don't talk stupid, the thought never crossed my

mind."

"Well, my mind is made up. I'm going home," said Lynda, while rolling up her sleeping bag and stuffing it in her rucksack.

While Lynda went round, collecting all her things, I sat on the step of the van. I thought that if Pat had turned up, she would not be going.

"Why not leave it until the morning," I suggested, as the rucksack was being buckled up.

"No, I'm gonna go now," said Lynda, reaching for her hat as she stood waiting for a goodbye kiss.

"Go on then, but take care. If you want to come back, I'll be back on the beach tomorrow night," I said resignedly, as I gave Lynda one short last kiss on the lips.

For a couple of minutes, I sat and wondered where I had gone wrong. Then realising the absurdity of the situation, I ran up to the road in one last ditch attempt to make Lynda see sense, but she was nowhere to be seen and had already got a lift. What the hell was R W Lewis going to say when, once again, I returned alone from the gorge?

I spent another scorching hot day at the gorge after a night alone in the van. I wondered how far Lynda had got and what had happened to force the non-arrival of

Pat and Maggie. Time passed slowly, as I lazed in the shade, only taking short dips in the lake, to cool down and have a leak. When all the other cars on the car park started loading up at the end of the day, I followed suit. Without really thinking about it, I joined the slow moving convoy heading back to the coast.

## Chapter Twenty-seven

Pat and Maggie were in the old ambulance, parked in their usual position, when I pulled alongside. Pascaline was playing poker with the family as I ducked under the mosquito net and sat next to Alice at the table.

"I had blue smoke coming from the exhaust," stated Pat, before I had said a word, " I thought it was a valve, I've had the head off and checked. In the end, I tracked it down to an oil leak in the brake servo. Hot oil in the exhaust, you know, blue smoke. I've been under that bonnet for two days. Just got it back together this evening. Where's Lynda?"

"She's decided to hitch hike home," I said dejectedly.

"Oh, that's good," said Pascaline happily "my old school friend called Agnes arrived today. I have told her all about you. You can meet her at the party tonight."

"Yeah, Lutfi is having a party on the beach tonight – everyone is invited," said Sean.

"He has invited all his friends," said Pat, "doesn't the guy know people are only friendly with him because he lets them park for free?"

"But you gave him our address last week, Pat, I hope

you know he could turn up on our doorstep anytime next winter," warned Maggie.

"I don't remember that," said Pat, as he peered into another empty bottle of Kronenbourg.

Lutfi was the young Moroccan student who collected the money for the council owned car park, where all the camping cars parked. Some people were charged but anyone who showed Lufti any kindness was allowed in for free. From me, Lutfi had a cup of coffee every morning and a lift anytime he was walking the way I was driving. From Pat, the Moroccan had an invitation to the first barbecue of the holiday and then was kept sweet with the odd packet of biscuits or piece of fruit. Most campers went for the evening meal approach, once they knew the score. Lufti's party was to show his appreciation for everything he had been given during the season.

Well over 50 people attended the party on the beach, far more than Lufti had expected or invited. The crisps, nuts and crackers did not go far, but with plenty of wine and a ghetto blaster turned up loud, there was a good atmosphere. Everyone told the host it was a great party, which is all he needed to hear. A surprise for me was to see Tarzan there.

"I found your English rose," I winced, after the usual painful handshake.

"Yes, my Mary. I think you and her go well together.

Am I right?" said Tarzan, with the air of an all seeing, all knowing mystic.

"Yes, truly an English rose.  What brings you back to Ramatuelle?" I said, swiftly changing the subject.

"I am here only for one night.  I have a project I am working on, but I cannot tell you about it," said Tarzan mysteriously, just as R'dub joined us.

"On your own, Chris?  No Lynda.  Haven't lost another one have you?" smirked R'dub.

"No.  She's gone back to Wales," I answered matter of factly.

"Year, if you say so.  I believe you.  Until they find the body, that is," said R'dub, in a manner that was intended to intrigue Tarzan.

But Tarzan did not bite;  he stared straight over the top of the diminutive R'dub, patted me on the shoulder and moved off to talk with somebody else. I then realised R'dub must have told Tarzan about my relationship with Mary;  but the super cool, former plagiste soon had labelled R'dub as a stirrer.

About the only person I did not know at the party was Agnes, who was eagerly introduced to me by Pascaline.  Agnes taught at a primary school and fitted the image of a typical French school teacher perfectly;

with neat bobbed hair, oval gold rimmed spectacles, long shapeless summer dress with flowery print and favourite old cardigan that always had her hands stuffed in the pockets, arms locked straight. The conversation between us was difficult, not because of the language difference, Agnes' English was excellent, but because of Pascaline's over enthusiastic match making. Neither of us knew what the other had been told, or what each other's feelings were, regarding a virtual blind date.

After shifting my weight from one foot to the other for about fifteen minutes, I suggested a walk along the water's edge, in the moonlight. Agnes agreed to a promenade and I thought we had slipped away unnoticed.

"Go to the Gorge du Verdun with that man and it will be the last thing you ever do," shouted R'dub playfully.

"Was that man talking to us?" asked Agnes demurely.

"No, I don't think so," I replied, hoping that the school teacher's English was not well tuned in.

The walk turned out to be a good idea. Although, at first, I was longing to pick up a flat stone and skim it out to sea; just for something to do with my hands. An impossible wish on a soft sand beach, but by the time we came to the rental hobie cat at the Cabane Bamboo, I was holding hands with Agnes. The catamaran held fond memories for me, as over the years, most of my late night shoreline strolls had finished with me sitting with someone on its canvas deck, watching the circling light of Cap Camarat. That night, it marked the spot where Agnes and I shared out first kiss.

There was a strange shyness to that first embrace, with no tongues and with our hands gripping each other's forearms. After losing Lydna, I felt I did not deserve such an instant replacement. Agnes seemed so prim and proper that any show of passion from me would probably be seen as an unwelcome advance. However, when we kissed again, Agnes' tongue made the first move and her hands slid down the inside of my shorts to pull the cheeks of my bum apart with unexpected power. I was still reluctant to force the pace, but when my offer of coffee, back at the van, was taken up without a moments hesitation, I began to wonder if my first impressions of Agnes might have been wrong.

After coffee, the classic school teacher turned into the classic lover and stayed all night. It seemed like a fantasy as the long all covering dress came off to reveal an unexpectedly well proportioned body that only needed a light tanning to bring it to a standard that would equal any on the beach. I had a tigress in my hands; once I realised exactly what sort of person Agnes was, my initial shyness was forgotten as passions ran riot on a first night that not even Pascaline could have foreseen.

The matchmaker was our first visitor in the morning; over a coffee, Pascaline told Agnes how worried about her she was, after finding the tent empty in the morning. It soon transpired Pascaline had also found somewhere else to sleep that night, but she would not say with whom.  As things turned out, Agnes never slept, even one night, in the tent at Les Tournels Camping during her whole holiday.  She soon moved all her gear into the van;  saying that it did not matter because Pascaline had not told the campsite reception about her arrival and she was not being charged.

The days with Agnes brought a distinct change of routine;  looking back, I can see that I was subtly manipulated.  The trio of Pascaline, Regine and Agnes dominated all those around them.  The whole day was planned by the three young women at the tables outside the Café L'Ormeau, where they held court every morning.  Any number of people came to sit and drink coffee with the English teacher, the Latin teacher and the primary school teacher.  While similar, in that they all possessed sharp scheming minds, each of the girls were physically different and had individual style:  Pascaline was the youngest and tallest, she wore sandals tied up above the ankle, cut off jeans so short that there was no room for the back pockets and tee-shirts which had been re-styled with a daring pair of scissors;  Regine, the eldest and the shortest, favoured high-heeled ankle boots with voluminous multi-pocketed shorts and white frilly blouses that were never buttoned up, but just tucked into her shorts, leaving a two inch gap, showing her suntan all the way up from her naval to her neck;  Agnes maintained her frumpy image, with the long dresses and the cardigan, but the secret of her body was soon out as no one wore anything on the beach.

Regine and Pascaline's favourite sunbathing spot had always been on the rocks between L'Escalet and Cap Cartaya; I was soon talked into spending my afternoons there. Amongst the rocks, little patches of sand were dotted along this undeveloped part of the coast, offering a high degree of privacy for those wanting an all over tan. The rocks also offered the chance to do some snorkelling and it was here that I had a problem with my right ear.

"Does anybody know what it's like when you burst an ear drum?" I asked after coming up in pain from one particular deep dive.

"Close your mouth tight, hold your nose and blow. If you can hear a whistle, then you have a burst ear drum," said Eric, demonstrating immediately afterwards.

I did what he said and heard a whistle.

"I think I've burst an ear drum," I said dejectedly.

"Don't go under water again, go and see the doctor, he will give you eardrops and antibiotics. When I burst my ear drum it took two weeks to heal, but you must keep it dry," said Eric, confidently.

The Dutchman was right, as usual. After a two minute medical examination that cost 200 francs, a bottle of drops and some tablets that cost another two fifty; I resigned myself to keeping my head above water and the windsurfer on the roof of the van. My days of rehabilitation were spent exclusively on the rocks with Agnes and the others. With the imminent return of Olivia, it seemed a good idea to keep out of the way until Agnes went back to Nancy.

In avoiding Olivia on the beach, I also avoided the problem of having to choose between her and Agnes. The autumn school term was only days away, so the school teacher would soon be gone.

When it came to sex, there was not much to choose between them. Both were in my top three of all time lovers; Olivia was sensually super smooth, while Agnes brought a certain kinkiness to proceedings which, given her outward demeanour of near Victorian correctness, was a hell of a turn on. One night, I was laying back, while Agnes gave me head, when one of her fingers pushed into my mouth, having made itself wet, her hand then went down between my legs and she slid the finger up my bum.

"What do you think you're doing? How would you like it?" I gulped.

Agnes said nothing, but came up to kiss my mouth and then as she lay beside me, she took my hand, put my middle finger in her mouth, then guided it up her own arse.

"Do not think of trying anything else, you are too big," said Agnes, with a smile.

After the trio from Nancy returned home after their holiday, I never looked at a school teacher again without thinking what they were like in bed. The conservatively dressed who, like Agnes, seem to be hiding a fit body, never failed to fire my imagination. Also the same can be said about bank cashiers, under their company issue blouse and skirt, I always wonder if they were wearing expensive, exotic lingerie, like that worn by Olivia.

With Agnes gone and the eardrum healed, I returned to the sandy beach of Pampellone, where I found Olivia starting the second week of her holiday.

"I've had a burst eardrum and haven't been able to do any windsurfing," I said, after we had exchanged the little kisses on the cheek.

"Yes, I know, the man who collects the car parking money told me. He also said that you were with a school teacher from Nancy and went to the beach of L'Escalet," said Olivia, with a tilt headed smile that gave me hope that our relationship was not over.

"Yeah, she's gone back to work now and the ears alright again,  Do you want to go out on the board?" I asked, hoping to get an excuse to end the conversation and do something.

"No, you windsurf, I will swim," replied Olivia, who then rolled up the top half of her one-piece swimsuit and went off into the water.

Olivia was well over 300 metres off shore by the time I had put the windsurfer together and sailed out to her. I wondered if she would be angry about me avoiding her in order to be with another woman, but the easy-going Parisienne made nothing of it whatsoever.

"What is it like at L'Escalet," asked Olivia, as we rested on the board, half a mile out to sea.

"It's very rocky, no good for windsurfing," I replied.

"Where else have you been since I was last here?" continued Olivia.

"I went to the Gorge du Verdun, great windsurfing, fresh water, and the mountains. It's a beautiful place. Have you ever been there?" I asked.

"No, but I have seen photographs in books and magazine," answered Olivia.

"Would you like to go there for a few days with me in the van?" I asked casually.

"Yes, that would be nice. I will speak to my parents," said Olivia.

So the van left the beach with a lone female, one more time and headed into the mountains. I could not remember how many different passengers had made the journey with me, but I never tired of the spectacular scenery, fresh water and hassle free parking. Olivia enjoyed herself, too. I was a bit worried that the lack of toilet facilities would be a problem for her, as she was not used to roughing it, but she never complained. We did the trip up the gorge with the windsurfer and like Lynda, Olivia swam a lot of the way in her effortless style, that mixed surface dives with everything, including back stroke, which gave her a unique view of the canyon walls.

At the waterfall, Olivia dived from a greater height and with far more artistic merit than I had ever done. Her technique even overshadowed that of a group of German guys, with their girlfriends in a flotilla of pedalos. I was glad that the excuse of a recently headed eardrum saved me from showing myself up. When we continued upstream I wondered if Olivia would want to be a statue. Somehow I could not see her agreeing to be covered in mud from head to toe. Unfortunately, the opportunity never arose, as there had been a rise in water level since my last visit; the mud bank was now knee deep underwater and the navigation limit was 200 metres up-steam with only rocky outcrops.

In our two days away from the beach, we did all the other gorge tour bits: the drive round the top road to the Pont d'Artury; the visit to Moustiers Ste Marie, with the climb up to the church under the star and the evening stroll to the bridge at sunset. Thankfully, Olivia did not ask me to jump, but if I had thought about it, I could have asked her to dive. The lovemaking was as good as ever, although our attempts to do it in the lake at midnight did not work out. The water was half a metre deep for about ten metres, but then there was a steep drop, off which put us out of our depth. All along the lake shore, it was either too shallow or too deep. In the shallows, the gravel bed made it too painful for the knees and although we had fun trying to get it together while treading water, we really needed a gently sloping sandy bottom. But it was all good foreplay; Olivia and I were straight onto the bed without drying off. I ended up sleeping on the biggest wet patch ever, I could not blame Olivia, because she slept on one too.

On the way back, we took a detour at Vidauban in order to visit the Domaine de St Genevieve and have a look at the vineyards. Francis Boi, the vendangeur, was out in the yard, servicing the tractors in readiness for the imminent harvest. When Olivia and I pulled up in the van, he seemed pleased to see me, after a handshake, his first question was to ask if I was looking for work. The grape picking was due to start in ten days' time and Olivia had too weeks holiday left. I thought about it for a minute or so, confirmed that I would be driving the tractor; then I told Francis that I would do it. The vendangeur offered Olivia a grape picking job, but she graciously declined. I agreed to turn up for work on a week next Monday, at 8.00 o'clock; as we drove away it started to rain.

The storm was with us all the way back to St Tropez. There was no point in going to the beach, so I took Olivia back to the apartment. She insisted that I come up and have dinner with the family. I did not want to go, as I knew nothing had been arranged with her parents, but as I had nowhere else to go, I reluctantly accepted the invitation. Meeting fathers, socially for the first time, after sleeping with their daughters, had never been a favourite pastime of mine. In the three years I had known him, I had never said anything more than "Bon jour" to Olivia's dad. Luckily the difficult situation that I anticipated did not materialise. There were no questions on how I was going to keep Olivia in the style and manner to which she was accustomed. Which would have been a tricky one to answer, then the guy knew I only worked half the year. Olivia's father, who was an engineer and spoke surprisingly good English was thankfully more interested in my experiences in eastern Europe than in my relationship with his eldest daughter.

However, it was not all plain sailing. Olivia's mother had planned a Chinese meal; there was enough to go round, but it was not like any Chinese meal I had ever eaten before. Chop sticks were never my favourite tools, so I was relieved when my struggling brought the offer of a spoon and a fork. But I really showed myself up when it came to the bit where you had to wrap up the roast duck in the lettuce leaves. Was French home cooked Chinese cuisine really that different from the English chinky-bars that I visited, half drunk, at 11.30 on a Friday night? But then I always had an omelette and chips anyway.

By the time coffee had been served, the rain had stopped, so Olivia, who had sensed my unease, suggested a walk around the port. The whole episode had become embarrassing for her too. Now that her sister, Sabine, had started to make remarks such as, "What sort of job could Olivia expect to find if she lived in England?" In the end we were both glad to get out on the street. That night and every night afterwards until I left St Tropez, Olivia slept in the van. I never had another dinner invitation, which was a good thing, as it would have been difficult to refuse. When I left to go to Vidauban, there was no talk of when Olivia and I would see each other again, but I knew it was probably my last summer on the beach. A lot of the international crowd said they would return again, but I could never see things being the same. There would be no Tarzan; Rupert was well ensconced on the farm; R'dub, Karen and the boys were going back to England, and the unprofitable occupation of beach seller had been abandoned by the unemployed English and Irish.

The grape picking at Ste Genevieve was totally different from all the previous years and was the wettest in living memory. The picking team was made up of local French teenagers and north Africans, which left me as the only non-fluent French speaker. I did not have a conversation with anyone for a month; in the end, I just ground out the days until it was all finished. Where as before, I had cooked for over 20, each evening I cooked and ate alone; except for the night that I went to the local transport café and pretended to be a transcontinental truck driver. At Les Routiers on the RN7 in Le Luc, I had the duck, which was off. I ended up with sickness and diarrhoea, which laid me low for three days, although I worked through it. The camaraderie of previous years was non-existent; the only things that were the same were the tractors and trailers.

After the four weeks at Vidauban, I drove back to England and telephoned Mary, Tarzan's English rose. For Christmas, I bought her an alto-saxophone. By May, we had set up home together in a brand new two-bedroom flat. I had a £43,500 mortgage. My beach days were over.

7433666R0

Made in the USA
Lexington, KY
21 November 2010